Civic Realism

The MIT Press   Cambridge, Massachusetts   London, England

Peter G. Rowe   Civic Realism

5744

This book was set in Bodoni Book by Graphic Composition Inc.

Printed and bound in the United States of America.

Library of Congress Cataloging-in-Publication Data
Rowe, Peter G.
    Civic Realism / by Peter G. Rowe.
        p.   cm.
    Includes bibliographical references and index.
    ISBN 0-262-18180-0 (hc : alk. paper)
    1. Public spaces.   2. City planning.   3. Architecture and
state.
    I. Title.
    NA9053.S6R69   1997
    711'.4—dc21   97-663
                                                          CIP

711.4 Row

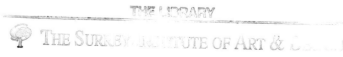

For Mor, *in memoriam*

Contents

Acknowledgments

Both the substance and structure of *Civic Realism* first emerged during a seminar conducted at the Graduate School of Design, Harvard University, in the spring and fall semesters of 1994. To all those students participating I owe a huge debt of gratitude, as I do to my two research assistants, Felicity Scott and Marie-Danielle Faucher. Early ideas also came from discussions with Deborah Torres, Pedro Cardona, and Aysen Savas, as well as with Hashim Sarkis, with whom I have shared the instruction of several design studios at Harvard. My colleagues Rafael Moneo, Rodolfo Machado, and Jorge Silvetti, unwittingly perhaps, also acted as sounding boards for various ideas at various times.

Books like this are inevitably autobiographical, and many friends, family members, acquaintances, neighbors, and colleagues in different places added immeasurably to my understanding of local contexts. To the following I owe special thanks. In Barcelona there was Joan Busquets, Manuel de Solà Morales, José Acebillo, "Pep" Parcerisa, and Elias Torres. In Ljubljana there was Davor Gazvoda—also my teaching assistant at Harvard—Ana Kučan, Dušan Ogrin, and Aleš Vodopivec, as well as Aleksandra Wagner here in the United States. In New York—my new home town—there was Richard Plunz, Peter Ballantine,

Ron Bentley, Sal La Rosa, David Moos, and John Loomis, and in Paris, Isabelle G. de Plenar, Marie Vag Lugosi, as well as François Vigier, more locally in Cambridge, Massachusetts. In Rome my local guides were Pietro Barucci—with whom I also shared a course at Harvard—Rosario Pavia, Gianfranco Palma, and Donatella Vinciarelli, who I should also thank for her good-humored forbearance and sense of exploration.

To Neil Rudenstine, the President of Harvard University, and to Al Carnesale, the Provost, I also owe a special note of thanks for their constant understanding and support during these campaign years. Likewise I must recognize Celia Slattery, my assistant at Harvard, for her loyalty and effectiveness, as well as Maria Moran for her assistance with the manuscript. Frankly, without them none of what follows would have come to fruition.

Finally, my undying respect and admiration goes to Gradoli, a small town in central Italy, where this project began. And last but not least, I wish to express my affection and esteem to Anthony Rowe, for all his encouragement, and to Lauretta Vinciarelli—my constant intellectual and ordinary companion in life—for all her timely suggestions and unstinting support.

Civic Realism

1

Reexamining the Public Realm

The Piazza del Campo and the Palazzo Pubblico in Siena (page 2).

*"Everyone knows, tortoises are slow! Everyone knows, tortoises are slow!"
chanted Giacomo mockingly, emboldened by the relative strength in numbers
offered by his fellow* contradaioli, *even though they were now far afield in Pan-
tera territory. "We will soon see on Sunday," came a reply from the first-floor
window overlooking Via Tommaso Pendola. "Go back to your filthy dens, you
sly Lupa bastards!"*

*Hot though it was, Giacomo eagerly pulled on his velvet doublet for one final
fitting before the big day. "Zia Giuliana really should buy an air conditioner,"
he mused. "The trouble with older people is that they are set in their ways . . .
Oh well, I shouldn't complain," he went on to himself with a certain amount of
pride. "When she gets done, I will look exactly like zio Umberto in the old photo
on the sideboard."*

*"Shit! If I hadn't closed my eyes I wouldn't have dropped that damn flag during
the* alzata. *Stupido! And there in the Campo for all to see . . . My God, what
will zio Umberto say?" "Don't worry, Giacomo," yelled Gianni at his side, as
they were carried by the swarming crowd away from the piazza. "There is always
next year!" "Yes!" thought Giacomo, taking at least some heart. "There is always next year."*

—Pietro Lupino, *Festa**

This book is about attitudes and an orientation toward the making and reshaping of urban public spaces that are civic in character, belonging to everyone and yet to nobody in particular. Of importance is how such places were created and the specific social, political, and cultural circumstances that brought them into existence. Also of importance is the shape and appearance of these places and how that was used to simultaneously represent, constitute, and enhance the daily lives of citizens. In short, this is a book as much about the broad processes and attitudes behind civic place making as it is about urban architecture per se, and it reflects a concomitant belief that civic place making cannot occur successfully without a propitious conjunction of local opportunity, community wherewithal, and design capability.

A good place to start examining both the social and physical aspects of viable civic places is with an incontestable example that has contemporary pertinence and has stood the test of time. Arguably, among all the likely candidates, Siena and its Piazza del Campo stand out as a place where civic life, civic aspirations, and civic responsibilities have been inscribed indelibly, encapsulating the themes that will run through the remainder of this book. To begin with, even during the thirteenth and fourteenth centuries, Siena presented an array of social, political, and cultural dimensions of importance to any discussion of public and civic realms. Broadly, the political functions and suffrage of the city-state were divided into three broad categories. First, there was the government of elected officials, magistrates, and other bureaucrats. Then there was civil society formed by the nobility, the well-to-do, and the remaining middle and working classes—literally the citizens of Siena. Finally there were the populations marginalized within civil society and without the full rights and protections of citizenship, including foreigners and itinerant laborers. Far from being fixed, this three-part arrangement in the sharing of power and responsibility and the creation of mutual dependency was dynamic. Governments came and went. Regimes changed hands, and the fortunes of prominent and not-so-prominent families waxed and waned. Uprisings were fomented and the rights to representation were both increased and decreased accordingly. The institutional character of the three major social divisions also changed. Sometimes the government ruled with a full complement of offices, and at other times it did not. The guilds, the university, confraternities, neighborhood organizations, and other gatherings were both more and less influential, and the livelihoods available to both the poor and the prosperous typically varied with the economy and with changes in technology. Correspondingly, alliances within and between the sociopolitical divisions also shifted, as did the distinctions that could be made between the divisions themselves.

The most remarkable aspect of Siena during this period, however, was the overall continuity of the republic, ultimately formed by the give-and-take relationship among constituents of civil society, and, perhaps most important, by the relationship between civil society and the state. More germane still, the Piazza del Campo—or simply, *Il Campo* ("the field") as the primary setting for Sienese social, political, and cultural life, reflected and continues to reflect these relationships, as well as some of the changing alliances. In the authorship of its overall layout, spatial definition, decoration, and use, the Campo was a mixed enterprise, involving both the government and civil society. Yet it expressively captured the life, times, and civil circumstances of Siena, as well as reminding the Sienese—should any reminder have been necessary—of who they were and what was expected of them. In this last respect the Campo was more than public, more than a matter of access or of the right of expression and display. It produced an aura, recalled fine moments from the past, and provided palpable guidance about what form of public behavior was not only acceptable but preferred. In short, it was *civic*.

What is also clear from the case of Siena and the Piazza del Campo is the directness with which civic life and expectations were and continue to be represented. Again the design of the open space, the architecture of the buildings, the provisions made for use, and the general adornment were and remain clearly understandable without being seen as nostalgic, trivializing, or overly picturesque. The Campo both was and is, in a word, *real*. It had and still has a realism that encompasses everyday life, occasional events, solemn occasions, and extraordinary celebrations. Nevertheless, like many great civic works the realism also extends to the expressive means themselves. Architecturally, the Campo remains somewhat contained or autonomous in this respect. It may be strikingly beautiful like an illuminated script from the early period, but it also requires contemplation, knowledge, and a sense of architectural form to be interpreted thoughtfully. The realism is thus removed and representational in one sense, and alive, literal, and constitutive in another. Certainly in strictly architectural terms, it extends beyond the usual stylistic label of realism— nowadays often confined to either state or corporate interests, such as "socialist realism," "photorealism," or "neorealism." Furthermore, the appearance of the Piazza del Campo involved many contributors, not only reflecting ideological aspects of the public and private sectors, but fundamentally expressing the common ground between government and civil society, including some inherent tensions and contradictions. In short, the realism here did more than merely illustrate and promote a particular class-based or political point of view. Unlike many other historical places, it also did more than augment the trappings of despotism, theocracy, or a manifest personal image. These generalizations, however, require the telling of a longer and more detailed version of the story before the underlying themes of this book can become clearer.

Following this clarification, the book proceeds with a definition of the civic aspects of places and useful distinctions that may be drawn with public spaces in general. This is followed, in chapter 3, by a discussion of realism and, in particular, of pertinent aesthetic and architectural dimensions of that concept. In chapter 4, the possibilities of individual spatial practices to define and reshape collective places are introduced, followed in chapter 5 by an exploration of how civic places must have the capacity to constitute as well as represent the civic aspects of our lives. To conclude, various interactive arrangements of by-then familiar concepts about civic realism are presented in chapter 6, along with balancing tests for sorting out good from not-so-good aspects of viable civic places. Ultimately this book is about enabling design practices, whereby any apparent decline in the presence of viable civic realms might be redressed constructively. In contrast to narrow definitions of what is or might be called civic in our cities—often corresponding to equally narrow definitions about the conduct of political life—the broad message of this book is that many publicly accessible spaces can have and should have a civic orientation that is direct, palpable, and there for the purposes of reminding us both of who we are and who we might become.

AN ORGANIZATION OF PUBLIC AND CIVIC LIFE

During the thirteenth century, against the backdrop of what must have seemed like an interminable political struggle for power between the papacy and the Holy Roman Empire, there emerged a remarkable and even more durable civic phenomenon—the *comuni* or communes of northern and central Italy. These republican city-states not only played pivotal roles in the broader struggle of the Guelfs and Ghibellines, but also established a new benchmark in civil rule and popular government, the likes of which had not been seen since the Roman republic before Caesar Augustus.[1] Populous, highly urbanized, wealthy, and enterprising, these communes and the exploits of their citizenry are well known, especially through the two most influential, the republics of Venice and Florence.

Yet it is in Siena—the City of the Virgin, the smaller and less prodigious rival of neighboring Florence through much of this period—where probably the most extreme form of popular government, committee rule, and communal municipal administration could be found. Considered politically unruly to the point of being untrustworthy by many would-be allies, Siena for a period of some three hundred years—roughly between 1255 and 1555—clung tenaciously to its republican independence and belief in civic virtue. In the final years of the republic, during a terrible siege that brought the city-state to

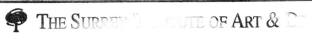

its end, Siena fought on heroically and paid dearly for these beliefs. The city's population was quite literally decimated to about one-tenth of its original number in earlier more peaceful and prosperous times.[2]

The thirteenth century was a period of bewildering economic development and profound social change in northern and central Italy: the time and place bore witness to the dismantling of the feudal system, freedom from a subsistence economy, agricultural reform, and a significant rise in the importance and largesse of urban areas. Indeed, towns and cities renewed their functions as centers of exchange during this period, as consumers of agricultural products on the one hand, and as providers of services and manufactured goods on the other. Gone, or in a distinct minority, was the rampant and parochial exploitation by local lords, whose former fiefdoms could barely sustain their indigenous populations, even during the best of times. On the ascent was a mercantile class and a mercantile culture, together with peasant ownership of small farms and rural land holdings. The commune that emerged was an administrative fusion between city and countryside, covering unprecedentedly large expanses of territory. In practice what occurred was subjugation of this territory by city interests, the imposition of laws and administrative practices, along with the dismantling of the castles and fortresses of local nobility. The whole region was melded into one political entity. In short, the countryside (*contado*) and city (*città*) became one, with smaller towns and surrounding rural areas effectively replicating the political and social qualities of the larger city-state.[3]

This was also a period of high rural-to-urban migration. Invariably, urban areas were dense. In most places there was one townsperson for every one-and-a-half country persons, and in some towns, like San Gimignano, this ratio was reversed, with three townspersons for every two country persons.[4] No doubt the practice of requiring Sienese citizens to purchase property and build a house in town of a certain cost, as a prerequisite for suffrage, contributed to these urban densities and the rural-urban pattern of migration. Economic incentives of better jobs and potential advancement also played a strong role in reinforcing the trend. By contrast, the new less servile relationship that emerged between those who worked the land—the *contadini*—and those who owned the land maintained productively sizable numbers of the peasantry in the outlying territory. Contracts replaced the former feudal system of servile relations and there was considerable encouragement, especially for ordinary citizens, to own land.[5]

During the period of entrepreneurial growth in the late thirteenth and fourteenth centuries, Siena was both bourgeois and enterprising, as well as land owning and profitably territorial. In particular, this era saw the rise of many mercantile ventures and of banking. Moreover, Siena was at the forefront of these enterprises, although the Florentine florin emerged as the chief currency of Europe. For many years the Bonsignori family ran from Siena their *Great Table*, a banking interest of considerable breadth and dependability, until its collapse in the late 1290s and eventual bailout by the commune during the early fourteenth century.[6] The Sienese Chigi family were also heavily engaged in the banking business, eventually establishing themselves prominently in Rome, where their former palazzo now serves as the government headquarters for the contemporary Italian republic. In fact, the Monte dei Paschi, founded in 1624 and one of Italy's oldest existing banks, began life in Siena, where its main offices were located in the former Salimbeni palace on the main street running north and south through the city. Later on, and not altogether for the better, a system of agricultural sharecropping emerged, allowing these and other wealthy Sienese families of rentiers to exploit peasant farmers.

Geographically, the territory or city-state of Siena, especially at the height of its expansion around 1337, encompassed a sizable area of central-western Italy, roughly 50 kilometers in every direction. With Florence close by to the north, Sienese influence extended south as far as the Monti Volsini—approximately the modern border between the regions of Tuscany and Lazio. To the east, the Sienese encroached into the rich Val di Chiana, and to the west lay the Tyrrhenian Sea.[7] Although in those days precise boundaries were never clear and often contested, the metal-bearing hills immediately to the west of

Siena constantly remained a part of the city-state's dominion, whereas increasing sections of the Maremma to the southwest, with its valuable pastures and impressive salt and mineral deposits, were gradually subjugated and incorporated. The broken terrain of the Sienese contado made dominance over local landlords, such as the Aldobrandeschi of Sovana in the Maremma, difficult.[8] The lack of extensive waterways and a general shortage of fresh water were also constant problems, along with the absence of a home port, in spite of ill-fated efforts to develop Talamone on the Tyrrhenian Sea for this purpose at great public expense during the early fourteenth century.[9]

Administratively, the contado—the larger territory of Siena—was subdivided into three parts, each with different legislative requirements and responsibilities. At the center was the city itself or the commune proper, under direct rule of commune authorities. Next lay the *masse*, or suburbs—known then as *burgi* or today as *borghi*—incorporating the shantytowns that grew up outside the walls of Siena and surrounding townships dating from earlier periods.[10] The masse were also administered directly by the city, although often taxed separately. Finally, the remaining contado, or mosaic of towns and countryside, made up the third broad administrative unit, in many cases with some autonomy. Towns like Grosseto and Massa Marittima, for instance, were awarded special status and relief from taxation in return for allegiance to Sienese authority.[11]

The city of Siena was located about 300 meters above sea level along a westward spur of the Chiana hills. With a land area in 1300 of some 50 hectares, it was roughly half the size of Florence. Unlike some central Italian cities, such as Viterbo to the south, Siena was not an expanded Roman town, but was built from the sixth and seventh centuries A.D., along the ridge lines of prevailing terrain and adjacent to major roads, especially the Via Cassia, linking Rome to the south with France to the north. Eventually subdivided into three *terzi*—Città, San Martino, and Camollia roughly in that order of development— the first settlement at Castelvecchio occupied a prominent hill for obvious defensive reasons. Subsequent expansions favored other hills and high terrain. A successive walling in of communities with *castellacce* also occurred as the city expanded along and across neighboring hillsides. Adjacent to these walls and some thirty-five to fifty fortified gates were located the *carbonaie*—deep trenches with wood piled up for fires—to discourage rampart storming by anyone laying siege to the city.[12]

By the mid-thirteenth century the population of the city of Siena was about 30,000, growing rapidly to 50,000 in the first half of the fourteenth century, a peak not exceeded until well into the modern period, and then only barely. Another 15,000 people were added by the shantytowns that sprung up along the roads and up the hillsides on the outskirts of the fortified town, in addition to other settlements in the masse, with the surrounding countryside and annexed territories contributing a further 35,000 people. In all, the population of the Sienese city-state was about 100,000 before the Great Plague or Black Death of 1348, with the vast majority concentrated in and around the city itself. Not at all unique in these characteristics, Siena reflected the typical pattern at the time. Bologna, for instance, had some 12,000 people in the city and an additional 17,000 in the countryside.[13]

Unfortunately, this population expansion and concentration could not be supported, as the precarious balance between demands for food and agricultural production at the time could not be sustained, leading to recurrent famine and pestilence. With declining populations and corresponding incentives to maintain former territorial expanses, many of the civic works of the thirteenth century were undone. The Sienese marshes, for instance, lost around 80 percent of their earlier population during the last decades of the fourteenth century. Moreover, Siena was not alone in these losses. In San Gimignano fully two-thirds of the population perished in the plague, while in Pistoia the population was almost halved, from 36,000 to about 19,000, and the population of Orvieto, just beyond the southeastern outskirts of the Sienese contado, was reduced from about 3,000 at the turn of the fourteenth century to only 1,300 less than a century later.[14]

Far from homogeneous, Siena's population around its peak in the early fourteenth century was composed of nobles, merchants, tradespeople, industrialists, day laborers, clergy, and others from a broad range of callings, as well as foreigners and immigrants from outside the city and its territories. Nevertheless, in a form very similar to Livy's class division of republican Rome, Siena's civil society was stratified into four reasonably distinct groups.[15] First, although not necessarily foremost, were the *casati*—the noble houses and families of aristocratic bearing such as the Tolomei, Salimbeni, Piccolomini, Ugurgieri, Sansedoni, Bonsignori, and Malavolti. Next were the *popolo grasso*, composed of upper-middle-class bankers, merchants, wool manufacturers, and other industrialists, as well as retailers, goldsmiths, and most professionals like doctors, judges, and academics. The majority of citizens—the *popolo minuto*—included master craftsmen, clerics, and farmers, together with other wage earners such as masons and soldiers. Finally, there were noncitizens, without complete rights and protections, such as servants and retainers of large households, foreigners, and some day laborers—in short, the majority of the population.

Full citizens of Siena, as Bowsky describes them, "were men who possessed a specified minimum of wealth, resided within the city, and demonstrated the ability and willingness to pay taxes and to perform real and personal services that the commune demanded of them."[16] In return they received the full and not inconsiderable measure of both privilege and protection that Siena and its commune could offer, with relatively minor liabilities. Indeed, histories of commune life are replete with references to the physical and economic safeguards offered to citizenry, including the Bonsignori bank stabilization mentioned earlier.

Within the ranks of citizens, the casati were expressly precluded from holding high state or municipal office through most of the period under discussion, for fear of a return to feudalism. By contrast to, say, Florence or Venice, long-standing rivalries between casati effectively meant that a monolithic *signoria* could not be easily established. Instead, the rival magnate families of Tolomei and Salimbeni, or of Malavolti and Piccolomini, could be balanced off in practice with great houses of the upper-middle class at the time, like the Montanini and Petroni.[17] Furthermore, it would be a mistake to think in modern class-conscious terms. The new bourgeois families did not see themselves as at odds with the older magnate families. For both there was a profound concern for peace and for limiting any magnate bellicosity and, if anything, accord was required. Other overlaps of interest also existed between the two groups. In commerce and industry, for example, guilds and other business associations flourished, although the commune, unlike the Florentines, took a dim view of guilds, largely because of their monopolistic tendencies and concomitant abilities to raise the prices of goods and services. Somewhat drastically (and wrongfully, as it turned out), all guilds were outlawed in 1305, except the Arte della Lana and the Mercanzia, an association of Siena's five major guilds.[18]

Family life, first and foremost, was patriarchal. Wives and children were expected to do their master's bidding. In practice, however, as we see from the delightful example of the Merchant of Prato, husband and wife could also be joined in a partnership of considerable give-and-take, mutual respect, and common direction.[19] Typically she was in charge of the household and he took care of the family business, although the interests in both domains often overlapped. Families of the well-to-do were also very large and extended to include relatives, retainers, servants, and even business associates, in addition to the immediate family. Child bearing and rearing was a priority, particularly in favor of male children who could carry on the name and traditions of the family. Lending assistance to needy or less fortunate family members was also a duty and thus commonplace. In addition, piety, especially in old age, was widespread, countenancing strong ties with the church, even over otherwise secular matters. In short, medieval families of Siena, particularly among the well-to-do, were very large, primarily preoccupied with their own destiny and day-to-day business, although certainly not to the exclusion of service to the larger community. They were also pious, formal, and even stern in outward public appearance, and, although not uncaring, much the same at home.

The predominant impression of the city of Siena, apart from the Duomo, or cathedral, and a few other ecclesiastical buildings, was one of dwellings with towers belonging to the casati. By the mid-thirteenth century some fifty-six such defenses and symbols of rank were in existence, although this number varied as towers could be destroyed by the commune in punishment for transgressions by a noble family, or erected as part of a new dwelling.[20] Over time, fire and sheer neglect also took their toll, toppling most remaining towers of noble houses. Probably originally based on the watchtowers and fortresses of the countryside, these urban counterparts were mainly proud signs of power, ownership, and wealth. By contrast, dwellings of ordinary citizens were comparatively low, at two or three stories, and built primarily of timber and adobe, often with masonry front facades and protruding wooden balconies, or *ballatoi*. Generally, municipal buildings lagged behind private property improvements, with the result that council meetings and other governmental deliberations commonly took place in private palazzi, such as the Alessi palace, or in nearby churches. Other public works were often pursued vigorously, especially the aqueducts and channels—or *bottini*—which conveyed precious water from distant streams into the city. The duct feeding Fontebranda, for instance, a large neighborhood fountain near one of the gates to Siena, involved a 1,600-meter underground excavation.[21] In 1267, the commune even seriously considered a project to bring water from a spring some 25 kilometers away, abandoning it in the end as too expensive. The Florentine Dante Alighieri probably had a point when he mocked the Sienese about their constant search for the "Spring of Diana"—the mythical underground water source that would have solved all their problems.[22] Instead, numerous fountains and grottoes, both large and small, were scattered at low points in the terrain serving surrounding neighborhoods. These also became places for community gatherings, particularly in the evenings and on holidays, a tradition kept alive to this day. Dispersion of fountains throughout the city also served to help fight fires, a constant threat in medieval Siena, which were also contained by destroying buildings and creating firebreaks. Subsequently the commune paid property owners compensation for damages, although less so in the masse where they were trying to discourage makeshift and shanty settlements.

Overall, among the public works and the private buildings there was a sort of dialogue between the architecture of the commune and the proud display of palace-owning patricians, merchants, and industrialists. Public taste and the setting of standards was of mutual concern, as was the more general source of pride and self-respect that came from the city's appearance. To both ends, legislation and special municipal authorities proved to be quite effective. From 1290 onward three selected public officials, or *praetores*, controlled all new construction in the city, and routine inspections of streets for general cleanliness each Saturday could bring substantial fines for violators.[23] Sometimes sanitary legislation was also enforced through all-purpose denouncers, who were paid a small wage for being vigilant about matters of theft, garbage disposal, illegal activities, and the like. Municipal commonplaces of today, such as a fire department, were also organized during the late thirteenth and early fourteenth centuries. Legislatively, community good usually overrode private interests. Demolition of old dwellings and reconstruction, for instance, had to be completed to the commune's satisfaction in a timely manner, and the taking of property for public purposes was an acceptable and well-respected practice. Again like today, debt financing was common in Siena, as elsewhere in Tuscany, as the commune pressed ahead with ambitious plans and public improvements to the city's and the contado's infrastructure. The last three decades of the thirteenth century, for example, saw massive concentrations in roadway improvements, bridge construction, street widening, and so on, not only to improve appearance but to better access and thus maintain the timely provision of relatively inexpensive foodstuffs and other consumer goods throughout the city-state. Similar motivations can also be found for justifying the extensive land reclamation and pasture improvement—or *bonifica*—that occurred at much the same time.[24]

Politically, the terzi—or tripartite divisions of the city mentioned earlier—were further subdivided into *popoli* and *contrade*. The popoli were administrative districts, drawing their names mainly from parish churches. In 1318 they numbered thirty-six, largely corresponding to the spatial distribution of population.[25] Overlapping these administrative units were the more numerous contrade or neighborhoods, reaching as many as sixty in number before the Great Plague of 1348, and before formally becoming rationalized to seventeen in 1729 by decree of Princess Violante of Bavaria.[26] This division into contrade also gave Siena a bona fide sense of factionalism, unlike most other places, replete with symbolic references to birds and animals such as the goose, panther, tortoise, and caterpillar. Even today for a Sienese, one's first allegiance is to one's contrada and then to the city. Rivalries among *contradaioli* from different neighborhoods are fierce, and there are numerous stories describing family feuds over where children are to be born to couples from different contrade. More formally, contrade are social as well as political entities, with clubs, local bars, and even museums. Throughout the emphasis is on mutual aid and support for the contradaioli. Dues are levied and other fund-raising activities regularly take place to support the welfare of the contrada. Although remarkably classless in the deference and respect paid among members, the governing organization— Società di Contrada—is presided over by a top official or *priore*. Membership is by birth, or through bloodline relationships, and every major right of passage for a Sienese from birth to death falls within the contrada. Even today many baptisms, for example, are performed at the fountain of the contrada.[27]

By the middle of the thirteenth century a populist government emerged in Siena.[28] It was not strictly democratic—certainly not by today's definitions and standards—but antimonopolistic, broadly representative, republican in spirit, and a strong departure from the earlier feudal seignorial system. For at least the first one hundred years or so, and with different specific organizations and ruling hierarchies at different times, regimes consisted of several basic components. There was, for instance, a broadly based council—the Council of the Popolo, or Council of the Bell—with citizen representation from the terzi and popoli. The post of Capitano del Popolo was created in 1252 and paid for by the commune. Often there was a Podestà who headed the Council and was the commune's supreme magistrate. By constitutional prohibition the Podestà was non-Sienese and typically served for a relatively short six-month term. Over the years Podestà were successfully recruited from other communes like Bologna, Modena, and Parma, where a similar experience in government could be found, but never from Florence, Siena's great rival close by to the north. There was also usually a war captain—the Capitano di Guerra—hired to lead Sienese mercenaries and other armed forces on defensive as well as extraterritorial campaigns. This became a permanent office in 1323, and was first held on an intermittent basis from about 1298. Again the term of service was relatively short, although perhaps the most famous holder of the office—Guidoricco di Niccolò da Fogliano of Reggio—served for six and a half years from 1327 and was recalled again in 1351, eventually dying in office in 1352. With the issue of civil order and peace uppermost in the commune's collective mind, all three of these offices—the Capitano del Popolo, the Podestà, and the Capitano di Guerra—assumed responsibilities and, especially during the conditions of famine, resulting civil unrest, and family feuding of the 1330s and 1340s, all three offices conducted regular searches for weapons, mounted patrols, and organized watches. In addition to these offices, there were other magistracies, including the Maggior Sindaco, or guardian of the constitution. Among other things, this magistrate conducted an audit of city officials dating from about 1270, held jurisdiction over building codes and other legislation, and informed the Council and other city officials about constitutional issues involved in their deliberations. Finally, there was the ruling oligarchy, priory, or *monti* itself, with responsibility for formulating policy and directing the affairs of the commune. Members of this group were drawn from numerous eligible citizens in the popoli and terzi, again serving relatively short terms during which they were frequently sequestered in the Palazzo Pubblico to avoid bias and corruption. Members of the casati, as mentioned earlier, were usually expressly precluded from holding these high offices. In contrast to the Florentines, who saw their politics in terms of groups, guilds, and business associations, or the Venetians with their closed-book seignorial form, the Sienese were conspicuously broad and inclusive in their legislative and administrative conduct.

Over the years this form of government evolved, but was invariably elected. Moreover, in spite of many tests of strength and will, it resisted overthrow and provided Siena with long periods of stability and prosperity. Beginning around 1236 there was the Regime of the Twenty-Four Priors, a

Ghibelline-dominated organization primarily of the bourgeoisie or popolo, with strong alliances to the Hohenstaufen and the Holy Roman Empire. In those days the Council was composed of fifty men from each terzo and headed by a Podestà. Failure of the Hohenstaufen regime brought about the eventual collapse of Ghibellinism in Tuscany and a return to Guelfist power. The death of Manfred, the Hohenstaufen Frederick II's son, in 1266, and the defeat of the Ghibellines at Colle Val d'Elsa in 1269, further accelerated the rise of Guelfism. In a transitional step toward a more stable and representative government, the nobles and popolo grasso seized power in 1271, abolished the office of the Capitano del Popolo and installed the Thirty-Six Governors and Defenders of the Commune of Siena. Shortly thereafter, the Capitano del Popolo was reinstated and the Regime of the Nine or Noveschi began in 1278, lasting the following seventy-seven years. These Nine Governors and Defenders of the People of Siena, as they were officially called, were given sweeping powers and responsibilities, and quickly became involved in all aspects of government. Over the years some five hundred citizens were office holders in the Noveschi, some serving as many as six to eight times, while the majority served at least two or three times. Consequently, some families, such as the Petroni and Montanini mentioned earlier, became closely associated with high office of the commune, and the specter of a ruling class system or hierarchy emerged. Peace was broken, however, in 1355 on the occasion of Charles IV's entry into Siena with some thousand knights and the successful revolt of magnates and popolo minuto against the Noveschi. The treasury, or Biccherna, was sacked along with the Palazzo Pubblico and the Mercanzia. Prisoners were set free and government records publicly burned in the Campo. A new regime of seven syndics and a Podestà was then selected, eventually becoming the twelve, and ushering in a period of political instability that lasted until the early fifteenth century. Subsequent communal rule by a monti, drawn from the city's three leading citizen groups, returned Siena to stability and relative prosperity, in spite of the political crisis and repression of the conspiracy lead by Antonio Petrucci in 1456.

This regime was eventually replaced, toward the end of the fifteenth century, by a political aristocracy of nine monti, leading, finally, to the decline of the Sienese republic in the early sixteenth century and passage into Florentine hands.

For many years, the governmental style and administration of Siena was most strongly influenced by the regime of the Nine or Noveschi. In spite of their eventual deposition in 1355, most of their legislation and ways of doing things remained in practice for many years to come. Generally, the success of the Sienese government can be attributed less to innovation than to what Bowsky refers to as "pragmatic experimentation." Institutionalization and regularization of government actions were emphasized, and effectiveness and efficiency in resolving issues and providing services were frequently overriding aims. There was also the Nine's legacy of direct participation at all levels of government and in all manner of public offices, both high and low and with or without potential renumeration. To give some idea about the extensiveness of this partic-ipatory process, consider an outline of government office holding, say, in the first part of the fifteenth century.[29] At that time 9 men, plus a captain, were elected from a 42-man contrade to serve bimonthly terms between elections. The result was that a total of some 480 people were elected in an eight-year period of the regime. In short, 60 citizens ruled the commune in a year and, considering the number of eligible citizens, probably around one in six were in government at any given time. In addition there were many other official posts to be filled, especially outside of the city proper, in the contado. Small wonder that the magnates and the popolo grasso backed the regime during the rebellion of 1218. Their influence was pervasive. Nevertheless, this outbreak did broaden representation within official circles as the government continued to live in harmony with various elements of what today we might call civil society. The Noveschi in particular used to regularly consult business and opinion leaders through so-called secret councils, involving as many as fifty men per terzo. Through these consultations political ideas and plans could be explored prior to any official action. Finally, success came from a strong if not sustained record of keeping the peace and providing food, shelter, and a sense of pride to Sienese citizenry.

Needless to say, civic values and aspirations permeated practically all aspects of Sienese life. Not only was civic duty required of all citizens—if nothing else, to keep the machinery of government running—but it was usually rendered with pride and enthusiasm. The three civic values of *iustitia, libertas, et honor*—justice, freedom, and honor—were paramount in the lives of most Sienese, even to the exclusion of many facets of private life.[30] While the first two of these values have already been elaborated upon, the last—*honor civitatis*—can be seen clearly in the symbiotic relationship between government and culture that flowered during much of the republican period. Artistic and intellectual development, for instance, flourished through special offices and supervisors of public works, such as the *operarii* of the cathedral, who were appointed for life. In addition, the University of Siena was founded in 1224 and, together with similar institutions in places like Padua and Modena, it remained independent of the church for some time as a center of Aristotelianism and objectivity.[31] Furthermore, for practical as well as cultural reasons, the role of the growing intellectual class became important and even vital to the commune, which often paid handsomely to attract scholars to Siena. Clearly as governance and administration became more complicated and far flung, the specialization that often resulted required new skills and knowledge. Also, by frequently traveling from one center of learning to another—an activity that became customary at the time—intellectuals could exchange information and keep the community of their employ abreast of current learning, cultural affairs, and other matters of the world. The moral and social consciousness of religion should not be underestimated, however, especially given the civic Christianity that grew up around Saint Catherine of Siena, in the middle of the fourteenth century, for instance, and around both San Bernardino and the blessed Ambrogio Sansedoni sometime earlier. Consequently, confraternities—societies of piety—were quite

Il Campo, the field, with the Casino dei Nobili and the Palazzo Sansedoni in the background.

common in Siena and the city's devotion to the Virgin Mary only emphasizes the reciprocal relationship that must have existed there between church and state.[32]

Not unexpectedly, over the years, much has changed in Sienese life. Both the city and the countryside around it have become truly modern in outlook and in many accouterments. Still, a specialized food industry flourishes, as it did in the past, as does banking and the city's fine university. Most notable, though, has been the persistence throughout of the contrade and the hold this form of local factionalism still has over the Sienese. It remains both a defining aspect of life and a driving force behind Siena's strong sense of civic pride.

SIENA'S PIAZZA DEL CAMPO

Of all the places in Siena, the Piazza del Campo remains in a category by itself—one usually reserved for only the most venerable of religious sites. Even from antiquity, when it was still architecturally a relatively undeveloped site, the phrase *Campum Fori*, or Forum in the Roman sense, was reserved for it as a term of special dignity.[33] In fact, through much of its medieval past, a special office, known as *procustodia campi fori*, kept the piazza clear of stones, bricks, timber, dirt, and other rubble, and prevented unwanted activities from occurring, such as animal slaughtering and skinning; the prohibition extending to nearby streets.[34] Like many temporary marketplaces, proper stalls could be erected at appropriate times within the Campo for the sale of all manner of commodities. After marketing, however, all was to be removed. Even bankers were discouraged from operating in public for fear of an unseemly display of usury in this city of piety and civic virtue.

According to an authoritative statute of 1262, the Campo was originally divided into two parts—a lower Campo del Mercato, or marketplace, and the upper Campo di San Paolo.[35] At that time, the original church of San Paolo and a thin row of houses ran roughly through the middle of the present piazza. Nearby, today's Palazzo Pubblico is located on the former site of a customshouse and gate in the city wall, which provided access from a long valley stretching to the south between the hilly mass of the Castelvecchio and the developing ridge line of San Martino. Nevertheless, even in its early piecemeal form, the Campo was the meeting place of the terzi—the three major political divisions of the city mentioned earlier—and literally the symbolic and geographic center of Siena. Work to clear the site and extend the Campo began in 1290, culminating in most of what we see today by the middle of the fourteenth century.[36] This period also roughly coincides with the rule of the Nine—Siena's most influential government regime—and corresponding displays of public wealth and grandeur. For the first time, the building program of the commune and other state-sponsored cultural activities began to rival and outstrip those of the nobles and the church. These distinctions are less important, however, when we remember the mixed scheme of government and participation largely without reference to class. Clearly the Sienese magnates, along with the wealthy *popolani,* identified strongly with the commune and even sought personal satisfaction in its glorification.

The statute of 1262 also set out nineteen articles indicating the manner in which the Campo could be developed. Gradually restrictions were placed on the height and other appurtenances of surrounding buildings, as well as conditions of entry and egress. Later, in 1297, a further public prescription was made requiring bifurcated windows and other architectural features around the piazza.[37] By now the Piazza del Campo was quite large, measuring some 140 meters by 100 meters, and surrounded in an almost semicircular arc by the palazzi of the Chigi, Sansedoni, and Elei, together with the Casino dei Nobili, which formed part of the Mercanzia. These buildings also accommodated a substantial grade change of at least one story from the Via Banchi di Sotto and Via di Città immediately to the north. In fact, far from flat, the Piazza del Campo slopes over 2 meters in the north-south direction and is inclined upward from the center of its radius over 4 meters in an easterly direction and over 3 to the west.

In 1343 the Fonte Gaia—fountain of joy—was constructed on the northern edge of the Piazza del Campo, fed by an aqueduct measuring some 20 or so kilometers in length and underlining Siena's capacity to overcome its almost total dependence on external sources of water supply. The present Fonte Gaia is a copy made by Sarocchi in 1868 of an original version installed by Jacopo di Pietro (or Jacopo della Quercia) between 1409 and 1417.[38] The fountain's sculpture celebrates the two primary symbols of Siena—the *lupa*, or she-wolf from the founding myth, not unlike Rome's, and the Madonna. In 1346 the surface of the piazza was paved in a fishbone pattern of brick, divided into nine segments radiating from a sculptured central drain—*gavinone*—at the lowest point on the site. Not coincidentally, the Fonte Gaia was relocated in the middle of the radiating segments of paving opposite the gavinone. Before that it was located on one of the *costole,* or ribs, dividing the paving into segments. Clearly the nine-part divisions is a direct reference to the Noveschi. Only a little less directly, it also reflects the symbolic and geographic joining of the terzi at this central location within the city.[39]

The adjoining Palazzo Pubblico forms the frontispiece to the piazza along the south and the focal point for the radial paving pattern and general layout of the Campo. It was originally occupied by offices of the Podestà, the Nine, the Biccherna, and other magistrates, with adequate courtyard and reception areas to conduct audiences with Siena's citizenry. The building was completed between 1297 and 1310 and remains a splendid example of medieval civic architecture. Fittingly, inauguration of the project was, in the words of the day, "for the honor of the Sienese commune and the beauty of the city."[40] Some time later, in 1325, the cornerstone was laid for the elegant tower rising over 80 meters to one side of the palazzo—the Torre del Mangia—reputedly named for Giovanni di Duccio, popularly referred to as the "profit eater" or simply *mangia* (eater) for his role in ringing the tower bells, with was thought to be a superfluous ceremonial frill by many at the time. The square brick chimney of the tower was built by the brothers Minuccio and Francesco di Rinaldo from Perugia, after which rises the travertine and marble crowning piece affording views over the city and off into the distance, as far away as Monte Amiata.[41] Later still, the elaborate Cappella di Piazza was constructed, adjoining both the tower and the palazzo, to commemorate release from the Great Plague of 1348. Begun in 1352 by Domenico d'Agostino, work on the chapel was completed around 1376 by Giovanni di Cecco, who saw to the final positioning of the pillars and the roof.[42] Throughout the early stages of planning and construction, Giovanni Pisano, the head of works for the nearby Duomo from 1284 until 1295, was influential in advising on the layout and design of the Campo and the surrounding buildings.[43] In spite of the grandeur of the fourteenth-century building program, however, the original two-part division of the public space remained, with the Palazzo Pubblico separating the Piazza del Campo above from the new marketplace and customshouse further down the hillside. Understandably, project costs were high, although justified to the aim of glorifying the commune, and included adequate compensation for owners of dispossessed property.

In addition to this external celebration of commune life, the interior rooms of the Palazzo Pubblico were adorned with paintings of heroic moments from Siena's rule of the contado, such as Simone Martini's magnificent landscape depicting Guidoriccio da Fogliano riding victorious over rebel forces in 1328, and political allegories calling attention to civic virtues. No less a place than the Sala dei Nove—the meeting room of the Nine—contained Ambrogio Lorenzetti's three extraordinary frescoes: "Effects of Good Government," "Effects of Bad Government," and "Good Government in the City and Good Government in the Countryside."[44] In the first of these representations of civic political philosophy, the ruler of Siena, dressed like the city's coat of arms in black and white, can be seen flanked on the right by the seated figures of "Magnanimity," "Temperance," and "Justice," representing cardinal virtues, and on the left by other figures depicting "Prudence," "Fortitude," and "Peace." The figure of "Justice," on the far left, balances scales with the aid of angels and the oversight of "Wisdom," representing "distributive justice" on the one hand and "commutative justice" on the other. Clearly these are Thomistic and Aristotelian themes. Beneath these eight main figures are other symbolic references to Sienese civic life, including the she-wolf suckling two infants—an obvious connection to

Roman republican virtues. Also under the figures on the left-hand side are twenty-four citizens representing the pious rulers of Siena during the Ghibelline Signory between 1236 and 1271. On the right-hand side are soldiers holding bound prisoners and other noncitizens of the city. Even without the written explanation across the base of the frescoe—the *cartello*—the Noveschi undoubtedly would have had the cultural insight necessary to enjoy the intellectual game posed by Lorenzetti's frescoes as they deliberated on the matters of state before them.[45] Noticeably, Siena was different in these regards from other Tuscan and northern Italian communes, with its insistent institutional orientation away from individual aggrandizement and toward *bonum comune*—the common good.

The uses of the Piazza del Campo were and continue to be numerous and varied, commensurate with its significance and central role within the city. It was, for instance, an open-air hall or church where clergy like San Bernadino would conduct discussions and give sermons. Similarly, it was frequently used for secular ceremonies and as a political forum. Certainly throughout much of the thirteenth century the piazza was large enough to accommodate Siena's entire urban population, which it did on occasions of severe duress, when the populace prayed together for deliverance. As mentioned earlier, the piazza also served as a regular marketplace and more informally as a meeting place for individuals from all walks of life. Today the Campo maintains a similar character and serves a similar function as the site for cafe life, as a venue for promenading by well-to-do Sienese women in their finery, accompanied by escorts, or simply as a refuge amid the crowd. In spite of the paving, it also preserves in use its original fieldlike quality, with tourists often found picnicking on the Campo floor as they might in an open field. As we might expect from such a large and venerable place, it remains the site of festivals and public ceremonies.

The Piazza del Campo also served, for a time, as part of a vast underground storage for grain, desperately needed during periods of siege and famine.[46] A depiction from a Biccherna tablet shows the allocation of grain from pits below ground in the Campo, managed by the city treasurer. In addition, records show that the custom of selling flour *a le tine*—by the tub—to the poor at low prices in the Piazza was very common, especially during times of duress. More generally, enclosed spaces beneath or within public rights-of-way, as well as warehouse facilities in institutions like the Hospital of Santa Maria della Scala, or even in private palazzi, were used to store grain as part of *monizione*—a universal set-aside program contributed to by citizens. The practice of subterranean storage, began at twenty-five points around the city in 1460, came at the suggestion of Pius II, a native of nearby Pienza, formerly known as Enea Silvio Piccolomini and a member of one of Siena's great magnate houses. Test results were so favorable, with preservation up to seven or nine years, that storage was expanded to 200 locations under piazzas and streets, with a total capacity of some 32,000 bushels of grain.[47]

In the everyday life of the medieval Sienese, the Piazza del Campo was also the site of "war games"—a ritualized "blowing off of steam" on the part of an often otherwise restless population, especially among the youth. In one game—*Pugna*—a sort of organized fistfight took place between sparring factions, invariably representing different contrade or neighborhoods.[48] Each faction, at a prearranged signal, would enter the piazza, usually from the main streets on the lower side, and try to force the opposing faction to retreat from the Campo, thus "abandoning the field," so to speak. Afterward, participants would all join hands and dance as a sign of camaraderie. Similar war games with sticks and lances, called *Elmora*, or stone throwing, called *Battaglia de' Sassi*, also took place, as well as ball games, such as *Pallone*, where the ritual would start by dropping a ball from the Mangia tower high above the Campo. Indeed, a French mercenary captain was astonished to discover at the height of a siege that Sienese youth dropped their arms and engaged in a game of Pallone. The ritual of Pugna continued at least until 1816, although the Elmora and Battaglia de' Sassi were banned as being too dangerous certainly by the end of the thirteenth century. Pallone, by contrast, was played as recently as 1904 and

1909. In keeping with similar rituals in other places, the Campo was also the site of bullfights—*caccia de' tori*—and bull races, as well as other live spectacles involving men and animals.[49]

Finally, the Campo is probably best known for its horse race—the *palio*, or more specifically the *palio alla tonda*, as distinct from the earlier *palio alla lunga*, which was not run around the piazza but from point to point through city streets.[50] The term palio derives from the latin *pallium* and refers to a rectangular piece of cloth, honoring a patron saint or, in this case, The Virgin, and offered as a prize in a tournament or race. In Siena the two remaining regular palios both honor the Madonna in different ways. The first, held on July 2—the day of Visitation—celebrates the time in 1594 when, during famine and pestilence, the Sienese turned for deliverance to the Madonna in the Via dei Provenzani (also an area notorious for prostitution at the time), where miracles had been witnessed. The palio was first run in 1659. The second, held on August 16—a day after the Assumption—is a part of that traditional celebration and was first run in 1709, becoming a regular event after 1802. Over the years additional palios have been held to celebrate extraordinary events for the Sienese, such as the end of World War II, the 600th anniversary of Saint Catherine's birth in 1947, the lunar landing in 1969, and the 500-year anniversary of the Monte dei Paschi bank in 1972. The earliest palio run in the Campo seems to date from 1583, although there is some disagreement about that fact. Certainly, regular events took place from 1656 onward, and in 1935 Mussolini decreed that the term "palio" would be reserved for the Sienese event.[51]

As a competition the palio is contested, nowadays, among ten of the seventeen contrade in a horse race run three times around the Campo in a centripetal clockwise direction. The event begins, however, three days earlier with the assignment of horses by lot—the *Tratta*—among the competing contrade. Several trials, or *prova*, are then conducted before the final event, in order to judge the likely outcome of the race and, therefore, the tactics to be employed by each competitor, as well as allowing the jockeys, or *fantini*, to become familiar with their mounts. The piazza is also transformed for these events and the race proper into a sand-covered track around its perimeter with barricades and viewing platforms to mark out the course and bring some semblance of order to the enormous crowd of spectators. Race day begins with a spectacular parade of young men representing each contrada, the *alfieri*, along with the horse, its jockey, and other symbol bearers. As they move slowly around the track, pairs of alfieri perform very graceful and yet acrobatic moves, in unison, with large flags bearing the crest of their contrada. In moves like the *alzata* the flags are thrown some two stories in the air, while in others like the *sottogamba* the flags almost brush the surface of the Campo. At the end of the parade the palio banner, depicting the Virgin and symbols of each of the ten competing contrade, is displayed before the public on an ox-drawn cart. After a sequence of complex starting procedures the race is under way, the combatative jostling for position begins, and an eventual winner emerges, sometimes without its rider. Intrigue among competitors is so intense that the fantini are hired from outside of the city as independent agents of the contrade. This arrangement also avoids the internal discord of blame being placed on another Sienese for failure to achieve an acceptable result. Interestingly, second place in the race is usually considered the greatest loss because presumably the horse could have won, and teamwork often takes place among representatives of strongly allied contrade, especially when one is claimed to have a better chance of winning.[52]

As a metaphor, the palio sums up many aspects of Sienese life, character, and tradition. Among other things, it represents processes of constant renewal, the triumph of life and death and with it, the longevity of the republic, as well as a reordering of prestige among the competing contrade.[53] More literally, with the surrounding suckling symbolism of the pacifiers worn and used by winning contradaioli, the ever-present images of the she-wolf with the two sons of Remus and the Madonna del Latte, rebirth is an essential part of the ritual, together with closely associated gender-specific themes involved with rites of passage and courtship. This is clearly evident during the competition itself and the preceding *passeggio*, replete with phallic and other sexual references. Related aspects concerning the sacred and profane are also not inconspicuous.[54] The "Virgin-harlot" association, for instance, is present in the origins of the celebration of the Madonna of Provenzano; in addition to being called the City of the Virgin, Siena was also known as *Civitas Veneris*—the city of carnal love. Finally, the "principle of limited good," referring to a type of civic virtue whereby one gains but only at another's expense, is intrinsic to the competition and the bragging rights that go with winning. Quite apart from being an engaging event, the palio is a ritual of rejuvenation for the city and a reconfirmation of its civic tradition.

The shape and appearance of the Campo—the setting for all these events—can be accounted for by several interpretations. One explanation is simply evolutionary. Available property parcels were assembled by the commune. Selected buildings were then removed or refurbished to create a space that was eventually paved and architecturally adorned in a sequence of building operations over time. In most respects, this explanation closely follows what is known to have transpired. Another explanation would portray the Piazza del Campo and the Palazzo Pubblico together as simply a larger and more grandiose version of the common practice among well-to-do Sienese of building a palatial residence, a tower commensurate with position and rank, and a fine piazza, with adjacent interior courtyard, setting off the whole composition. Again the typological argument involved befits the time and was certainly well known and accepted during construction of the Campo. It is also consistent with the underlying communal idea of a close association between civil society and government, as well as simply repeating the two-part division of the Campo that existed before—albeit at a much larger scale.

At a more detailed level though, the reminders of republican rule and republican virtue are expressively incorporated within the Campo and the facade of the Palazzo Pubblico. The nine segments of paving, for example, converging at the center of the piazza's composition, clearly invokes the sociopolitical idea of a model of unity built on diversity. This interpretation is further underlined by the elaborate architectural rendering of the drainage

The running of the palio in Siena's Piazza del Campo.

opening, where all the separate flows of water from across the Campo converge and become one. It is also an obvious direct reference, as already noted, to the Noveschi, and the constant expressive reference to "threes" immediately recalls the locational logic of the piazza at the merger of the terzi and, therefore, at the center of Sienese life; the accepted civic practice of well-to-do women enjoying the passeggio with two servants walking in front and behind; the Holy Trinity, and so on. Finally, the shape of the Campo can be seen as the symbol of a single event, in this case the unlikely triumph of the Sienese and their way of life against the Florentines during the Battle of Montaperti in 1260. At one point in this conflict, or so it is told, a heavenly light appeared above the City of Siena, as seen from the battlefield, which was immediately attributed to the protection of the Madonna hovering overhead. The iconography immediately calls to mind images of the Madonna della Misericordia with her outstretched cloak sheltering the populace and City of Siena below, as well as the shape of the *mantello* in part of Lorenzetti's masterpiece, the *Maestà*. As at least one historian has pointed out, there is a strong correspondence between the arched outline of these cloaked figures and the plan shape of the Campo.[55] Eventually, in a reversal of fortune from Montaperti, time, circumstances, and an independent way of life ran out for the Sienese. Between 1555 and 1559 the republic collapsed and the Florentine Medicis were installed in quite a different form of government. Fortunately this course of events did not end there in downfall and ignominy. Many of the institutions and civic artifacts of that republican period persist today, including a fine university, a continuing legacy of good government, and socially cohesive neighborhoods with their own symbolic identities— not to mention the unusual horse race.

UNDERLYING THEMES OF CIVIC REALISM

The rest of this book is also about what appropriately might now be called *civic realism*—a concept based on the belief that it is along the politico-cultural division between civil society and the state that the urban architecture of the public realm is made best, especially when the reach of both spheres extends simultaneously up to a civilization's loftier aims and down to the needs and aspirations of its marginalized populations. By contrast, the other alternatives, which have been operating for some time in many parts of the world, are not very attractive. On one side there are the enclaves, exclusive precincts, and private realms commonly found in corporately dominated urban and suburban circumstances. On the other are state edifices and places of authoritarian rhetorical splendor. Frequently the state bungles when it builds exclusively in its own image or at variance with the rest of society—an error that is painfully evident, for example, in public housing. Unsatisfactory results also often occur when the city building process is turned over to the market forces of civil society. Consequently, the current perceived crisis in public space making is often less a matter of inadequate design technique as it is a muddled uncertainty about appropriate relationships between the state and civil society. In some places and at certain times, the private sphere appears to be on the ascendancy, whereas in other places and times it seems to be of diminishing influence. By contrast, during more exaggerated moments of interaction between the two spheres— either through the resurgence of one relative to the other, or because of comparable strength—the making of public space seems to have been that much easier and more obvious than at other times. As we shall see, this was definitely the case in post-Franco Barcelona and, for different reasons, in Mitterrand's Paris, as well as in New York City both before and after the turn of this century. Certainly the aftermath of great sociopolitical conflagrations, like revolutions and World Wars I and II, can become such moments, as was the case in both Ljubljana and Rome, respectively.

Nevertheless, clearly it would be wrong to put everything on hold or to use past formulae for making public places. These are, after all, different times, but times with needs nonetheless. Nor does it seem appropriate to retreat into the rapidly expanding virtual worlds of information and communication, in spite of their superficial egalitarian appeal and apparent ideological freedom.[56] It is not at all clear, for instance, that many of the present disparities between "haves" and "have nots" in society won't become exaggerated further. By contrast, it is reasonably obvious that particular regimes control these information-based worlds, thus not structurally altering the existence of power arrangements and their expressive needs. Furthermore, the "talking heads" aspect of this mental habitat effectively denies the bodily engagement with public space so essential to a full liberating and edifying experience of the public realm.[57] Even if this partial experience was to change appreciably, the question of what the public realm should be like would still remain open. Therefore ways of seeing, speculating about, appreciating, and even guiding the cultural politics involved in shaping civic places are always useful and, given the alleged disappearance of the public sphere, quite timely.

Having laid claim to the idea that civic realism can be both inherent to the public realm in general as well as specific to particular times, places, and arrangements between a state and its people through civil society, the rest of this book explores relationships between urban architectural expression and democratic sociopolitical practices, ultimately arguing against the idea that as the world changes, so somehow organically does architectural expression. Rather than simply being a matter of from a set of forces to a form—consistent with some positivistic doctrines—there is usually a discontinuous cultural development at work. Until relevant and coherent aesthetic principles are devised or appropriated, new expression cannot be given to broad and perhaps mounting societal pressures, even when the arbitrariness of architectural signs can be overcome in the first instance. Instead, nothing much will happen, or there will be simply an extrapolation of past aesthetic practices, often with strained effects like the classical postmodernism and reduced modernism of recent years. In short, cultural activities do not march in lock-step fashion with sociopolitical and economic orders. The urban grid of New York City, for instance, was convenient, utilitarian, and somewhat abstract until given more palpable and visceral meaning during, say, the Victorian period. Similarly, as we have already seen, the populist government in Siena was firmly ensconced before the Piazza del

Campo was constructed. By contrast, the planning strategy and design concepts for the urban public places of Barcelona, as we shall discover, were well developed long before they emerged publicly with the end of Franco's Spain. No doubt a certain amount of avant-gardism can be useful in expanding design thinking and pushing it along, although it is by no means fully consistent with other requirements of civic realism. In the case of Paris, Mitterrand's challenge of the *Grand Projets*, for instance, was already in place well before the designing began.

Both the physical character and program of the Piazza del Campo clearly reflected aspects of what might be looked for in good civic realism. First, while expressing many changing aspects of government and civil society, certain long-lived and transcendent qualities remained common, thus providing a civic face for Siena that markedly influenced generations to come. The strong overall shape of the piazza, for instance, with its relatively plain surfaces, as well as historical and mythical references, formed a robust framework for all manner of uses. The wide-open and semi-abstract pavement continued this theme by allowing many events to take place without functional constraints, yet requiring each of them to adhere to a certain decorum. Even the exuberance and pell-mell of the palio was ordered, ritualized, and enabled by the space of the Campo, and the surrounding architecture with specific decorative programs, icons, and heraldry provided a broad historical narrative of the place, a common thread of which was civic pride, independence, and duty. Second, the self-same size, scope, grandeur, public iconography, and program of the Campo was and remains a constant reminder to future governments and societies of their civic responsibilities. The literal homilies to good and bad government offered explicit advice and criticism, yet clearly affirmed the veracity of community rule and the role of different constituents of civil society. In other words, the urban and architectural expression of the Campo presented an interpretable and rather constant challenge to governments, while holding fast on the very idea of civil rule itself. Third, the program, form, and symbolism of the Piazza del Campo embraced everyday life, provided an appropriately formal setting for government, projected a sense of civic well-being, and yet, at the time anyway, was innovative while somehow remaining familiar. Further, the Piazza del Campo amply provided a place for collective practices and rituals, like the pugna of old, the palio, and the passeggio, as well as a place for individual habitation and experience.

Setting Siena aside for a moment, it is also clear that locations and sites for civic realism can be varied and should not be expected only in overtly state-oriented circumstances or by contrast, in prosperous semiprivate situations. As we shall see, the scale and scope of sites and programs will vary, including the overall streetscape and public squares of a city. They cover scattered public places of different sizes and types, such as those found recently in Barcelona; the development of new quarters on the urban periphery, as in post–World War II Rome; central places within cities, like the Piazza del Campo or Rockefeller Center in New York; renewal of abandoned or deteriorating urban precincts, as in contemporary Paris; and improvements in public infrastructure, such as those so clearly evident, for instance, in post–World War I Ljubljana. Nevertheless, one of the important lessons of the Campo is precisely this issue of size and scope. The Piazza del Campo served as the principle civic realm for a relatively local population, certainly in the central Italian context. By contrast, many other large metropolitan public spaces may have had aggrandized state or corporate sponsors, but failed to become truly civic realms in the very necessary senses of sustained local use, collective comprehension, memory and, therefore, attachment. Indeed, Siena is a very pointed reminder that a strong sense of community and civic pride is first and foremost a local phenomenon. The fiercely partisan behavior of the contradaioli still provides and promotes the sociopolitical rationale for the Piazza del Campo, as it did in the past, allowing the Campo, in turn, to become the common property of all seventeen contrade. Clearly, without this factionalism Siena would not be the city it is today and the Campo would not be the place it is either. The lesson to be learned is the necessity of an indivisible localism and an immediate sense of neighborhood or local turf in any larger civic enterprise, suggesting the idea of both practical and conceptual limits in the physical expanse and other related characteristics of viable civic realms. Without seeming to contradict earlier comments about virtual worlds, this notion of local physical participation might be combined with the not too far-fetched concept of virtual communities, operating with comparable civilizing tendencies at a broader urban, megalopolitan, and international scale. In any regard, civic realism is also about different populations within civil society, as well as on its margins, and this is part of their story.

"Things haven't really changed all that much," said Umberto Montadini to himself during a break in proceedings. "It's all a matter of how you see it, and following a few basic principles of good government. . . . Those old farts in the picture had it right. You balanced things on one side, then on the other, and wherever the balance falls, you decide." The council chamber was now full, with various claimants waiting expectantly. "What also hasn't changed is our business," Umberto thought to himself. "It's all about who gets what and where. Take that proposal for the tourist camp on the outskirts of town. . . . The trouble now, though, is how to decide. . . . Is a tourist camp worth a field of olives, a month's maintenance on the Campo, what? I wish Giacomo hadn't dropped the damn flag for his own sake," he mused, changing subjects abruptly. "But he is still young. There's lots of time."

—Pietro Lupino, *Festa**

2

Civic Realms and Public Places

The Plaça dels Països Catalans in Barcelona by Piñón and Viaplana (page 42).

The din in the Plaça de Catalunya was deafening, and the situation was made even worse by car exhaust and the casual use of fireworks. Golden banners, symbolically marked by the bloodied fingers of a fallen hero, waved majestically overhead in the hazy night glare, together with Barcelona's club colors of blue and maroon. "My God, look at the size of the crowd!" yelled Josep to his friend Joan, as they elbowed their way forward. "What did you expect? We did win, after all—and over Real Madrid!" Joan screamed back, getting into the mood of the jubilant crowd swirling around him, in spite of his fatigue from a long day's work.

"Dammit! With this crowd and the oddball shape of this place, I can't figure out where we're going," exclaimed a frustrated Josep as they struggled on. "It's okay! I think I parked over there," said Joan, gesturing to his left. "It just goes to show, they still can't get anything straight, even with the big plans," Josep went on, ignoring his friend's apparent calm and good humor. "Nobody's yet figured out how to bring all the neighborhoods together, even in the middle of town," he continued, defiantly. "They will! They will!" said Joan. "But then again, perhaps not," he reflected, stopping. "After all, remember that we are all born with seny!" "That is," interrupted Josep, "unless we are overcome by rauxa." They looked at each other, laughed, and jumped into the car.

—Pedro A. Lupo-Garcia, *Gent de bé**

Civil society, *sensu lato*, usually denotes political entities, including the state under rule of law; social institutions, such as markets and other associations based on voluntary agreements among citizens; and a public sphere where citizens can engage in public activities and debate among themselves, as well as with the state about matters of public interest.[1] In a more modern and restricted sense, the term normally refers to social organization apart from the state per se, thus opening up the idea of power sharing and a pluralism of interests among government and various elements of civil society.[2] At the best of times there is often a convergence of these interests, as numerous institutions and other entities find something in common across the boundaries that usually separate the state and civil society, and therefore are in a position to create something civic. Naturally enough, the identity and quality of urban spaces are also at stake during these moments of social and political interaction, although less frequently, unfortunately, with the same sense of mutual purpose and élan as one finds, say, in the contemporary city of Barcelona. There an uncommon balance was struck between the undeniable need for a diversity of urban space on the one hand, and an overriding sense of places belonging to a new Barcelona and *Catalunya* on the other.

THE URBAN PUBLIC SPACES OF BARCELONA

Completed between 1981 and 1987, the urban public space projects of Barcelona represent a large and impressive body of public works at widely different scales, spread throughout a city of some 1.7 million people. The program officially began in December 1980 when the mayor, Narcís Serra, appointed a five-member town planning commission to assess the urban issues confronting the city.[3] The members were: Josep-Miguel Abad, the vice mayor; Oriol Bohigas, a legislative delegate; Signor Galofré, a consultant; Gairalt Puidgomènech, a planner; and José Antonio Acebillo, an architect. After examining the Outline City Planning Scheme of 1976, the commission strongly recommended the immediate development of highly specific and much needed open-space projects, both to establish a strong public presence and to help renovate the city. In addition, the commission recommended general adoption of the 1976 planning scheme— a broad metropolitan master plan—although largely as a medium-term reference tool and a normative device covering property transactions among businesses and the general populace within the city. By favoring adoption of a program of specific projects, the commission clearly recognized that the urban space needs of Barcelona were relatively well known and nothing would be gained from pursuing the abstractions of further master planning exercises. In these regards, the commission was also following in the footsteps of earlier contributions to Barcelona's urban realm, such as Idelfons Cerdà's remarkable nineteenth-century extension, the *Eixample* or *Ensanche*.[4] Moreover, the underlying rationale was much the same, namely the improvement of public health and alleviation of poorly serviced and overcrowded living conditions.

Under the direction of Acebillo, a special urban design team was formed in 1981 at the *Ajuntament*, or City Hall, known as the Office of Urban Projects.[5] The first commissions were then quickly conceived and constructed. During the early stages, all public improvements were confined to the project sites themselves, and there were no displacements of population or viable urban functions from surrounding areas. Furthermore, projects were undertaken in all ten districts within Barcelona: Ciutat Vella, Eixample, Sants Montjuïc, Les Corts, Sarrià-Sant Gervasi, Gràcia, Horta-Guinardó, Nous Barris, Sant Andreu, and Sant Martí. This was to be a program for the entire city, but one that would eventually operate in a decentralized manner, fitting the needs of particular geographic locales and groups regardless of their socioeconomic and physical circumstances. Apart from being a local jurisdiction, each district also corresponded to a distinctive area within the city that warranted special urban design consideration. Gràcia, for instance, like several other districts, was once a small town on the outskirts of Barcelona, which eventually became engulfed by urban development during the nineteenth and early twentieth centuries, as Barcelona made its way north from the sea to the hills. Gràcia has an irregular arrangement of small streets and modest-sized buildings for which small paved plazas and pedestrian areas are most appropriate. Sants Monjuïc, by contrast, is more open and diverse in its physical conformation, thus warranting larger-scaled open-space projects. In the beginning, design personnel within the Office of Urban Projects were assigned specifically to each district to become familiar with local needs and to work with citizens, businesses, and other interest groups.

In addition to the Office of Urban Projects, numerous other designers, particularly young architects, were commissioned to carry out projects. Pasqual Maragall, Mayor Serra's socialist successor in 1983, enthusiastically embraced the urban space program and continued to expand its influence. Joan Busquets, a faculty member of the University of Barcelona, also joined the City Hall staff at this time in a supervisory role.[6] By 1987, when Barcelona began to focus its attention on hosting the 1992 Olympic Games, more than 100 urban space projects had been completed, beginning with small-scaled urban plazas and ending with extensive improvements to the Moll de la Fusta along Barcelona's waterfront. Today the number of completed projects stands in excess of 140, as each of the separate districts undertakes its own projects, following the lead of the earlier public works program. Attention has now been turned toward other sorts of related public improvements in housing and transportation.

Three kinds of urban public space projects—plazas, parks, and streets—were completed under the initial program. Some, such as the Plaça Reial and the Parc Güell, were renovations or restorations of existing urban places, whereas many of the others, such as the Plaça dels Països Catalans and the nearby Parc de l'Espanya Industrial, were new improvements within the city. Some plazas, such as the Plaça de la Mercè to be found in Ciutat Vella, or old town, as well as those found in the district of Gràcia, were relatively small, discreet, and hard surfaced. Others, like the Plaça dels Països Catalans, or Sants Plaza, were far more extensive with more dynamic boundary conditions, although equally hard surfaced. Neighborhood parks, such as the Parc del Clot and the Plaça de la Palmera, contain a variety of recreational activities, as well as public artworks by major international artists like Bryan Hunt and Richard

Serra.[7] In the Plaça de la Palmera, for instance, Serra's curving walls are an integral part of the park's life, creatively dividing serene, well-planted, and contemplative spaces from the active terrain of youngsters' games. Other parks, such as the Parc de Joan Miró, on a site formerly occupied by a slaughterhouse, are more extensive and were intended for citywide use. Here varied settings of well-planted areas, open plazas, and sports facilities are found within a single site. Street projects such as the Avinguda de Gaudí, focusing on the well-known Sagrada Família, and the multilevel Via Júlia—the main street of a low-income neighborhood on the outskirts of Barcelona—have created well-appointed pedestrian environments where only vehicular traffic congestion and dilapidated storefronts once existed. Others, such as the early Passeig de Picasso, provide straightforward definition and pedestrian relief on heavily traveled streets, whereas the Moll de Bosch i Alsina, or Moll de la Fusta, extending along much of the city's harborfront, is both a park and a street system combined, simultaneously rerouting traffic, providing a public face to the city, and accommodating leisure-time activities.[8]

Throughout the urban space program, a shared intellectual idea of Barcelona accompanied the strong conviction that the city was in large part something tangible, objective, and capable of renewal. Given this common agenda, however, there was also a tolerance of formal design diversity reminiscent of other moments of Catalan modernism, such as the earlier periods of Antoni Gaudí and Luís Domenech i Montaner, or of Josep Luís Sert. Among the contemporary projects, this diversity extended from the minimalism of the Plaça del Països Catalans, by Piñón and Viaplana, to the expressionistic contexturalism of the Parc de l'Espanya Industrial, by Peña Ganchegui and Rius, as well as more prosaically from softly planted surfaces to the traditionally hard-paved plazas. In the final analysis, a broadly based and authentic Catalan style of place making emerged.

Most of these shared intellectual ideas centered around the University of Barcelona during the 1970s, and teachers such as Manuel de Solà-Morales, author of the Moll de la Fusta, José Rafael Moneo, and particularly the head of the School of Architecture at the time, Oriol Bohigas. Throughout the school, and in special units such as the Urban Planning Laboratory founded by Solà-Morales, the city became a preoccupation. No project rose above the city in importance, and all contributed to what became a shared urban idea. Central to this idea was the perception of Barcelona as an aggregation of different and distinctive quarters or districts, as noted earlier, rather than as a general system of functions. Considerable emphasis was also placed on continuing the significance of the city's traditional morphology, but in new urban-architectural ways, and on a shared regional past of considerable architectural merit. Through a process that Bohigas likened to metastasis, local projects were to be deployed as catalysts for upgrading the overall quality of the city.[9] Thus the value of public improvements could be leveraged substantially and the interaction between elements of the government and civil society stimulated accordingly.

Also underlying Barcelona's open-space program was a strong commitment to diversity in the social arrangement and expression of projects. Indeed, physical and expressive variety among local projects, once broad norms and intentions had been established, was seen as a matter of both progress and survival. In these regards the urban public spaces of Barcelona embraced a broad range of functions, with many of the parks equipped for specific recreational and leisure-time activities. The architects and public officials were keenly aware of the plurality of interests confronting them as various groups in civil society began to assert themselves. The Parc de l'Escorxador or Parc de Joan Miró, by Antoni Solanas in conjunction with the Office of Urban Projects, for example, provided facilities for organized basketball and football games within its expansive landscape. Less formal but nevertheless significant venues were also established within a garden setting on the same site for other organized recreational pursuits such as bowling. By contrast, many of the small plazas within the city, such as those in Gràcia and within Ciutat Vella, simply provided the opportunity for respite from the bustle of daily city life and were far less programmatically specific. More often than not, these paved spaces provide outdoor public "rooms," as it were, within the otherwise private realm of the city and are conformed to enhance the surrounding architecture. The small plaza alongside the venerable Santa Maria del Mar, for instance, admirably achieved both civic purposes, while serving in its own right to memorialize the Catalan martyrs of 1714. In addition, considerable emphasis was placed on multiple uses of public spaces. Almost all in some way accommodate the daily rituals of meeting, strolling, and simply being together in a public place—all strong cultural characteristics of Barcelona's life. Indeed, among various parks, plazas, and streets, these straightforward yet crucial activities were provided for amply. Many, including the Plaça de la Mercè and the Plaça Reial, for instance, also now accommodate and were designed for more formal collective gatherings of commemoration, political expression, and celebration.

Two other related aspects of this functional and formal diversity also deserve special note. First, throughout the urban public space program, an inventive and productive awareness was apparent concerning differences between various open-space functions and the degree to which those differences should be reflected in design. Sometimes, unfortunately, the formal variation of urban space, in general, can be accomplished too readily for its own sake, rather than as a reflection of vital cultural interests. Conversely, social diversity can be denied, in principle, through an overly monolithic insistence on a particular style or approach. Fortunately, in Barcelona a sensitive awareness of appropriate design difference in various links of the roadway network, for example, is spatially very apparent. Here one immediately confronts essential differences among streets for traffic, avenues that accommodate both traffic and people strolling, and the *passeig* or *paseo*, which accommodates both activities and yet has a higher-order civic role to perform as a gathering place. Within the physical realm of Barcelona, for example, the new versions of Via Laietana, the Avinguda de Gaudí, the Passeig Colom, and the Passeig de Picasso can hardly be confused, although on the city plan they may all appear to be nothing more than major roadway segments.

The second important aspect of formal and functional diversity was realization of an appropriate level of indeterminacy in design. Once again, a proposal can be so specific as to rule out reappropriation of public spaces for other desirable yet unforeseen uses, or designs can be so vague and bereft of ideas about use that they become alienating and intimidating. Fortunately, in places like the Parc de l'Espanya Industrial, for example, by Peña Ganchegui and Rius, the stepped inclined edge that forms an exuberant backdrop to the park itself is routinely used by spectators at outdoor events as well as by a plethora of more informal users for sunbathing, reading, lounging, or simply socializing. Similarly, the surfaces of the Avinguda de Gaudí, by Quintana, are a haven for skateboard riders, hopscotch enthusiasts, street vendors, strollers, and delivery men on lunch breaks. Likewise, the Via Júlia clearly demonstrates that the traditional repertoire of streets can be cleverly rejuvenated to accommodate many modern exigencies of both transit and repose. Large portions of Via Júlia, for instance, are nonspecialized areas, allowing for a considerable amount of local invention to occur. The trellis area above the train station, partially buried beneath the project, contains a large sitting area for afternoon conversation, a market held at least once a week, and a festival site or area for community gathering and public functions. Dominated by a large lantern tower that marks its intersection with the adjacent high-speed ring road, the Via Júlia has become both a *rambla* and a center of neighborhood activity in a dense, low-income area of the city.

For a process of urban refurbishing and remaking to take hold among an urban populace, and to become adopted as a fundamental part of a new image for the city, those in government and civil society naturally must find the right level at which decision making matters most. In urban design, this invariably means identifying the scale at which there is sufficient congruence between city form, social purpose, and cultural values to make a palpable difference in the daily life of citizens. Unfortunately, such decisions often vary between the abstractions of plan making and broad social programs that attempt to satisfy everyone and yet often end up enfranchising very few, and the construction of favored local projects that have become the pet causes of powerful interest groups. Fortunately, the City of Barcelona appears to have avoided the pitfalls of both positions. From a social perspective the urban public spaces program addressed one of the city's most pressing problems—namely the need for viable open spaces within what was a dense urban fabric of buildings. Whether it was in fact the most pressing need could be argued, although an obvious competing issue like housing appears to be more one of distribution than of sheer insufficiency. From a political perspective, the program offered the important potential of relatively quick, prominent, and tangible results from public investment. Furthermore, the relative cost-effectiveness was high, allowing projects to be distributed throughout the city, leaving few of its citizens unaffected. Even large improvements, such as the Plaça dels Països Catalan and the citywide parks, were relatively inexpensive to construct, and the effect of the design results on urban space users was almost instantaneous.

Along with the creation of an appropriate vehicle for making public improvements, however, comes the need for strong political will and vision. On both counts it is clear that the local government administration was formed and aggressively led by Mayors Serra and Maragall. Not only did they enthusiastically endorse the urban public spaces program, even during times of controversy, but both men also had an unusual tolerance for experimentation. Narcís Serra, for example, was directly responsible for the prolific installation of contemporary public art. However, without diminishing the central role of public officials, an interest in novelty and experimentation can partly be explained by the larger historical circumstances of the urban space program. For some time during the Franco regime, very little renovation had occurred in Barcelona. The democratic elections of 1979 signaled a strong break with the past, not to mention the dawn of a new political era for which there was enormous popular enthusiasm. Under these circumstances it is little wonder that a return to traditional approaches would be eschewed in favor of confidently striking out in a new contemporary direction. Moreover, technically speaking, no adequate indigenous precedents existed for many of the spatial conditions that had to be resolved. Thus in most cases, invention was the only recourse.

One of the most noteworthy innovations was the extensive use of hard paved and masonry surfaces, the *plaza dura*.[10] Although controversial, particularly when expressed on the vast scale of the Plaça dels Països Catalans, there are several reasons behind this rather consistent choice of surface for public open spaces. First, immediate and pragmatic use could be made of available materials and an available craft tradition, which obvious cost and socioeconomic benefits. Second, the hard surfaces were durable, relatively easy to maintain, and symbolically gave an immediate appearance of project completion. Third, a broader culturally based decision was made that Barcelona belonged to the tradition of no trees, rather than vice versa. Among the intelligentsia of the design community at the time, there was a preference for hard urban plazas in a Mediterranean tradition, such as those found in Italy, and skepticism expressed about the image of trees in the presentation of an emphatically public plaza.

In keeping with other broad themes of the urban space program, this new tradition of the plaza dura also allowed for considerable expressive variety among separate projects, partly promoted by specific design circumstances. The Plaça Reial, by Federico Correa and Alfonso Milá, for instance, concerned the restoration of the original plaza created by royal decree beside the Rambla and originally designed in 1848 by Francesco Daniel Molina. Incorporating several civic monuments, the plaza was paved throughout, with furnishings forming an inner plaza parallel with the surrounding building facades. Tall palm trees were planted at regular intervals, conforming in plan to a complex axial arrangement. Unlike the original, however, the entire plaza can now be comprehended immediately as a singular spatial entity. Similarly, the nearby neoclassical Plaça de la Mercè, by the Office of Urban Projects, is a renovated space. Modestly understated and civic in outlook, the plaza is paved simply, with a fountain and a nineteenth-century sculpture found in a nearby warehouse serving as a central focus. Finally, the controversial Plaça dels Països Catalans, by Helio Piñón and Albert Viaplana, was also a new installation, although unprecedented, as noted earlier, in its minimalist expression. Formerly the site of a large parking lot in front of Barcelona's major commuter rail station, the new plaza was designed to avoid interfering with surrounding traffic systems, including the rail lines underneath. Under these conditions the paved surface and skeletal structures are understandable, yet the result accomplishes far more than a basic material utility. The dynamic formal abstractions of frames, bollards, benches, and light stanchions bring order to an otherwise vast and disparate space in an extraordinarily parsimonious manner. The result is at once functional—providing shade, places to pause, and a certain definition for pedestrian traffic—yet sculpturally engaging, drawing attention to the material conditions surrounding its genesis and the capacity of frames in a field to articulate, effectively command, and volumetrically define the space.

Another noteworthy innovation of Barcelona's urban spaces program was the emergence of a regionally distinctive type of park, involving a strong sense of enframement that simultaneously distinguished the park from surrounding areas and provided for an expressive autonomy within the frame itself. In planimetric terms, it resembled a carefully framed painting on which various overlays were rendered, and in almost all cases where the contrast between hard and soft surfaces, between water bodies and land, and between sculptural installations and their field were often accentuated. Moreover, one geometric order, such as the planting of trees, was overlaid on another, such as systems of pathways, so that differences between the two orders remained intact rather than being resolved into a third. This process further gave the affected areas of the parks a heightened abstract, three-dimensional quality that they might otherwise have lacked. Specific elements within the overall composition tended to be finite and discontinuous, serving as accents and foci within the normally ordered field of the park. Invariably, one or more of the boundaries took on an irregular, organic shape in stark contrast to the orthogonal and linear forms of surrounding features. In fact, this emerging genre of modern park has become perhaps even more distinctive in Barcelona than the better-known plaza dura.[11]

Less abstractly, in the Parc del Clot, by Dani Freixes and Vicenc Miranda, for instance, enframement was delivered by retaining the outside masonry wall of the large factory structure that formerly occupied the site. A rough division was made on the east side of the park with a bermed, well-planted, and predominantly grassy area, and on the west by a partially sunken paved plaza. Undulations in the ground plane, from the prospect at the top of the berm, provided a singular well-defined sweep of space. The predominant building elements in the composition were bridge structures that literally spanned the berms and paved areas. Other features, such as an aqueduct-like water body and public art installation by Bryan Hunt, completed the improvements. In another instance, the Parc de l'Espanya Industrial, which also occupies the site of a former factory complex, was carefully enframed by a steeply inclined wall of steps, rising from a sunken area of the site. Again, there is a substantial interplay between soft grassy and well-planted areas. The pervasive imagery of the park, though, differs greatly with the Parc del Clot. It has an idiosyncratic, expressionistic quality, especially in details such as the huge light and observation towers that help define one edge. In addition, both the Parc de la Creueta del Coll, by Martorell, Bohigas, and Mackay, in the hills overlooking Barcelona, and the Parc de l'Estació del Nord, by the Office of Urban Projects, closer to the center of the city, possess many of the same general spatial features, as does the Vil-la Cecília garden complex by Elias Torres Tur and José Antonio Martinez Lapeña.

Understandably, problems have been encountered with such a definitive design approach, even with considerable local district participation. Administrative naiveté and oversight, for instance, prevented the allocation of adequate resources for project maintenance, leaving several of the earlier projects in need of considerable refurbishing. The piecemeal character of project organization, in the absence of a more coherent overall plan, sometimes led to a lack of design coordination. Novelty and experimentation also had their prices. The absence of immediately identifiable furnishings in several parks has been a point of contention with neighboring residents. At the Parc del Clot, for example, banners draped from upper-story windows in surrounding apartment buildings ask, *When will a real play area be built?* Nevertheless, children enthusiastically continue to play, apparently oblivious to distinctions between contemporary and traditional building practices. It was also not the first time that Barcelona's leaps of civic design came under criticism. No less an architectural

The Parc del Clot in Barcelona by Freixes and Miranda.

figure than Josep Puig i Cadafalch, for instance, strongly objected to Cerdà's plan for the Eixample as being far too abstract, egalitarian, and uninteresting for Barcelona's needs, preferring instead Antoni Rovira's less undifferentiated and hierarchical proposal.[12]

Another aspect of the historical circumstances surrounding the urban public spaces program that warrants closer examination is the timing of economic cycles. During the Franco regime, the 1960s and 1970s in Barcelona were periods of private economic boom in which a considerable amount of speculative development occurred, especially on the outskirts of the city. Until recently, however, the immediate post-Franco period was a time of relative economic downturn, during which little private-sector development occurred on any scale. Because of the strong initiative taken by city government during this lull, public works could regain an exemplary status and be presented as models for action. In fact, the local administration was practically the only investor in urban development at the time. A situation in which the economy was sluggish, therefore, was successfully converted into one of considerable public leadership. Subsequently, when the economic pendulum swung back again in favor of private investment, a new administrative posture of joint public-private participation in urban development was established, with the local government acting from a position of strength and vision that it probably could not have attained without the earlier public works projects. This was certainly apparent during the Olympic Games preparations, which catapulted Barcelona, although not without further criticism, into another scale of urban improvements, including completion of a ring road, large-scale housing development, and 5 kilometers of public beach and adjacent park improvements.[13]

CIVIC INTERACTION BETWEEN THE STATE AND CIVIL SOCIETY

By now it is evident that at the core of Barcelona's successful urban revitalization lay a viable expression of the common purpose of local government—or the state—and the diverse needs and senses of identity of ordinary citizens and of civil society. This was all the more remarkable or perhaps even facilitated by the relatively novel appearance of this kind of productive tension in post-authoritarian Spain. After all, Francisco Franco's predominantly fascist dictatorship had lasted from the end of the Civil War in 1939 until his death in 1975, and was preceded only a short time earlier, between 1923 and 1930, by the dictatorship of Miguel Primo de Rivera. In effect, Spain had enjoyed a mere half dozen years of any form of democratic republican rule in the past half century. This was all to change, however, during the years of rapid development—*años de desarrollo*—which took place between about 1961 and 1973, as Spain's economic miracle and the early reorganization of civil society created a robust urban middle class for the first time, making the country ripe for democracy.[14] At the very least, it made the transition between dictatorship and democracy much smoother, and the typical Spanish jump from the lower to the upper classes far less abrupt. During the años de desarrollo, in the hands of the technocrats, the economy expanded 7 percent per annum, faster than any other country in the noncommunist world except for Japan. Material prosperity among Spain's citizenry also increased at a spectacular pace. Car ownership, for instance, rose from a ratio of about one in one hundred inhabitants in 1960 to around one in ten by 1970—a tenfold increase in just ten years. In comparison to the rest of Europe, however, Spain remained comparatively poor, with per capita income in 1973 slightly less than half the average of E. E. C. countries, and only 30 percent of U.S. figures. Imports still outstripped exports, only to be offset economically by earnings sent home by Spanish laborers working abroad and by receipts from tourism.[15]

From the outset, Franco's authoritarian regime was heavily reliant on other elements of society including the army, the Catholic church, parts of the business community, and large numbers of peasant smallholders, as well as urban and semi-urban middle classes and other elements of an emerging civil society. In the age-old Spanish tradition of the *pronunciamento*—a process of favoring particular sociopolitical groups on the part of the military—Franco's regime overtly favored the fascist Falange, although more broadly dominated practically all aspects of Spanish civil society.[16] Strictly speaking, it was not a completely totalitarian government, as it gradually opened itself up to other influences. Nevertheless, after 1940 the aims of Francoism were clear. The regime stood for a homogeneous Catholic society, the organization of economic and social life along corporate lines, and the advancement of Spain as an industrialist power. Success in most if not all of this program depended to a very large extent upon a neutral relationship between Spain and the outside world. In name this was certainly the case at the time, although the situation was to change abruptly in the post-World War II era, after a period of isolation that almost brought the country to a standstill economically. The *años de humbre*— years of hunger—effectively began with the United Nations-sponsored blockade of Spain in 1946, lasting until 1950, during which time real income plummeted and shantytowns sprung up around major urban centers.[17]

In the subsequent period of development, as Victor Pérez-Diaz tells us, at least five factors began to change, irrecoverably, the relationship between Spain and the outside world, and with it the relationship between the state and an emergent civil society.[18] The first and perhaps foremost was economic. Not only did the economic miracle of the 1960s raise material standards of living, but it also opened up markets, creating an influx of foreign capital and, quite naturally, related outside influences and prompting a significant weakening of state control. Tourism, one of the chief components of the burgeoning Spanish economy, brought further contact with the outside world and exposure to other cultural norms and kinds of institutions. Vast migration from rural to urban areas and regionally from south to north transferred the conservative Spanish peasantry and agricultural laborers into an urban proletariat with much more liberal views. The church, split largely along generational lines by the Second Vatican Council, became less homogeneous in outlook. The liberal Catholic intelligentsia also offered fierce resistance to the ultraconservative and shadowy *Opus Dei* movement. Finally, universities had developed a political culture hostile to Francoism and began permeating professional ranks with graduates who challenged established patterns of conduct. Certainly by the mid-1970s the economic, social, and cultural institutional makeup of Spain—in effect, much of civil society—was close to that of Western Europe. Consequently, as scholars like Victor Pérez-Diaz, Jean Cohen, and Andrew Arato seem to conclude, the steps to democracy were that much quicker in coming, although not without their own drama.[19]

In Barcelona, what followed was dramatic on another score as well. Many in Catalunya had been implacably against Francoism, and somewhat more abstractly, against Madrid as a symbol of external domination. During Franco's regime, Catalan as a language was forbidden, and the region was deprived of practically any support. A virulent resurgence, then, of Catalan regionalism—if not out-and-out nationalism—was understandable during the post-Franco period. This tendency was at least partially counteracted, however, by the re-emergence of broadly based political parties, outlawed during the dictatorship, especially by those on the political left. The Socialists who eventually gained and continue to hold municipal power in Barcelona are more universal in their social, political, and cultural vision than are their conservative opponents on the political right. Thus, in a fashion analogous to controversies surrounding the open-space projects, a tension exists between a sense of unity (belonging to Spain) and a sense of being somehow separate and unique (being from Catalunya).

Understandably, the role and scope of the emerging civil society expanded and flourished dramatically with the dictatorship's downfall. A cultural renaissance, as we have already seen in the architectural world of Barcelona, was almost immediate, in part because of the "rehearsal," so to speak, that had been going on earlier in a somewhat clandestine fashion. Economic conditions for many Spaniards also improved, although there have been recent problems and a substantial slowing down of the march toward full European participation. Perhaps less readily measurable, although just as pervasive, are the changes in social mores—including gender roles—and the general permissiveness of society, now out from under the puritanical thumb of the earlier regimes.[20]

Elsewhere in the western world speculation about the role of civil society, the state, and the public sphere was taking other turns. Some even doubted whether the public sphere existed in any identifiable singular conception, particularly as the lines between private and public were constantly shifting, and as identity politics among minority and special-interest groups raised legitimate questions about whose public was under discussion anyway.[21] In the inevitable balancing of public and private life, many saw the scales being tipped deliberately in favor of the private. For some, like social historian Richard Sennett, this came from the general rise of an "intimate vision of society" during the nineteenth and twentieth centuries, whereby the social-psychological basis of understanding private individual behavior was extended too far into public life.[22] The result was a confusion between public and intimate life in which the criteria and procedures for assessment of the latter were used for the former. One upshot was a strong emphasis on family as the pillar of society and the hyperextension of notions of personality into the public domain, where they were quite incompatible with modern forms of social diversity, cosmopolitan life, difference, discontinuity, and so on. Others, like David Harvey, described the occlusion of a truly public realm amid rampant consumerism, continued leisure-time activity, and a general degradation of socially rendering values.[23] The philosopher Hannah Arendt found mass society difficult to bear, not so much because of its scale or tastes, but because of the lack of sufficient common ground, or way of truly relating to one another and of being gathered together.[24]

In his major work on the subject, the eminent contemporary German philosopher Jürgen Habermas readily acknowledges the multiplicity of meanings that have been given to the terms *public* and *private*.[25] Indeed, from his historical-etymological account, both concepts have gone through at least three major changes from Greco-Roman times to the present. Within the modern scheme of things, according to Habermas, the private world embraces the intimate sphere of the household, matters of personal moral religious conscience, as well as the liberty of making economic choices. Public authority, by contrast, is bound up in state policy, the courts, and government. The public sphere— *öffentlichkeit*—is a place of appearance, representative publicness and publicity among private citizens, including: the public sphere of politics, the public aspect of club life or other voluntary associations, as well as "town life" in general.[26] Civil society is an organizational construct within this public sphere, depicting the banding together of people with common interests, and "as a corollary of a depersonalized state authority."[27] It is in essence a public part of the private realm necessitated, according to Habermas, by the alienation of the state and usually existing potentially at odds with organized authority in a critical capacity. In Habermas's account of the relationships among these components he adopts a "transactional model" of bourgeois society—also referred to as a "discourse model"—based on traffic and intercourse among commodities, news, mail, and other forms of communication, as well as stock markets, and role playing among various classes and types of individuals or groups.[28] The essential analytical power of this model is that it goes well beyond the traditional opposition between majoritarian politics and the liberal guarantees of basic rights and liberties, at least to the extent that the normative or defining conditions of transactions and discourses are neither fixed nor fixable. In short, the "rules of the game," can be contested within the game itself, closely approximating idealized democratic debate where everything is contestable. Others, such as Cohen and Arato, adopt a not dissimilar stance, but define civil society as a sphere of social interaction between the economy and the state, composed above all of intimate relations—for instance, the family—and the sphere of voluntary associations and social movements.[29]

For Hannah Arendt the concept of "the public" also signifies publicity or the space of appearance where one can be seen and heard by everybody, but the term also brings with it the idea of a world of things held in common.[30] Furthermore, as she puts it, the common world not only gathers us together, but it "prevents us from falling over each other." Also explicit in Arendt's conception of the public is a permanent or transcendental quality. In her words, "If the world is to contain a public space, it cannot be erected for one generation and planned for the living only, it must transcend the life-span of mortal men." Here she draws on the Greek *polis* and the Roman *res publica* in creating a model of republican virtue. Also implicit is the idea of a moral project—to paraphrase Pérez-Diaz again—that gives the state its authority or moral suasion, usually by way of some master fiction or mythos.[31] When such a fiction or mythos loses its plausibility, as it often does today, then the role of the state is usually diminished. In addition to having things in common, members of society must also actively entertain a simultaneous awareness of social and cultural diversity. "Only where things can be seen by many in a variety of aspects without changing their identity, so that those gathered around them know they see sameness in utter diversity," writes Arendt, "can wordly reality truly and reliably appear."[32] As one might imagine from this, the topography of Arendt's public realm could vary considerably. A dining room where dissidents meet, for instance, could be just as much a public place as a town hall.

In the liberal tradition, the justification of power and authority in terms of individual rights and freedoms is of paramount importance.[33] Relations between the public and private spheres of life tend to revolve around the public accountability of major institutions in a democratic society. At work, ideally, is a principle of action—a supreme pragmatic imperative—under which any member of society must be willing to discuss and debate the concept of "good" with anyone else, regardless of relative advantages, differences in social position, and so on. From a liberal perspective, unbridled majoritarian rule is seen to be corrosive precisely because it cuts off or avoids this type of debate and therefore tramples on individual liberties. In principle, certain general aspects of social conduct, like individual freedom and the rights that guarantee this freedom, are held to be more important than other aspects of a more communitarian kind. Consequently, the idea of "public" per se is synonymous with government and the state, whereas the private realm includes all aspects of civil society and the household. Indeed, within this institutional complex, a primary role of civil society is to facilitate debate on matters of public good and benefit.

Hegel in his *Philosophy of Right* also makes a distinction between family and civil society, while stressing the need for both.[34] Civil society, as it has become commonly recognized, was the sphere of choice where the ruling principles were ones of agreement and contract. Furthermore, these agreements and contracts, while undoubtedly controlling economic and other businesslike transactions, took on tacit dimensions as well. Codes of manners, for example, became finalized expressions of the accepted or ruling virtue of civil society. Clearly these were of practical value by defining the manner of respect with which one would hold another person, so necessary to the bringing together of strangers for other transactions. The niceties of these tacit dimensions of civility also reveal further ways by which the institutions and activities of civil society might be understood better. Language and dialect, for example, as well as the habits of leisure-time activities, and manners of imbibing food and drink, can become powerful descriptive dimensions. The cultural theorists Nekt and Kluge, for instance, stress the ideas of fantasy and the difference between standard and colloquial language as means by which the alienation of official versions of life experience can be dealt with and expressed effectively.[35] In cases like the Australian dialect *strine* and its usage, both ideas converge sharply. The utterances of Banjo Patterson's ballad *Waltzing Matilda,* for one, are not only officially unintelligible and deliberately so, but describe a fantastic if macabre release from the trials of British colonial oppression. "You'll come a waltz'in matilda with me" actually describes a state of incarceration that the vagrant bushman escapes by committing suicide.

Building on Hegel's foundations, the sociologist Talcott Parsons, in his theory of social community, saw civil society or its equivalent as mediating between traditional forms such as tribal kinship or feudal bands and a modern condition, where pluralism is encouraged and, indeed, legally secured.[36] To Parsons, citizenship in a modern sense signifies equal access to membership in a social community rather than in the state. In other words, equal rights guarantee autonomous forms of action like free speech, the right to assembly, etc., vis-à-vis the state. Antonio Gramsci, by contrast, working from the same Hegelian foundations, first adopted a three-part conceptual framework consisting of civil society, economic development, and state power.[37] He then viewed the particular form and substance of civil society as the outcome and object of class struggle. For instance, when the middle class is hegemonic in this struggle, civil society takes on middle-class values and cultural norms. In spite of this rather schematized view of civil society as either bourgeois or socialist, Gramsci's tripartite scheme does avoid the economic and political reductionism that usually befalls simpler distinctions between the public and private sectors.

In most, if not all of these speculations, the concept of something being *civic* lies somewhere between the private realm of one's existence and the public domain of officialdom. More important, it is produced by both spheres of activity and influence. Just as a totally private matter hardly can be civic, so a state function like defense can be entirely devoid of civic virtue. Publicity is also an important aspect of a civic realm. They are places of appearance, just as one finds today in Barcelona's urban spaces. From an Arendtian perspective, things civic bring people together and give them a sense of something permanent in common, while also maintaining in this convergence, or expression of sameness and significance, a human plurality and diversity of viewpoint. In fact, as pointed out, this twofold aspect is one of the great strengths of the Barcelona experience, which was at once Catalan and tailored to meet the needs of specific neighborhoods and locales within the city. Furthermore, the boundaries between what is public, what is private and, therefore, what is civic are also shifting as society changes and evolves. Catalan *modernisme* and modernism, for instance, were certainly related through time and place, but addressed, appropriately, different institutional complexions of city life.[38] From the transactional model, a negotiated character to the civic dimension emerges, potentially embracing official as well as unofficial versions of experience and rather constant processes of interchange, transaction, and discourse. Coming to terms with Serra's wall and use of the Plaça de la Palmera, for example, has something of this aspect to it, relying as much as anything on a certain amount of improvisation and turf negotiation. Finally, the civic dimension of life is entirely necessary for holding public institutions accountable and for ensuring a diversity of individual rights and freedoms. Helping to define the moral project that moves society forward— again a process clearly evident in Barcelona—is a paramount civic responsibility. Prominent United States Senator Daniel Patrick Moynihan once put it: "Buildings should not make private citizens realize how unimportant they are,"

A folie at the Parc de la Villette in Paris by Tschumi.

but instead should create "a public architecture of intimacy, one that brings people together in an experience of confidence and trust."[39]

CIVIC PLACE MAKING AND THE PARISIAN *GRAND PROJETS*

Even given Barcelona's accomplishments, finding a correspondence between urban-architectural public space and political public space is not altogether straightforward, either conceptually or practically. Political public space is abstract and primarily concerns categorial distinctions, and the processes for making those distinctions between the public and private realms of citizens' lives in society. Urban-architectural public space, by contrast, is far more narrowly tangible and inherently static. Consequently, finding direct correspondences between one domain and the other is highly improbable, and yet definitions of what is civic applied to both political life and to architecture are clearly possible. It would be difficult to argue, for example, with the civic import of Barcelona's urban public space program. Nevertheless, it is equally difficult to relate this experience directly to philosophical discussions of the public sphere, the everyday manifestations of which were significantly influential in Barcelona's urban renaissance. How, then, can a correspondence be made between one kind of public space and the other, and what are the consequences?

A fruitful mapping of one kind of public space on the other generally involves three analytical dimensions. They are programmatic, representational, and constitutive. First, under the programmatic dimension, the earlier central question becomes rephrased. In what circumstances—functionally and urban-architecturally speaking—do legitimate politico-cultural distinctions between public and private realms of people's existence become either impeded or enhanced? In other words, what happens or might happen, civicly, in a particular place? Placement of a courtroom inside a supermarket, for instance, may severely impair the aura of authority necessary for judicial proceedings or, depending on degrees, make that process more approachable. Second, under the representational dimension the question becomes slightly different. How are relevant distinctions and overlaps between the public and private aspects of life best represented and articulated in a spatially iconographical, symbolic, or other architectural manner? In short, what is the spatial appearance of the civic realm or, in the simple case of a household, how might a domicile not look like a public building, and vice versa? Third, under the constitutve dimension, how can an urban-architectural project suggest, or otherwise create, further distinction and elaborations of the public and private realms, thereby enhancing the civic experience of life? By putting a grand public front on private industry, for instance, the late nineteenth-century lofts of New York, as we shall see in chapter 4, significantly expanded the civic scope of that city. This dimension also implies a reciprocal relationship between the civic enterprise—politico-culturally speaking—and urban architecture. Good civic space, in other words, is accessible and allows expression and an equal sense of belonging to all participants. It is also devoid of suppressive references and encourages unofficial as well as official interpretations of meaning and use. Furthermore, it reminds individuals of larger senses of responsibility and presents something that could be passed on to subsequent generations. In these regards, both the *miranda* and *credenda* of power expressed by good civic architecture are tempered. While this process certainly uses symbolic instruments and appeals to reasonableness, both the choice of symbols and what is reasonable should be open to negotiation.

The Parisian *Grand Projets* of François Mitterrand, like the urban spaces of Barcelona, are fine examples of civic space making with considerable affinity with these criteria.[40] Begun with a public announcement in March 1982, the grand projets quickly established Mitterrand's high regard for the cultural role of the city and materially helped his socialist government improve the quality of life for many Parisians, especially at a time when further wealth and income redistribution was difficult to envisage. Over time, the projects also allowed Mitterrand to leave his own personal mark on Paris—not altogether out of keeping with earlier French leaders—and to promote the international function of the metropolis. Projects varied in both location and type, although most were concentrated in the eastern and central portions of Paris, as well as at La Défense on the western periphery. The Sainte-Geneviève project, for instance, was concerned with renewal of one of the most picturesque districts of the Latin Quarter, whereas Tête-Défense was concerned, by contrast, with an almost entirely new, high-density commercial district. Parks figured prominently among the projects, as did single public buildings, like the Opera House by Carlos Ott at Bastille in 1982, or conversion of prominent existing structures into an alternative public use, such as the museum at Gare d'Orsay, dating from 1977, by Gae Aulenti. Unlike other times in the past, most projects were awarded on the basis of competitions, which often attracted large numbers of foreign participants. Indeed it was estimated during the late 1980s that something like 2,000 designers were working at once on Parisian projects in various parts of the world.

Both Mitterrand and Jacques Chirac, the mayor of Paris, had an interest in good modern design, in spite of their political differences.[41] Moreover, their collaboration was to be decisive on several projects, including the Louvre addition by I. M. Pei and the Gare d'Austerlitz redevelopment. Unlike Georges Pompidou, a predecessor as head of state in the Fifth Republic, Mitterrand did not play a personal stylistic role in shaping the various projects, nor in attempting to devise some kind of consensual design philosophy. Instead, he was interested in attracting the best architects in Paris and leaving questions of design in their capable hands. During an interview in 1984, however, Mitterrand did come out strongly for modern architecture and a liking for pure forms, such as the "cube" at La Defénse (the arch by Johan Otto van Spreckelson of 1985 to 1989) and Pei's "pyramid" of 1986 at the Louvre.[42] Above all, he seemed to value the combined characteristics of scale, location, form, efficiency, and visual integration in defining the overall scope and appearance of each of his regime's public improvements.

The interaction between civil society and the state was also clearly evident in forging the appearance and program of the grand projets. A tension between modern and traditional architecture had existed throughout much of the Fifth Republic, beginning with Charles De Gaulle's plans to modernize Paris and to symbolically pull it into the postwar era.[43] In fact, Delouvier's strategic plan for the city of 1963 did just that, reversing plans for decentralization inherited from the Fourth Republic and aiming instead to open up Paris for development as a conurbation with new towns on its periphery. Later, in 1970, Pompidou—also with a taste for modernism as an appropriate symbol of the French Republic—embraced high-rise tower developments, expressways, and large-scale urban renewal. This tendency was quickly halted, however, through mounting public outcry and, in particular, the *scandales* surrounding Montparnasse, Défense, and Les Halles—three districts either undergoing or slated for further modernist renewal and expansion.[44] Valéry Giscard d'Estaing, the liberal president elected in 1974, quickly called for a review of all large-scale projects in Paris and just as quickly showed a preference for tradition and conservation. The land-use plan for Paris of 1974 combined careful zoning with sensitive building regulations and stressed continuity and harmony with the inherited building fabric of Paris. Soon after *architecture d'accompagnment,* an architecture linked to adjacent older structures, began to emerge. Public tempering of the doctrinaire manifestations of modernism was truly afoot, leading to the integrative symbolism of "new modernism," a humane and by and large contextual contemporary interpretation of prevailing architectural conditions. "Postmodernism," by contrast, was relegated to the suburbs. Thus by the time of Mitterrand and Chirac in the 1980s, this "new modernism"—to the extent that there was one—became the "official" urban architecture of Paris.[45]

One of the other conspicuous features of Mitterrand's grand projets, implicit in some of the earlier theoretical definitions of the civic realm, was the idea of a moral project. Not only did Mitterrand value Paris for its palpable cultural role, he also saw in its transformation a way of rallying civic pride and, perhaps even more important, of setting Parisians examples to follow. This didactic quality—criticized by some as a superimposition of high bourgeoise taste on the rest of the populace—was purposeful and, in the end, very effective. As in Barcelona, a common response to the public projects was emulation on the part of others in civil society. The seeds were sown, as envisioned by Bohigas, for more wholesale and localized renewal. Development in the Manin-Jaurès district in the XIXth arrondissement, with its mix of public and private sector activities, is a clear case in point.

Following in the tradition of Napoleon III and the Second Empire, Paris under Mitterrand and Chirac was again to be graced with a series of park improvements. In fact, green areas generally were to be found in almost all the larger district-oriented grand projets, as well as more specifically in the so-called greening of the Seine, in conjunction with the redevelopment of disused or underused and obsolete sites. Prominent early on in the latter regard was the Parc de la Villette redevelopment of the old historic slaughterhouse areas on the northeastern edge of Paris in the poorer XIXth arrondissement.[46] Since its creation in 1979, the *Etablissement Public du parc de la Villette*, a local public body, has progressively defined and managed the construction of the park and all its facilities, including the science and industrial exhibits (*Cité des Sciences et de l'Industrie*), the grand hall, and the extensive music facility (*Cite de la Musique*).[47] The site covers an area of some 55 hectares (137.5 acres) and surrounds the old Ourcq canal, which together with the adjacent St. Denis and St. Martin canals originally opened up the entire area as a center of river trade, in addition to la Villette's historic role as a transit point and city toll, especially for merchandise en route to Flanders and Germany.

In 1982 an international competition was set for the Parc de la Villette, explicitly calling for the creation of an urban park for the twenty-first century and accommodation of a complex program of cultural entertainment, education, and sports, as well as acting as a "social field" for contemporary Paris. Bernard Tschumi's winning proposal clearly rose to the occasion, creating an exciting new prototype, synchronous with contemporary concepts of order and disorder in urban life. Drawing upon the *Manhattan Transcripts*, an earlier exhibition of drawings that explored relationships between architectural concepts such as space and use, object and event, set and script, as well as type and program, Tschumi created a scheme organized by the architectural apparatus of points,

lines, and surfaces.[48] Among other things, superimposition across the site of
these three spatially organizing constructs allowed many of the disjunctive,
noncoincidental, interchangeable, and potentially contradicting aspects of contemporary cities to be reflected, in addition to a feeling of life and openness,
which according to officialdom is the common denominator of the park. Technically, the project was comprised of a neutral point-grid underlying spatial structure, established at 120-meter intervals, parallel with the Canal de l'Ourcq,
which roughly bisected the site in an east-west direction. To the north lay the
Museum of Science and Industry and to the south both the grand hall and the
City of Music. Many of the points—eventually to be twenty-five in all—were
physically occupied by red buildings of various shapes (*folies*), each based on
a cube of 10.8 meters on each side. Sometimes they were merely decorative,
and sometimes they were devoted to specific functions, such as the *Café folie*
and the *Quick folie* for eating, as well as the *Belvedere folies* for observing
other aspects of the site, and the *Music* and *Jazz folies*, which were places of
entertainment. The steadfast lack of unification between the physical form of
the folies and their function was both deliberate and polemical. Tschumi was
arguing strongly against the unification of one with the other—a strong orthodox
modernist trait.[49]

The other two systems of "points" and "surfaces," respectively, mark
paths and various gardens with specific themes. There was, for instance, the
garden of mirrors, conceived by Tschumi to cleverly present a "false-real landscape" in which reality and reflection combined through the presence of twenty-
eight monoliths, 2 meters in height, each with a polished steel mirror. At night,
hidden projectors light up the mirrors and create disturbing effects and shapes
that further accentuate the strangeness of the place. Further on is the *garden
of mist*, by Alain Déllisier and Fujiko Nakaya, where microjets form nebulous
horizontal curtains. This effect was also further enhanced at night through pro-
jection of lasers. The *garden of bamboo*, to describe yet another landscape, was
located on the eastern extremity of the terrain to the south of the park, described
as the *prairie du triangle*, near the *Café folie*. Designed by Alexandre Chemetoff,

Daniel Buren, and Bernhard Leitner, the garden was embedded in a wide hollow space, 6 meters in depth, supported on one side by a large heat-reflecting concrete wall. Within this environment grow something like thirty different species of bamboo—the second largest collection of this sort in France—combined with amplification of their sound, so that movement and sound lie at the core of the composition. In general, each garden was located in a domain along the sinuous path that zigzags through the park, punctuated at regular intervals by the red folie structures.[50]

Very evident in Tschumi's conception of the Parc de la Villette are the qualities of arguing over and making up rules, implicit in Habermas's concept of civil society and the state, as well as the other communicative features of the "transactional model." Clearly one can negotiate the "points," "lines," and garden "surfaces" of the park in a variety of different manners. The nonconsequential overlap between one spatial system and the others calls further attention to this disjunction, or discontinuity, between an official version of things and more private, unofficial trajectories. In addition, the rather humorous iconographic qualities of the folies, in particular, divert attention from any official or otherwise loaded meanings. Instead, the symbolic references are almost antiauthoritarian and obviously toylike, immediately opening up the idea of play and with it, improvisation. Interestingly enough, each folie is rather large and denotes a space around it, where usually are located chairs and other informal seating arrangements. Clearly the message here is that a certain monumentality and boldness of scale need not carry any of the expected authoritarian or official symbolic references and have a distinct absence of miranda and credenda, as discussed earlier. Instead, these elements can be invitations to play and, in the process, to discover—if nothing else—oneself.

The Conservatory or Museum of Music, by Christian de Potzamparc, the *Zénith*, which houses many popular concerts, the grand hall, and the Museum of Science and Industry by Adrien Fainsilber all attract vast numbers of visitors. In fact, for the year 1992, La Villette received 8.4 million visits, of which fully

5.9 million were for the indoor activities.[51] There are something like 7,000 daily visitors, many from the adjacent neighborhood of Manin-Jaurès in the normal course of child-minding and daily leisure-time activity, but also from outside in the general vicinity of Paris. La Villette is, after all, a substantial concentration of broadly appealing cultural activities for all Parisians. And, as such, it is part of Mitterrand's and Chirac's overall plan to remake and redistribute Paris's civic activities.

The more recent Parc André Citroën-Cevennes is another major open-space improvement with local as well as citywide ambitions. Located in the XVth arrondissement in southwest Paris, alongside the River Seine, the park was also the subject of a design competition that enlisted a multidisciplinary design team in a cooperative venture with public officials and the public at large, especially nearby residents.[52] The team included the architects Patrick Berger, Jean-Paul Vigieur, and Jean-François Jodry, together with the landscape architects Gilles Clement and Alain Provost. The site had an irregular shape, incorporating spaces between and around existing buildings, covering an area of some 35 acres. Work began in 1992 amid a larger renewal project consisting of about 2,500 new dwelling units—primarily of mid- and high-rise buildings— two hotels, two schools, a hospital, a large public garage, and about 3,000 square meters of artists' studios, mainly in the form of loft space.

The final design of the park was dominated by a large rectangular open lawn, or *parterre*, running north-south orthogonally from a boat landing and small canal, parallel to the River Seine. An underlying gridlike spatial structure, based on the geometry of the parterre, was then extended into the adjacent garden and used to locate pathways, entrances, and a series of glass and teak-wood pavilions along the eastern side, overlooking the parterre. A prominent diagonal pathway transects this spatial structure, including the parterre, linking an outlying garden segment, the *Block Garden*, with the rest of the composition. In all, there are fourteen botanical gardens, several pools, playful fountains, and multiple pathways running through the site at different levels. Indeed, the three-dimensional quality of many of the improvements is what makes the park such a strong feature in the landscape and offers such high perceptual variety to the user. The six small gardens, for instance, that run along the parterre on the opposite side from the glass pavilions are devoted to the senses of sound, touch, and sight.

The idea of pluralism and individuality within a large communitarian social system—a recurrent theme in this chapter—is amply portrayed at the Parc André Citroën, which in its public and civil aspects is also a joint venture. Clearly there are formal systems of spatial definition, primarily to be found in the many orthogonal and axial pathways, together with far less formal and idiosyncratic ways of traversing the park. Interactive individual experience is also encouraged by the different smaller gardens, although the impressive overall presence of the parterre quickly provides a synthesis and common focal point. In general, the minor paths and different gardens provide an irregular heterogeneous outer layer to the project, enabling the park to be well integrated into the surrounding neighborhood. Meanwhile, the extensive parterre is simultaneously of a sufficient scale to be readily recognizable as a distinctive place within the city. Symbolically and spatially, a codependence between opposite or complementary conditions crops up throughout the project (grand versus local, city versus neighborhood, formal definition versus idiosyncratic experience, and established history versus current use). In the last regard the grand parterre, canal, axial arrangement of elements, and so on is entirely reminiscent of Le Nôtre and others in the French landscape tradition, even though the games people play and the manner of use is entirely contemporary and often extemporaneous. Another feature deserving special comment is the line of tall glass and teakwood greenhouse pavilions, each standing on a concrete podium above the park's general ground plane. At one level they are almost entirely public, appearing as they do as prominent edifices in the landscape. At another, they are almost private gardens capable of being occupied only by individuals or very small groups. The inherent transparency on almost all sides also effectively denies any sense of seclusion, while simultaneously providing sweeping vistas to occupants of the city beyond. Indeed, the issues of transparency in the grand projets was taken up recently by the architectural critic Anthony Vidler as "a strange notion of public monumentality that is more reticent . . . even as it represents the full weight of the French State."[53] Given planning progress in Paris through civil action, however, and since the intemperate modernism at the beginning of the Fifth Republic, such a notion is less strange. It sums up, among other things, a well-balanced relationship between the state and civil society on matters of Paris—France's collective cultural ornament.

"Plaça Jaume is quite lively these days," remarked Isabella, looking out the window at the by now familiar sight of the two guardia, ceremoniously decked out in uniforms with red and blue markings, lounging against their cars, hardly looking at the citizen group with their banners and placards, nor at the tourist group pointing up at the tower and clicking away with their cameras. "Yes, but I hope it will last and that things won't become too pat and, somehow, expected," responded Josep, deliberately misunderstanding part of what his colleague was indicating. "What do you mean?" she inquired, arching an eyebrow in a gesture of genuine perplexity. "Well, I dunno. . . . You see, there's us and there's them," pointing across the square, "and now there's these others. . . . Look, I certainly want the Ajuntament to be effective—don't get me wrong—but not by just going through the motions. Somehow people—like that lot down there from Nous Barris—must begin to fend for themselves," he went on with a serious gesture. "You're still the idealist, eh Josep!" she smiled, patting him on the arm. "But remember, this is politics, and every vote counts," she continued somewhat ad- monishingly. "Yes, but whose politics?" he shot back quickly, although not of- fended by the superior tone of her voice. "When push comes to shove, Isabella would be down there with them. . . . I know her," he thought to himself. "But that's the dilemma nowadays, isn't it?" he continued to think, although this time out loud, again not entirely in synch with her train of thought. "Oh, stop this! Let's go, or else Settes will be full like last time," she said, now with a certain amount of exasperation, motioning Josep toward the door, just as the chimes began to ring three o'clock.

—Pedro A. Lupo-Garcia, *Gent-de bé**

3

Realism and World Making

A memory wall and community park in New York's Lower East Side (page 80).

"Nonna, have you always lived here?" asked the girl as she watched her grandmother at the kitchen window feeding the sparrows. This was a daily routine that seemed to have gone on forever, or at least as far back as Lidia could remember. "No, cara," her grandmother replied. "Your grandfather and I came from the countryside over the mountains. First we went to live with zio Nino in Tiburtino, before we got this place. Those were the hard times. Not much work, nor good food—Still, I'm not complaining! We have made out alright."

"Tina, Tina, come quickly!" whispered Adalberto. "What is it now?" she said, waking with a start, although weighed down by her pregnant body. "At last we have our own place—casa nostra!" he replied gleefully, hardly able to contain his enthusiasm. "But Adalberto, it won't be good for the baby, riding on Italo's motorino!" "It's alright, it's not far."

"Oh, how nice—it really is like Campli!" exclaimed Tina, involuntarily clasping her hand to her mouth. "Look at all the tiled roofs . . . and chimneys . . . and balconies!" "Well, it's still a bit rough. The streets need to be fixed, and a few trees wouldn't hurt," replied Adalberto, smiling inwardly at his wife's obvious pleasure.

—Piero G. Monteverdi, *Tornare a Casa**

What is real and what is not has preoccupied people's minds for centuries. Certainly by the time of Plato and Socrates, subject matter handed down in pictorial and narrative form no longer had the same veracity as before. Art ceased to be self-evident, even when involved in the relatively straightforward presentation of biblical themes within the western Christian tradition. When Hegel declared art as a "thing of the past," he was not so much referring to the end of this tradition as saying that artistic presentation of the divine could no longer be made in quite the same unproblematic manner as earlier.[1] The common language and cultural bearing that stretched back, for instance, to the populist *Biblia Pauperum* no longer exercised the same hegemony, or held the same explanatory power.[2] Science now provided a new and exciting depiction of reality, although with time there appeared to be limits here too.

Today when asked what is real, we usually say that it depends, quickly betraying the contextual and relativistic orientation of our conceptual apparatus. Even philosophers do not agree. Some like David Papineau hold that reality, as a thing in itself, is independent of thought and that realism with a capital *R* exists independent of human judgment.[3] Others like Nelson Goodman are far more skeptical and relativistic. He argues that "one world may be taken as many, or the many worlds taken as one; whether one or many depends on the way of taking."[4] Moreover, these ways of taking depend on "frames of reference" belonging, in turn, to systems of description. Given the apparent impossibility of describing something fully independently from these frames in some essential way, we are thus confined to our ways of describing. Analytically, Goodman reaches much the same point as Ernst Cassirer did in his cross-cultural search for a single universal basis for things. Frames of reference are not given, but emerge from a rather constant process of world making, starting with those few references at hand. Less radically relativistic, Hilary Putnam argues for a pragmatic realism with a small *r*.[5] In so doing, he holds to the position that truth or reality depend on one's "conceptual scheme," but are nonetheless truth and reality. From a perspective of common sense, for instance, it is possible to be a realist and a conceptual relativist. Here conceptual reality specifies that there are several accounts of phenomena that have their own logic, practicality, and perhaps most important, usefulness.[6] They are not mere conventions, as Goodman might hold. They give rise to commonsensical truths and insights about the world, even though over time they too may be subject to revision.

STRAINS OF AESTHETIC REALISM

In its most specific sense, the term *Realism* in the figurative arts is usually reserved for a historical movement that attained its most coherent and consistent formulation in France roughly between 1840 and 1870 or 1880. The aim of Realism at that time, according to art historian Linda Nochlin in her classic work on the subject, "was to give a truthful, objective and impartial representation of the real world based on meticulous observation of contemporary life."[7] More broadly, however, Realism was and continues to be less a matter of style than a philosophical issue concerned centrally with the problematic concept of reality. Certainly not "mere appearance" or a "mirror image" or simulacrum, reality instead was perceived traditionally to lie beyond the realm of immediate sensation and the surficial facts of everyday life. Realism in turn was always conceived with a certain essentialism and search for truth in life and, as one might imagine, it quickly became ideological in its grasp for those essentials and quest for veracity. Times do change and so do the opinions, preferences, and attitudes by which prevailing circumstances are characterized, and what counts as being more or less important. Few areas of human activity are immune from these changes—perhaps least of all art. Indeed, artistic preoccupation with versions of reality, or truth, are often the precursors of much broader cultural enterprises in world making.

Artistic Realism of the mid-nineteenth century was a reaction against the sentimentality of Romanticism and an attempt to deal more directly with socially relevant subject matter.[8] So-called history painting and lofty esoteric themes were abandoned in favor of commonplace subjects from the contemporary world. Consequently, the spatiotemporal dimensions of art were narrowed significantly to the "here and now." In the hands of painters like Théodore Géricault, Jean Courbet, Honoré Daumier, and Jean François Millet, as Nochlin tells us, agricultural workers and the urban proletariat become preferred foci. Canvases such as *The Stonebreakers* of 1849 by Courbet and *The Man With a Hoe* by Millet of 1859 to 1862, together with Daumier's drawing, titled *The Third Class Carriage* of 1856, capture their subjects during a particularly characteristic moment of their existence and, indeed, very survival. Moreover, the few number of human figures within each work, together with the middle-ground perspective, heightens both the immediacy of the observational experience and the possible intellectual connection to the historical circumstances behind each social milieu. The sheer isolation and toil of *The Stonebreakers,* for example, was a telling commentary of their precarious livelihood within the emerging modern world, as well as a tribute to their stoic heroism.[9] James Whistler's depiction of figures clinging to the Old Battersea Bridge of 1872 also captures these modern senses of precariousness and isolation.[10] An essential feature of Realism was precisely this capacity for social criticism and a certain democracy in art, which eschewed any ready-made or hallowed artistic subjects. A little later on, Edgar Degas would sharpen still further this factual and socially committed character of painting with his almost instantaneous, even fragmentary, depictions of dancers, cafe life, and working people.

The issue of convention versus reality was also at stake among the nineteenth-century realists, in addition to contemporaneity and the pursuit of socially relevant themes. As Ernst Gombrich clearly points out, there was a struggle against "schemata" as well as habitual and normally accepted views of the world. In their place, realists pursued a more empirical investigation of reality based on direct observation rather than second-hand knowledge of a scene or event.[11] According to the English painter John Constable, one had to forget about what one had seen in the past and go directly to the phenomenon at hand. There was a kind of scientific empathy at work, stressing exactness, foundation in facts, and even a universalizing of truth. In accepted literary practice, for instance, conversations among protagonists in realist novels by Emile Zola, Gustave Flaubert, or the brothers Edmond and Jules Goncourt were interspersed by lengthy and highly detailed descriptions of surrounding circumstances. A certain detachment was also effected by constant reference to "he said" or "she said," and so on. Indeed, Flaubert was among the first to move the novel away from a certain theatricality, using the device of scenes to capture the concreteness of everyday settings and experiences.[12] Furthermore, while faithful to particular places and circumstances, the stories were also told as indicative of significant aspects of modern life in general. Sincerity and a self-conscious objectivity were combined to illuminate the underlying conditions of contemporary existence, especially the plight of the socially dispossessed. Epics like Zola's *Germinal* were clearly aimed in this direction and indeed had considerable political and reformatory impact.

Later in the nineteenth century, again according to Nochlin, shifts occurred in both the subject matter and manner of realist depiction.[13] In concert with prevailing concerns for everyday life, suburban themes began to emerge alongside depictions of urban and rural conditions. Characters also came from middle-class as well as working-class backgrounds. The work of Claude Monet and the young Batignolles painters illustrate both these transitions, in the merger they effected between *plein air* techniques and contemporary recreational themes.[14] "The heroism of modern life," to use Charles Baudelaire's famous salon comment of 1846, also tapered off, becoming replaced by a more casual approach to both subject and scene. Contradictions in the realist position also became evident at this time, if they weren't so before. For one thing, the professed descriptive stance and exactitude toward nature substantially misunderstood the idea of natural science and underlying order. For another, the conformation of scenes, as if for the first time and without resort to past practices, was not consistent with many artists' adoption of well-known compositional principles and pictorial precedents. As Nochlin points out, Courbet's early portrait of *The Meeting* appears to be founded on an earlier illustration called *The Wandering Jew*, for example, even though the surroundings are clearly his native Montpellier.[15] Certainly the role of observation was emphasized more than that of convention, yet there was a rather persistent use of accepted artistic conventions nonetheless.

In the transvaluation and resurgence of various realist themes that followed, new strains of realism emerged. From about 1870 and 1920, the critical dispute over realism in literature focused primarily on the naturalism of Emile Zola. While readily accepting the social profundity of Zola's position, many reacted strongly against the overdetermination of a work of art by its content alone. Marcel Proust, notably, was adamantly against what he perceived to be an almost total passivity before raw phenomena. The more that free will was to play a role, and the more critical of prevailing circumstances realism was to become, the further it strayed from Zolaesque naturalist tendencies.[16] In painting, Impressionism emphasized the perception of light and movement, before work in the medium moved on to cubistic preoccupations with more radical insights about movement and the simultaneity of viewpoints. The American Ashcan School in the early 1900s, especially through the work of painters John Sloan, Robert Henri, and George Bellows, illustrated many impressionistic tendencies while maintaining a recognizably realist commitment to the furious energy of city streets and, as John Ward put it, "the expression of an especially brash, even vulgar, social and historical environment."[17] By contrast, in the decades that followed, artists like Edward Hopper and photographers like Walker Evans, while adhering to many of the techniques and the basic philosophy of realism, deemphasized and even challenged the central urban metaphor of brute force, noise, and action. In its stead was portrayed an almost literal silence and the stillness of those who do not move or speak.[18] Yet, here again, fidelity to circumstances can also be observed, as the mechanical power of the late nineteenth and early twentieth centuries gave way to the organization, specialization, isolation, and even alienation of the modern era.

Capture of the fleeting reality of the present was also accomplished, after Flaubert's earlier attempts, in the work of James Joyce.[19] In many ways, his internal monologues represent an apogee of this sense of "presentness."

Likewise, Ernest Hemingway admirably captured the concreteness of the present, especially, in his dialogues. Invariably these conversations are surrounded by a certain dailiness that interrupts them constantly, slows them down, distracts them, and makes extensive use of an unspoken context among the conversants. Repetition and disjointed exchanges—both features of everyday conversation—are also skillfully displayed to convey an immediate and concrete sense of being there. Artifice and kitsch, by contrast, obscure and tidy up these commonplaces in the name of some (unreal) propriety.[20]

Philosophical debates over artistic realism were waged well into the 1930s—mainly, as one might imagine given the socially critical content of most realist projects, on the political left. Georg Lukács in his *Essays on Realism*, for instance, showed a pronounced preference for orthodox literary works of realism like those by Honoré de Balzac, Walter Scott, and Leo Tolstoy, which appeared to him to contain solutions to the impasses presented by modern life.[21] Moreover for Lukács, Realist art's function was to *de-reify* reality, thus revealing capitalism's permeation of society and culture, especially through processes like machine production, the division of labor, depersonalization of individuals, the growth of cities, and the break-up and dissolution of small communities. In his classic essay of 1932, titled "Reportage or Portrayal," Lukács argues strongly that realism is not simply a matter of reportage or documentary.[22] Instead, realism requires revelation of the processes within society acting on the world. In short, realist works must move below the surface of things and events to get at the struggle involved. It is a form of essentialism that gets to the root cause of social and political phenomena. Furthermore, realism requires context and form to be in accord. Indeed, Lukács was critical of forms, or formal devices, that precede content and are defined a priori as a general response to sociopolitical circumstances. By contrast, his preferred artistic method was dialectical on at least two counts. First, while not denying the need to describe events and conditions with accuracy, he also argued strongly for poetic license and a sense of portrayal. Second, relevant content was constantly a matter of struggle between upper and lower classes in society.[23]

During the celebrated Lukács-Brecht debate that followed, the dramatist Bertolt Brecht stressed the urgency of a popular realism. Writing in *The Popular and the Realistic* of 1937, he said that "the words 'Popularity' and 'Realism' are natural comparisons. It is in the inherent interest of the people . . . that literature should give them a truthful representation of life . . . and to be useful to people they have to be suggestive and intelligible to them."[24] Differences with Lukács centered mainly around method. Brecht favored experimental methods and art based on documentary, whereas Lukács assaulted the work of modernists such as Erwin Piscator, seeking instead a broader, more conventional narrative structure. While Brecht attempted to demystify art completely, stripping it bare of any illusions, Lukács respected more the role of conventions and time-honored expressive norms. In the end, Brecht accused Lukács of being closed minded and of emulating earlier realist styles, to which Lukács countered that Brecht was predetermining the manner of portrayal in advance of the circumstances and ideas being portrayed.[25] As we will see, this distinction between mode of expression and content continues to be a central issue in the realist program. Certainly for Lukács and, even more so for Brecht, how the outside world was addressed by art determined what could be said about it. Realism for them lay in the dialectic between these two aspects of a work. Too much emphasis on the medium resulted in art for art's sake, whereas too much emphasis on subject matter about the outside world resulted in dogmatic, instrumental, and propagandistic artworks. The complete realist project required work to be performed on both aspects, but in a manner that carefully balanced the emphasis and interplay of one with respect to the other. This is a criterion, parenthetically, very similar to Putnam's notion of pragmatic realism described earlier—a *verisimilitude*, or affect of reality, in both genre and content.

Theodor W. Adorno took a similar position to that of Brecht, although he also saw art as a social labor arising from society through a dialectic of subject and object.[26] Fundamentally, Adorno recognized only one "historically advanced material" for a given epoch, representing, in effect, society. Here he defines musical material as something sociohistorical, made up of tones and tonal arrangements generated when composing and modified historically by other composers. In the early twentieth century, for instance, according to Adorno, the sociohistorical movement of historical musical material (i.e., tonality) began to run counter to musical works of art. Consequently, in his *Philosophy of Modern Music* he treated Igor Stravinsky harshly for his eclectic use of material from different periods, while supporting Arnold Schoenberg's atonal pieces as the epitome of a modern age.[27]

Several others also joined in the fray. Walter Benjamin, for instance, in his paper of 1934 titled "The Author as Producer," argued that it is the form of production out of which the art work is made, rather than its depicted subject, which guarantees its progressive radicalism.[28] For him it was absolutely essential that art continue to break new ground. Like Brecht, verisimilitude of genre was the most important issue, at least at the time. The central concern of Epic Theatre, for example, was not to take an audience out of itself into an imaginary world, but to instruct people about their own world in terms of capital and class. Debates at the Maison de la Culture in Paris, organized by the Communist Party in the mid-1930s, took up similar themes.[29] Louis Aragon, for example, championed the Socialist Realist position, seeing it as liberating and the timely accompaniment for a worldwide movement toward social justice. Le Corbusier, by contrast, argued for an abstract, nonfigural position, more in keeping with the facts of contemporary materials, fabrication techniques, and the like. Fernand Léger, by conceptualizing a third position, strove toward a *new realism* with its origins squarely within modern life itself. Instead of making illusions to daily life, however, as in the depictions of social realism, Léger called for "freed color and geometric form," whereby art would emulate, by analogy, the wider play of forces in the contemporary world.[30] For him new realism had to be won from a milieu of new materials, new projective techniques like film, and new forms of public display such as shop windows. This attempt to connect the social concerns of realism with the reflexive concerns of the artistic avant-garde brought Leger close to Brecht and the main left-wing critique of orthodox social realism between the wars. Indeed, among the political left in the 1920s and 1930s there was a real split between marxist modernists embracing surrealism, abstraction, etc., and the communist, popular front, action-oriented realists in whose milieu could certainly be counted Brecht, Benjamin, and only to a lesser extent, Léger.

The place where realism undoubtedly was most strongly tied to an official revolutionary impetus was in the Soviet Union.[31] During the 1930s it was also where the subject matter of the work, as well as the idea of social responsibility and state power, were much more in evidence than any exploration, for instance, of the limits of artistic media. In short, Soviet Socialist Realism quickly became an increasingly dogmatic doctrine about figurative art and its current relationship to society, in sharp contradistinction and even antagonism to avant-garde or modern art, which was seen in turn as being subjective and bourgeois. As earlier as 1928, Stalinist policy within the Soviet Union required social accountability in art, in spite of attempts by some, like the October Group, for reform. By this officials meant a heroic, even propagandistic celebration of state communism. Content thus became the sign of truth in an art work, usually embracing a didactic depiction of the heroic agricultural and industrial worker, as well as in many cases a return to nineteenth-century compositional and thematic precedents.

In the architecture that emerged, public works such as the Moscow metro stations clearly illustrate these trends.[32] For instance, the station for the Lenin Library stop, constructed in 1934–35 and designed by A. I. Gonckevič and S. M. Kravec, among others, was quite modern and functional in appearance. As such it could have been designed for almost any European city and was almost entirely devoid of any figurative references to the Supreme Soviet or state capitalism. The Sokol'niki station of the same date, by I. G. Taranov and N. A. Bykova, is clearly more monumental and hall-like in its spatial composition, with coffered ceilings and decorative lighting fixtures even over the railway tracks themselves. The use of chandeliers and noble materials of stone and marble was also prolific throughout. By the late 1930s, and certainly well into the 1940 and 1950s, both the monumentality and figurative program of decoration increased, often quite dramatically. The proposal for the Elektrosarodskaja station by V. A. Ščuko of 1938, for instance, incorporated a hallway on track level full of oversized statuary illustrating Soviet realist themes. Later projects, like the Komsomol'skaya station of 1951 by P. D. Korin, achieve an almost baroque quality with their monumentality, domed and vaulted hallways, and frescoed ceilings. Other public buildings, including the theatre of the Film Academy of the USSR, designed in 1936 by A. N. Duškin, and the pavilion of the USSR for the 1939 New York World's Fair, show similar trends, although also remaining in the realm of a sober neoclassical architectural tradition.

Other schools of realism emerged during the interwar years. *Die neue Sachlichkeit,* or "new objectivity" to be found predominantly in Weimar Germany, stressed, among other characteristics, a new matter-of-factness, a spirit of simplicity in function and form, as well as an interest in new technologies and materials. Often seen as largely a reaction to Expressionism and its celebration of individualism, Die neue Sachlichkeit art, especially in the *verism* of its left wing, displayed a strong and broad social concern and a commitment toward revealing underlying social truths.[33] In the work of adherents like Georg Grosz and Otto Dix, themes of social marginalization and exploitation within big cities were to be found consistently. For them, art was far from neutral or politically disinterested. Instead it must be tendentious and grapple with society's conflicts. Their paintings, particularly in the late teens and early 1920s, together with those of Rudolf Schlichter, were certainly not real in any naturalist sense, but rather allegorical and figurative, evincing a pictorial interest in avant-garde composition and gestural brush-and penstrokes. Grosz's *Friedrichstrasse* of 1918, for instance, is a clear reminder of this period. Later, from about 1925 onward, both Dix's and Grosz's pictorial technique became more objective; and as some have observed, the more realistic their art became, the blunter in turn became the social criticism and content. Unlike orthodox socialist realism, however, it never became didactic and remained far less optimistic in both theme and portrayal.

In architecture, Die neue Sachlichkeit was manifested soberly in the functional modernist works of some of Weimar's most prominent builders.[34] Ernst May, the *Stadtbaurat,* and chief architect for Frankfurt-am-Main between 1925 and 1930, deliberately fused a rational architectural interest in form, function, and new materials with Garden City principles in planning to promote new satellite communities around the city.[35] This "new objectivity" was to become an essential ingredient in what amounted to a sociopolitical attempt to literally establish a new living culture—*der neue Wohnkultur*—better suited to contemporary post-World War I realities of household formation and housing production. High on May's agenda, as in much of Weimar Germany at the time, was social stability through a return to basics and the expressive realism of a direct reckoning with functional needs and technological requirements. Similar efforts were pursued elsewhere in Germany and most notably in the capital, Berlin, through the architectural and planning work of Bruno Taut, Bruno Ahrends, Walter Gropius, Martin Wagner, and the like. Perhaps less wedded to the idea of such a direct connection between Die neue Sachlichkeit and radically new ways of dwelling, this group of architects, as well as others in *Der Ring* certainly equated rational, modern architectural expression with truth, honesty, and sincerity. In short, it represented for them the realism of the day.[36]

Returning to the art of the interwar years, a self-conscious form of realism began to flourish in Mexico during the 1920s and well into the 1930s, especially through the work of painters and muralists such as José Clemente Orozco, David Siqueiros, and most prominent of all, Diego Rivera. Educated from a very early age as a painter, Rivera also embraced the revolutionary spirit of his country, first as an anarchist and then as a communist.[37] Although he was well traveled, his work nevertheless soon displayed, in its subject matter and pictorial technique, his Mexican roots and a rejection of earlier cubist influences. In 1921, he began work on a wall mural at the National Psychiatry School of the University of Mexico, the first of many frescoes, including several at the National Palace, depicting social and nationalistic themes. By 1930 Rivera went to the United States to undertake work on a mural for the San Francisco Stock

Exchange Building, which in a controversial populist vein depicted the tennis player Helen Moody as the symbol of California. The allegorical and stylized qualities of Rivera's work were then amply displayed in the 1932 commission at the Detroit Institute of Arts, titled simply *Detroit Industry*. This large frescoe faithfully depicted the role of technology and the industrial worker in modern life—both by then almost the staple content of realist art. There were several compositional and narrative twists, however: no electric lights were depicted, for instance, in spite of the ubiquity and even celebration of the so-called electric age. Machines assumed an overall appearance suspiciously like huge Aztec gods, and the usual tension between managers and workers was downplayed considerably. The message of the work seems to go well beyond the usual realist concerns with class struggle and conditions of contemporary life, to suggest a kind of primordial role for technology, which is somehow larger than life and through which everyone stands a chance of being subjugated. Compositionally, the relative relationship between background circumstance and foreground figures is reminiscent of much earlier work by Courbet and Millet.

Many of the interwar strains and dimensions of aesthetic realm can be found to converge in New York at the Rockefeller Center.[38] Originally intended to shelter the Metropolitan Opera House—a project never realized—work on the midtown Manhattan site, located between Fifth and Sixth Avenues and bordered by West 48th Street to the south and West 51st Street on the north, began in earnest late in 1929. John D. Rockefeller, Jr., put the firm of Todd, Robertson and Todd in charge of development, and the young practice of Reinhard and Hofmeister was appointed as architects, with Morris, Corbett and Raymond Hood as consultants. Unlike the earlier opera house proposals, the development was to be primarily commercial and speculative, even if the timing of the project, on the eve of the Great Depression, could not be less favorable. With a long financial lease on the three-block site secured from its owner, Columbia University, Todd set about to secure General Electric's entertainment subsidiaries (RCA, NBC, and RKO) as major would-be tenants. The concept of *Radio*

City quickly emerged, including a complex of theaters, cinemas, and sound stages, all with a capacity to make worldwide broadcasts. This international theme was taken further with the eventual inclusion of the British Empire Building, La Maison Française, the Palazzo d'Italia, and the International Building. The project itself was officially unveiled in March 1931 to considerable public consternation and criticism. Some saw it as megalomaniacal and almost totally devoid of civic virtue, whereas others criticized it as being far too hermetic and insular. Nevertheless construction began, together with the purchase of needed additional lots along Sixth Avenue, and the first phase was completed by 1933.

The plan of the scheme as built owes a lot to the earlier design proposals for the opera house project, although ultimately most to the talent and perseverance of the Associated Architects, as the design consortium was now called. The centerpiece of the project was the seventy-story RCA building, rising like a great slab above the sunken plaza between 49th and 50th Streets. The plaza, in turn, opened up to an upper and lower concourse of restaurants, retail commercial outlets and finally, on the Sixth Avenue end of the project, to the main complex of theaters, including the Radio City Music Hall (designed by Edward Durell Stone) and the Roxy. Along Sixth Avenue, due deference was paid to St. Patrick's Cathedral opposite, with the British Empire Building and La Maison Française rising to a modest height of only six stories above the avenue, with an additional story added on the other side toward the plaza. These two buildings also flanked the relatively narrow slot of space—on axis with the RCA building and referred to as Channel Gardens—which sloped down from Fifth Avenue to the sunken central plaza. Unlike many other surrounding city buildings, the rooftops exposed by the stepped-back massing of the buildings were originally exploited as gardens for semipublic use. Ralph Hancock designed those for the buildings along Sixth Avenue, as well as the eleventh-floor garden at the RCA building. During subsequent phases of building activity— now under the designation of Rockefeller Center—the Palazzo d'Italia and International Buildings were added to the Fifth Avenue frontage in 1935, followed by the much bigger Time Life Building in 1938, the Eastern Airlines Building in 1939, and the U.S. Rubber Company Building in 1940. The skybridges, originally proposed to span across the streets from the RCA building complex, were eventually abandoned as impractical. After weathering the initial storm of criticism and a shabby start to the entertainment complex, Rockefeller Center began to become a successful business venture by about 1938, although it wasn't until the post–World War II era that it began to enjoy the kind of civic appreciation and affection among both New Yorkers and visitors that it does today.

Returning to earlier definitions, the program and form of Rockefeller Center, from its inception, had much in common with the content and expression one would expect to find in an aesthetic realist project. As one might imagine, historically this was never an issue on the part of either the developer or the designers, but some essential attributions can be made nevertheless. First, themes of contemporary and everyday life were clearly incorporated, and in a forward-looking manner. Indeed, celebration of the high lyric arts was replaced by the more popular and universally accessible arts purveyed by RCA and RKO. The commercial program itself was not only something of a breakthrough in convenience and access, but Rockefeller Center also became a symbol of what the critic Cram referred to as a "*too* faithful reflection of the age . . . and a self-assertion of the democratic multitude."[39] To be sure, this is not the social context of the agricultural worker or the proletariat, but it does embrace certainly the office worker, the middle class, and other segments of civil society, including the press and even horicultural societies. In Paris toward the end of last century, as we saw, realist art expanded into middle-class themes just as the social structure evolved. Certainly the critical aspect of verism or the new realism was lacking, although an obvious quality of Rockefeller Center, and especially its publicly accessible domain, was a very real civic character. It might even be called didactic in this respect, with a manner for constituting civic sensibilities similar to socialist realist projects and their preferred milieu.

The second and perhaps clearer coincidence with aesthetic realism occurred in the art and program of decoration incorporated within Rockefeller

Center.[40] The entrance portals along Fifth Avenue, for instance, were adorned with heraldic references and cartouches by René Chambellan, Paul Jennenwein, and Alfred Janniot, depicting within their particular national scheme of things symbols and scenes of social progress. Lee Lawrie's figure of *Atlas*, cast in 1936 and located in the forecourt of the International Building, is heroically humanistic in both content and form. Upon entering the complex, Paul Manship's sprawling golden statue of *Prometheus*, created as a part of the surrounding foundation in 1934, continues much the same theme. In fact, both Todd and Hood wanted a coordinated program of decoration around a coherent theme, making allusions to the Vatican and Versailles in these regards. The philosopher Hartley Alexander was commissioned to write a theme, which he titled "Homo Faber, or Man the Builder." This was later changed by the project management to "New Frontiers and the March of Civilization." In the interior murals that followed, various versions of this theme were executed. For the lobby and back walls of the elevator shafts in the RCA building, a limited competition was conducted. Among those invited to compete, Henri Matisse and Pablo Picasso refused and eventually Diego Rivera was awarded the commission for the large wall at the entrance, with José Maria Sert and Frank Brangwyn commissioned to do the side corridors. When almost completed, Rivera's frescoe, titled *Man at the Crossroads Looking with Hope and High Vision to Choosing a New and Better Future*, caused a sharp controversy within the project team and with Rockefeller himself, especially over the depiction of Lenin in the scene from a socialist country.[41] Work was summarily stopped and the mural smashed to pieces in February 1934, to be replaced sometime later by a far more insipid composition by Sert. The episode did not stop there, however, Rivera brought the "murdered painting," as he put it, back to life on the wall of the Palace of Fine Arts in Mexico City, this time inserting a portrait of Rockefeller in the debauched nightclub scene.[42] Other art work within the center included Ezra Winter's frothy mural, *The Fountain of Youth*, at Radio City Music Hall, a large wood-carved mural by Carl Milles in the lobby of the Time Life Building titled *Man and Nature*, and the magnificent plaque above an entrance to the Associated Press Building, created in 1938 by Isamu Noguchi.

Apartment building at the Quartiere Tuscolano by Muratori.

Finally, the architecture of much of the complex was direct and sincere in a manner befitting a realist project. The limestone and glass-clad towers were straightforward, modern, and unencumbered. Indeed, they were unfashionably so at the time. The RCA building in particular, with its narrow prow facing Fifth Avenue and its flanking clifflike sides, seemed to punch through the ground and shoot straight up toward the sky—so much so that Alice Toklas was moved to remark to Gertrude Stein that "it is not the way they go into the air but the way they came out of the ground that is the thing."[43] When choosing the massive slablike form for the RCA building, Hood was dramatizing the overpowering scale of the new skyscraper in Manhattan, a spatial dimension that would soon become synonymous with the island, replacing the ground-hugging overlay of buildings characteristic of former times. Refusing to adhere to requests by Rockefeller and others to reconsider a symmetrical tower, Hood felt that the slab form was more functional and consistent with the idea of a building made up of layers of stone facing. The forthright blockiness of the buildings also strongly expressed a businesslike attitude, well in keeping with the center's commercial program and optimistic new confrontation with the realities of post-depression America.

NEOREALISM AND ROME'S POSTWAR DEVELOPMENT

As Nochlin astutely observes in her book on Realism, a direct analogy can be drawn between the appeal of William Morris, August Pugin, and John Ruskin to medieval architecture during the later nineteenth century and more contemporary attempts to find vernacular and participatory approaches toward town planning and building that restore an intimate relationship between culture, shelter, and the individual.[44] For Pugin and Ruskin, the organic and apparently seamless connection between Christian virtue, common ways of life, and appropriate architectural expression—which they imagined existed in England during the middle ages—had a ring of truth to it and a sufficient moral weight to counteract the alienating forces of the industrial revolution prevailing at the time. Like more contemporary vernacular approaches, theirs was an attempt to offset a reality—at least in rhetorical terms—based on what was common knowledge, familiar and immediately believable. In short, it was an appeal to a traditional and popular basis for verisimilitude and a logic of persuasion founded on the use of figurative architectural devices that were readily recognizable and that could be embraced broadly with affection. As such, it was an approach to making architecture that stood in sharp contrast to later modernist concepts of reality, where the object of representation was so often depicted by the use of elements found outside of architecture per se, mainly in technology.[45]

The era of *Neorealism* in Italy shortly after World War II was a time during which a popular basis of verisimilitude was imposed extensively on architecture and other arts, including several soon to be well-known cinematic masterpieces.[46] Roberto Rossellini's *Roma città aperta* of 1945 and *Paisà* of 1946, together with Vittorio De Sica's *Ladri di Biciclette* of 1948—to name three—set new standards for apparent authenticity and a graphic directness of experience. Alberto Moravia and Giorgio Bassani accomplished much of the same thing in literature, as well as dramatizing the tragedy that often accompanied the lower class in their struggle for survival. In painting, Italian realism dated back before World War II and, in the lively canvases of Renato Guttuso depicting heroic working-class themes, extended well into the late 1940s. In fact, his studio in Rome on Via Margutta was the center of artistic and political debate between realists and the emerging abstractionists during the postwar period. Owing something to his acquaintance with Rivera, who had spent time in Paris, Guttuso's work also often showed a cubist influence in the fragmented background illustration of towns and countrysides. The photographer Alberto Lattauda in his book *Occhio quadrato*, published underground in 1940, clearly anticipated later neorealist preoccupations with the naked geometries of squalid tenements, southern agricultural exploitation, and the desolate outskirts of northern industrial cities. A connection with depression-era American photographers like Walker Evans and Dorothea Lange was also evident. Federico Patellani's *Sicilia* and the coal-mining series titled *Il Dramma di Carbonia* have the same immediacy, poignancy, and grainy quality as scenes from Rossellini's, De Sica's or Luchino Visconti's films. Indeed, the photojournalism of what became known as the *paparazzi* was conspicuous for its down-to-earth, hard-hitting style and instantaneous capture of the moment. Simultaneously, photographic images began to epitomize contemporary Italian life. Mario De Biasi's *Gli italiani si voltano* of 1953, for instance—the depiction of a statuesque woman walking toward a group of men in a street—vividly conveyed a kind of "Italianness" in the sexual tension and social mores of the postwar years, some would say, verging on the manufacture of identity stereotypes. Meanwhile, in architecture, neorealism was also asserted as an appropriate way of identifying with the mass movements sweeping Italy after the war, and of creating dwelling environments in a familiar, commonplace way.

One of the mass movements that began even before the war ended in Italy was interregional migration. Before 1960 well over 25 percent of the entire population had picked up their belongings and moved, often into cultural milieus very different from their own. Migratory flows to northern industrial cities and towns from the south, or *mezzogiorno*, were not only the stuff of cinematic chronicles like Luchino Visconti's *Rocco e i suoi fratelli*, but the primary vector of this human drama.[47] Rome, the nation's capital, in the central province of *Lazio*, also experienced massive immigration, although equally from the neighboring and, at that time, far less prosperous provinces of Umbria, Le Marche, and Abruzzo. Over the course of about ten years this influx of population amounted to around half a million people. Rome's population, which stood at 1,155,722 inhabitants in 1936, expanded to 1,651,754 people in 1951 and grew to 2 million inhabitants by 1960.[48] The reason for these migratory patterns was very rapid economic development and gross regional imbalances in that development. Italy in 1943, at the end of the war, was in many ways little changed outside of its major cities, since the time of the *Risorgimento*. It was still a peasant country and, especially in the south, was to remain that ways for some time to come. Yet in the relatively short span of forty years, Italy was transformed out of all recognition, becoming the world's fifth largest economy.

Per capita income, which in 1945 lagged far behind that in northern Europe, had all but equaled that in Britain by 1970, and the material standard of living improved accordingly. Automobile ownership, for instance, rose from around one car per 36.5 households in 1950 to around one car per 3.1 families by 1964.[49] Ownership of household appliances like refrigerators, washing machines, and televisions, also showed dramatic rises.

Demographically, the Italian family structure also changed appreciably during the postwar years, even if the family's hold over society was to remain for a while.[50] Overall, the average size of families decreased from 4 persons per household in 1951 to 3.3 in 1970. If anything, in a place like Rome, there was also a general trend toward smaller nuclear families and yet also a decrease in the number of single-person households and larger extended families. During the first quarter of a century after World War II, the percentage of the population that belonged to traditional nuclear families was to remain high, at around 55 percent, and more Italian women became housewives than ever before, especially in comparison to other industrially developed nations. The prominence of the middle classes—the families of the *ceti medi*—was on the rise, leading to a certain kind of familism, founded primarily on Catholic values of piety, love, and unity, as well as the primacy of the family unit within civil society. In some quarters, pressure to defend the family led to an integralist view, whereby all institutions of civil society were to be made in the image of the family and its reflection of Catholic values.[51] On balance, these social trends, especially during the 1950s, led to a victory for the communitarian spirit over individualism and, in the minds of some critics, effectively inhibited other modern forms of collectivization.

In retrospect anyway, the Republican system of government, which began in 1943, inherited many characteristics and weaknesses from the prior regimes of the Liberal State of 1860–1922 and the Fascist Government of 1922–1943.[52] Generally, decision making was highly centralized and held to be above local interests. State involvement in the economy was broad, and bureaucracies burgeoned in every branch of governmental activity. The linkage between the ruling elite and the masses was often effected through clientelism. These practices were particularly apparent in the south, although as many Italians have recently learned in the context of the *mani pulite* movement, they extended all over the peninsula. To these aspects of government the postwar Republic brought universal suffrage, a complex and highly representational democratic party system—at least prior to the recent Segni Amendment—and, as we just saw, rapid socioeconomic growth and change. The rights and privileges of civil society, including freedom of association, the press, and expression of opinion, were also expanded considerably, particularly in comparison to the repressive Facist period. Given this contrast between institutional rigidity and flexibility, the relationship between the state and civil society was often negotiated through a sort of hybrid world of political organizations, autonomous agencies like INPS and INAM, public bodies in industry, such as the energy combine ENI, as well as regional governments. In many instances, these entities were the control gates to resources, a quasi-state apparatus that had to be negotiated from both sides of public and private life.

Formal politics during the postwar period was controlled, with varying degrees of success, by right-wing coalitions, but always with the inclusion of the Christian Democrats (D.C.).[53] Between December 1945 and July 1953, Alcide De Gasperi was President of the Council of Ministers (i.e., the Prime Minister), and in the 1948 constitutional referendum he helped effect the historic compromise with the political left led by Palmiro Togliatti of the Communist Party (P.C.). Differences across the spectrum of parties were great and factionalism was rife. Nevertheless, no matter how positions appeared to change, the basis of power remained much the same. Laissez-faire policies abounded, particularly on matters of development, and the economic boom—often officially pegged between 1956 and 1963—really began not long after the new Constitution was put into place. The only town planning laws that remained—*piani regolatori particolareggiati*—dated back to 1942 and were effectively dead letters because of the inadequacy of local enforcement powers. In the case of Rome, a group of intellectuals including prominent architects Saverio Muratori,

Ludovico Quaroni, Mario Ridolfi, and Mario De Renzi began lobbying for a new *piano regolatore* midway through 1952.[54] They would have to wait, however, until 1962 before such an instrument would be drafted for the greater municipality. A prevalent explanation of Italian politics, certainly at the time, described political parties as necessary evils representing an anachronistic process in a modern economy. Other probably better informed views saw both aspects as interdependent and not wholly negative, certainly given the substantial degree of change and reform that was actually achieved in Italian life.

One figure who emerged forcefully onto the political scene during the late 1940s and early 1950s, was Amintare Fanfani, who would become President of the Council of Ministers for a brief time in 1954.[55] A dynamic university professor with some political associations in the fascist past, Fanfani was a subscriber to a brand of reformism embracing traditional Catholic social theory. He belonged for a while to Dossetti's faction of the Christian Democrats, which preached the need to safeguard Catholic values in a rapidly changing society. The ideology of *solidarismo*, as it was called, advocated charity, associationism, and the state's duty to protect the family as well as the weak and the poor. This position sparked sharp debate within the Christian Democrat party, particularly when viewed in contrast to other laissez-faire doctrines with considerably more emphasis on individualism. The liberal party faction, for instance, was for unfettered technological development, consumer capitalism, and a free play of economic market forces. In fact, during the late 1940s and 1950s, the D.C. party was constantly balancing capitalist interests with those of the urban *ceti medi* and the rural property owners. On par, the industrialists, through the organization *Confindustria*, enjoyed considerable governmental influence. Nevertheless, the internal party dominance of the 1950s of the *Fanfaniani* attracted considerable undifferentiated support within the D.C., both because of its appeal to Catholic cultural origins and because it provided a promising means for building up the new party—albeit along old lines—through the use of extensive state intervention. With unemployment running rampant in 1949, to almost 2.2 million workers, the construction industry was called upon to help resolve the problem, as well as helping to accommodate the overcrowding and housing needs of Rome and the northern cities. One result was that the INA-Casa (*Istituto Nazionale Abitazioni*) constituted by Fanfani and headed by Arnaldo Foschini went into effect and was responsible, during the next ten years, for the construction of 110,953 housing units, or about 8 percent of the units constructed in Rome between 1949 and 1959.[56] As a joint public-private venture, two-thirds of the financing was provided by a special payroll tax of 0.6 percent levied on employees, matched by a contribution of 1.2 percent by employers, as well as mortgage financing provided through an intergovernmental bank and monies donated through philanthrophic agencies. The other one-third of the financing was provided by the state.[57] Unfortunately perhaps, INA-Casa represented the only fully fledged attempt at public or quasi-public intervention into housing development and planning. Clearly though, with the title of *Provisions for Increasing Worker Employment and Facilitating the Construction of Labor Housing*, Fanfani's plan was to stem unemployment and, incidentally, to tie housing development to small businesses, and by holding housing firms to pre-industrialized levels of technology, to amplify the positive unemployment benefits.[58]

Postwar urban development in Rome quickly began occurring on its periphery, starting up approximately where development during the Fascist period had left off. With little room for practical expansion within historic areas and inner-city quarters, this was also a path that followed a course of least resistance. Between 1932 and 1940 considerable demolition and dislocation of housing occurred in Rome, principally to accommodate Mussolini's plans for an Imperial City.[59] Under Piacentini's plan, for instance, the *Borgo Pio*—a dilapidated yet still vital community next to the Vatican—was all but totally destroyed, and its inhabitants relocated, for the most part, on the outskirts of the city. The peripheral developments that resulted from the redevelopment of Rome's historic core in this manner became known as the *borgate*, a term used officially for the first time for the construction of housing in Acilia, a poorly drained area 15 kilometers from Rome.[60] In reality and as the term suggests, borgate—even if derived from *borgo*—referred to segments of urbanization that were incomplete with respect to services and nonresidential functions, certainly in comparison to well-established *quartieri*. They were, in effect, built-up areas isolated in the middle of nowhere, without the benefit of being part of either the city or countryside. Many new inhabitants were often transported to these barracks-like environments in military buses, no doubt stationed on the nearby army bases. In fact, the borgate were used as a dumping ground for antifascist troublemakers, a condition graphically depicted by Rossellini in *Roma città aperta*.[61] Even before enactment of the 1931 Plan of Rome, three borgate were being established at San Basilio, Prenestina, and Gordiani. Between 1935 and 1940 many more were to follow, including Primavalle (the recipient of many people displaced form Borgo Pio), Trullo, Tiburtino III (the subject of Rossellini's film), Tor Marancio, and Quarticciolo. The architectural quality of several of these later subdevelopments improved substantially, incorporating sound modern planning principles, openness to light and air, access to community space, and so on. Over time, streets were paved and the relative isolation of the communities was diminished by public transportation. By 1951, however, housing conditions in Rome had reached crisis proportions with almost 7 percent of the population living in cellars, under stairways, and in shanties, as well as another 22 percent living in dramatically overcrowded conditions.[62]

Three of the first INA-Casa projects constructed in Rome were the Quartiere Tiburtino, the Quartiere Valco San Paolo, and the Quartiere Tuscolano. All three were commenced in 1950 and quickly became the objects of discussion and debate about the role of neorealism in the Italian postwar architectural recovery.[63] The Quartiere Tiburtino, adjacent to the old Roman road of the same name leading east to the Adriatic, was located about 5 kilometers from the center of Rome on its developing periphery. The design group responsible for the project, headed by Mario Ridolfi and Ludovico Quaroni, was called L'APAO (*L'Associazone per l'Architettura Organica*) and included Carlo Aymonino, Cesare Chiarini, and Mario Fiorentino. The irregular-shaped site was 8.8 hectares in area, sloping up fairly steeply to the northeast away from the main road. Housing was provided by 771 dwelling units for some 4,000 eventual inhabitants, primarily in the form of three-, four-, and five-story row houses and several seven-story towers.[64] The street pattern was organic in layout, creating seven large land subdivisions and, where necessary, conforming to the topography. The overall effect of the urban spatial organization was, in the minds of the designers, to correspond to the essential psychology of the future inhabitants from rural areas around Rome and from the mezzogiorno. Although certainly not referred to as such, it was almost a Pugin-like and Ruskinesque appeal to common knowledge and familiarity. Or, as Quaroni put it, "while creating a city, in reality we made a village."[65] Indeed, the deliberately varied building masses, pitched tile roofs, stucco wall finishes, and shuttered windows gave the Tiburtino project a distinctly picturesque quality reminiscent of much older rural towns. The layout of dwelling units within one of the large land parcels was also usually varied, with an irregular arrangement in plan of row houses of different heights, counterpointed by tower blocks and small housing clusters. Each ground-floor unit was provided with a private garden, and those above with sizable balconies. Typically, street edges were walled, thus providing paved entrance courtyards and common garden areas within each block. Even when the geometry of a block was relatively regular, an organic irregular quality was superimposed through the alignment of buildings. This quality, in turn, was undoubtedly intended to give the appearance of an incremental, discontinuous process of development, also reminiscent in atmosphere to the middle-class Roman *palazzine*. In this concentration on housing there was also a marriage of sorts between neorealism and the conservationist attitudes of Fanfani and others in the D.C. toward family life, although, oddly enough, the design group was more strongly associated with the Italian political left.[66]

Underlying the neorealist architecture of the Tiburtino, and the Roman School of Quaroni in general at that time, was an encounter between intellectuals and mass movements made heroic by the Italian Resistance. Specifically, it was an encounter—or more accurately, the adoption by intellectuals of a role—that deliberately embraced a language of popular experience and action in order to annul an architectural past based on abstract intellectual considerations and internationalism. In short, it was a search for a new beginning in postwar Italian architecture rooted in the purity, vitality, spontaneity, and humanity—that is, realism—of peasant existence.[67] Poorly equipped for such a search, Ridolfi and others set about to document vernacular construction in detail. His *Manuale dell'architetto* of 1946 presented "little techniques," as he called them, suitable for vernacular reconstruction or, at the very least, vernacular reinterpretation, ironically somewhat similar in format to May's *Frankfortur Normen,* or building standards for Frankfurt-am-Main.[68] Typologically based, these studies of architectural fixtures and construction details were also regionally based, expressly introducing the idea of local traditions and craftsmanship into the discussions. Throughout, the value of the vernacular experience was extolled as an antidote, among other things, to a strongly felt sense of alienation experienced at the hands of international architectural modernism. Again it was a reaction similar to that of Pugin and Ruskin during the late nineteenth century. Closer to home, it was also an impetus that continued from work in the early Fascist period and before, concerned with "garden city principles" and concomitant eclectic, picturesque, and even romantic architecture. Garbatella of 1920 to 1930, for instance—*una borgata giardino*—initially planned by Gustavo Giovannini, a scholar of the garden city movement, and completed by Marcello Piacentini with architecture by Innocenzo Sabbatini, has several formal parallels to Tiburtino.

Needless to say, Ridolfi's and, at the time, Quaroni's unequivocal neo-realist position came under attack. Irenio Diotallevi and Franco Marescotti, in their *Problema Sociale costruttivo ed economia dell'abitazione* of 1948, for instance, were very critical and advocated instead a radically rational approach, explicitly returning in the direction of the prewar Die neue Sachlichkeit.[69] The approach pursued by Saverio Muratori and his partner Mario De Renzi at the Quartiere Valco San Paolo was also distinctly rational in outlook, although clearly neorealist in many of its motifs and aesthetic sensibilities. A relatively small housing project, Valco San Paolo occupied 5 hectares of relatively flat land south of the center of Rome near the eastern bank of the Tiber River in the direction of the prewar EUR sector. About 440 dwelling units were completed to house some 2,500 inhabitants, again like Tiburtino in three-, four-, and five-story row house configurations with some eight-story towers.[70] The street and block layout was rational and almost gridlike, and although the overall composition of building masses had a certain picturesque quality, it had none of the wantonly organic character of Tiburtino. The four parallel bands of row houses, for example, were straightforward blocks with spacious rear yards without any noticeable articulation in plan from one unit to the next. A central open space and organizing feature of the scheme was a long rectangular treed piazza, running east-west through the site and then bending northward as a paved strip in front of two lines of commercial stores and service establishments. Unlike the earlier borgate, both Tiburtino and Valco San Paolo were planned from the outset as well-serviced communities. The remarkable feature of the architecture at Valco San Paolo was the manner in which neorealist features, such as pitched roofs, chimneys, balconies, shuttered windows, and entry stoops were tightly edited into a rational modern architectural language. The resulting effect is certainly realist in both its import and impact, but without a great deal of vernacular mimicry.

A polemical contrast was thus established within Italian neorealist architecture between the two positions of Quaroni and Ridolfi with their group on the one hand, and Muratori and De Renzi with their followers on the other. The first stressed adoption of a strong vernacular language and an organic sensibility, whereas the second was more discriminant and rational. At about the same time as Valco San Paolo, Muratori and De Renzi, in collaboration with L. Cambellotti, G. Perugini, and L. Vagnetti, planned and designed the largest INA-Casa project in Rome, the Quartiere Tuscolano, extending themes began at Valco San Paolo.[71] The prominent prewar rationalist architect, Adalberto Libera, also was to add an unusual courtyard housing complex to the scheme, apparently influenced by his recent travels to North Africa. Overall, the project conformed to Rome's 1931 *piano regolatore* and the more recent local plan of 1949. In both plans a strong axial arrangement was specified through the center of the site, parallel to Via del Quadraro and Via Cartagine, and running roughly in a north-south direction from Via Tuscolano to Via Selinunte. The comparatively large site, located southeast of the center of Rome near the Via Appia Nuova and adjacent to the interregional railway line, was more than 35 hectares in area. In total, around 3,350 dwelling units were constructed for a resident population of about 19,000 people.[72] The overall plan, with the exception of Libera's parcel on the southwest side of Via Selinunte, was divided into four quadrants, although in reality the scheme can be best described as consisting of a strong central spine of buildings flanked on both sides like proverbial ribs with parallel rows of buildings, terminating with tower blocks along Via del Quadraro on the east and Via Cartagine on the west. Again three-, four-, and five-story row houses were deployed throughout the bulk of the scheme, making up the smaller community precincts. The more or less rational layout of buildings—strongly influenced by contemporary Swedish patterns of development—continued the approach taken at Valco San Paolo, although as already noted, many of the symmetrical and formal qualities of the plan derive from the original 1931 *piano regolatore*.[73] A remarkable spatial sequence was formed along the main central axis of the plan, beginning with a heavily wooded park and parabolic fero-cement entry by Libera, and then followed by a very long wall of row houses inflected outward in plan to form a large garden space, terminating in Muratori's V-shaped six-story slab block embracing the paved piazza in front of Via Tuscolano.

Again it is in the architecture of the housing complexes that the tension between the traditional vernacular and a modern rationalism can be found. Muratori's extension of the V-shaped apartment building creates an urban space that is at once familiar and commonplace like a traditional town piazza, as well as modern and functional for use as a bus stop and general-purpose open area. The architecture of the apartment building is clearly defined by a rational framework of vertical concrete columns and horizontal slabs, whereas the side profile is faced in *tufo* stone and features a pitched gable with a multitude of village-like chimneys. Panels within the concrete facade framework also feature tufo infill in a manner similar to local villages, together with shuttered windows and traditional balconies. Again a double reading of modern and vernacular is apparent. Similarly, in Libera's unusual and not altogether Roman courtyard housing scheme, old and new materials and methods of construction were combined to produce a time-honored and yet contemporary effect. Thick rusticated walls, also reflecting those to be found in nearby ancient Roman ruins of aqueducts, were joined by thin reinforced concrete roof shells over the single-story courtyard units. Gateway and entrance details, as well as overhanging roof gables, also lent an air of familiarity and tradition, as did the layout and planting of the adjacent community park. Meanwhile, the huge parabolic arched entrance to the complex was clearly traditional in its location and prominence, and yet highly technological in its specific form and substance. The overall composition was also something of a microcosm of the traditional Italian small town, although modern and functional in its layout. In retrospect, the neorealist tide that had buoyed Italian architecture after the war began to recede at Tuscolano and elsewhere, although not without having had positive transformative effects.

In the middle 1950s, INA-Casa entered a second phase under the government's Vanoni plan, which placed further emphasis on job creation.[74] By then the housing industry was booming, with annual estimates of production ranging around half a million units annually, or a very high normalized rate of 9.8 dwellings per 1,000 population. The construction industry in general was expanding at a rapid rate of 12 percent per annum—compared to about 8 percent for all industry—and employed almost 30 percent of the work force.[75] Unfortunately, the open collusion that developed between municipal authorities and building speculators resulted in what some termed "the sack of Rome." Apartments, often of poor quality, were built indiscriminately almost anywhere, with the result that almost one in six Roman houses by 1970 was not in compliance with local codes. Additional legal provisions to INA-Casa also resulted in a further shift toward smaller private entrepreneurs, through provision of credit and other special financial arrangements. Meanwhile, in architecture circles Quaroni became self-critical of his earlier attempts, moving away from "the poetics of neighborhoods," as he put it, to far more formalistic approaches.[76] This effectively ended the prominence of neorealism in Italian architecture, and in 1963 INA-Casa itself was replaced with GESCAL (*Gestione Case Lavoratori*), which soon became notorious for its clientelistic way of doing business.

Criticism of Tiburtino, Tuscolano, and Valco San Paolo typically occurred around three points of contention and was usually made from the political left. First, the projects, as free-standing communities on Rome's periphery, were perceived as aiding and abetting rampant property speculation. There was undoubtedly some truth in this, although Fanfani and his cohorts were against extreme forms of individualism as a matter of political credo. Moreover, similar approaches to building, conducted elsewhere in Europe both before and after World War II such as in Frankfurt-am-Main, relied on satellite communities to control outward expansion and speculation. Second, at least in Tafuri's eyes, there was a deliberate merger of public employment policy and the aesthetic inclinations of neorealism with its localism, populism, and craft orientations, ultimately resulting in a conspiracy toward the use of low technologies and away from more highly industrialized building processes.[77] These aspects of employment and relatively low technology are certainly true, and very similar to the orientation behind much of American housing policy in the wake of the Great Depression. Hindsight has shown, however, that unless the margins of utility and performance are dramatically reduced, housing is not something that lends itself quite so easily to industrialization. In fact significant advances were made in the efficient management of labor and materials, precisely because of the open-ended, relatively low-tech character of housing production. Furthermore, attempts at manufactured housing, again elsewhere in Europe, were to prove nothing less than disastrous. Third, criticism was made that nothing really new by way of a living environment was offered at Tiburtino, Tuscolano, or Valco San Paolo.[78] Again there is a ring of truth to this, although Libera's courtyard housing at Tuscolano was certainly unusual, if not entirely new. More generally though, the effect of novelty in housing—like newness in many things—has had both good and bad results in social terms. Part of the appeal of the neorealist program was quite the opposite: a quest for familiar, traditional living environments.

Finally, the often purported claim that neorealism, especially in the Italian context, was somehow new and revolutionary in itself can stand some reexamination. As Peter Bondanella points out, neorealism in film was actually not completely new, nor an original phenomenon. Indeed, for him "Italian film culture under fascism was a rich, multi-faceted, and highly heuristic spring-board for post-war cinematic production."[79] There was readily on hand a well-trained professional cadre, good studio facilities, and an orientation toward mass entertainment rather than propaganda per se. No less a figure than Vittorio Mussolini, himself a participant in the film industry of the Fascist period, held out for authenticity of landscape, scenes from everyday life, and a general search for cinematic realism. In both photography and other visual art, as we saw, realist approaches were also under way shortly before World War II, al-though in architecture, neorealism, at least in the sense of the Roman School, was essentially a postwar phenomenon. In spite of similarities between prewar and postwar rationalism, as well as deployment of figural expression on the part of fascists and republicans alike, the commitment of an architectural neorealism to vernacular references, organic compositions, and popular associations with the masses was a point of departure. Certainly the convergence of neorealist creative energy and the charting of a course toward social reform and prosperity was a break with the past, and a phenomenon that was to leave an undeniable impression.

Pier Paolo Pasolini, to name just one prominent artist and intellectual, was to continue in a similar vein in cinema work like *Accattone* and *Mamma Roma* and in literary pieces like *Ragazzi di vita* and *Una vita violenta*. For Pasolini realism was a way of attacking and criticizing what he called "false freedom" and "the false tolerance" of the bourgeoisie.[80] This he did effectively through an explicit sexuality that challenged accepted social norms, and through the celebration of borgate life as an alternative based on instinct rather than on

Dwellings at the Quartiere Tiburtino by Ridolfi and Quaroni.

accepting and following convention. For Pasolini the *borgatari* were authentic, essentially lying outside of contemporary history with its economic miracle, *La dolce vita*, polite commonplaces of the *ceti medi*, and antics of the proletariat. Simultaneously, as a realist artist he resisted strongly interpretations of a work of art solely in terms of the social message it conveyed, arguing instead that style does matter. In effect, Pasolini was neither for art for art's sake nor for art for the sake of politics.[81]

Populist brands of architectural realism also appeared elsewhere. In Britain, for example, Gordon Cullen's *Townscape* and related picturesque principles were used in the new town movement sweeping the country, shortly after the war.[82] Apart from the specific figural references that could be drawn easily to traditional townscapes, there was a certain "democracy of things" being applied to low- and moderate-income housing estates, similar in intent to Italian neorealism. Later attempts, during the late 1960s and 1970s, to make use of the reality of the contemporary and popular American building scene by architects like Robert Venturi were pursuing something of the same logic, although perhaps with considerably more irony and a less genuinely democratic motivation. Less obviously populist and vernacular—like Muratori and Libera's Tuscolano complex—the neorationalists, again in Italy, set out to recover the reality of a sense of history and continuity with the past through autonomous architectural forms. For Aldo Rossi and others in the *Tendenza*, architecture should be a representation of itself. Rather than an emphasis on populist content, theirs was a rhetorical effort aimed at a verisimilitude based on a concern with the logic of a genre and its convergence on architectural problems per se.

DEFINITION OF ARCHITECTURAL REALISM

By now the difficulty of pinning down precisely what can, or might, be intended by architectural realism should be obvious. As we saw, Realism in any form does not easily lend itself to definition. Fortunately, however, there are certain principles and characteristics that persist, regardless of other prevailing circumstances. The crux of realism is a probing concern with everyday life and a simultaneous interest in advancing the medium involved in its representation. Both a "verisimilitude of content" and "verisimilitude of genre"—to borrow again from rhetoric—are required. Realism, as we have seen, is not a concern with surface appearance or likeness. Nor is it synonymous with naturalism and, even when more than less abstract in its use of a medium, there is none of the wholesale commitment nor subjectivity found in modernism. Instead, both the "now" and "what" of a work must involve a certain detachment, even critical distance. This having been said, however, still leaves considerable room for interpretation, requiring a further sharpening of the concepts implied in these definitions.

A probing concern for everyday life—or a verisimilitude of content—immediately introduces two separate though interrelated aspects. First, what constitutes "everyday life"? Second, what is "probing concern"? The defining of everyday life, as we have seen already, immediately raises ideological issues about which scenes, what characters, and which environments are to be included. Clearly, subject matter must be generalizable, or part of a more widespread set of social concerns. Class struggle in art or a parallel appreciation of the mode of habitation in architecture are cases in point. The content of a realist project cannot be personally idiosyncratic: mass housing could be included, whereas a private home probably could not. The subject matter, or content, should also be representative of prevailing circumstances and not nostalgic in longing for some former time, or overly futuristic in advancing the cause of something not really part of this world. Under this requirement, Rockefeller Center clearly qualifies as a realist project, especially in the United States at a time when the office worker had begun to replace traditional working-class symbols of labor. The aspect of everyday life incorporated into a realist project must also be commonplace, at least in the sense of being accessible to all or many, and well within the domain of broadly shared experience. This should not, however, preclude ritual. Rather it is a matter of special commonplaces rather than all of them. Architecturally, the neorealist commonplaces in housing of entry courtyards, traditional shuttered balconies, and other popular references are the results of this kind of selection.

The idea of a "probing concern" in realism immediately equates with sociopolitical forms of criticism to be found in verism and, as we have also observed, in the illustration of movements of class struggle in socialist realism. As Lukács and Brecht both remind us, this is not criticism for criticism's sake, but an attempt to reveal underlying social processes—particularly those that might be oppressive to one group or another. Although putting it differently, Géricault and Courbet probably would have agreed. Presentation of alternative ways of making the world can also accomplish a similar critical stance, as we saw with the better socialist realism, and is much closer to the effect that architecture can have on an audience. The design of Central Park in New York, discussed at greater length in the next chapter, clearly recognized and yet deliberately transcended the underlying social differences and potential for conflict among New York's disparate population groups. The park became a remarkably successful project, precisely because of its capacity to harmoniously accommodate everyone. In addition, a "probing concern" for everyday life can also mean honesty and sincerity in outlook and a dedication to not simply take matters for granted. Again this kind of sentiment is difficult to translate directly into architecture, although a housing scheme, for instance, that explicitly accounts for the potential reality of urban violence in its design and yet provides positive community space, clearly embraces such an outlook. A recent project by the Nos Quedamos group in New York's South Bronx, at least in social terms, is just one such case.[83]

Verisimilitude of genre—or a concern for advancing the medium involved in a realist project—immediately introduces the question of how the medium should be regarded. In architecture, as we have seen, there was a rather significant difference between the Die neue Sachlichkeit position and that of the later neorationalists. Die Neue Sachlichkeit interests, in many aspects, lay outside of architecture per se, concentrating instead on parsimonious use of new materials and construction technologies seen in their own terms. Neorationalism, by contrast, turned attention inward to an existing world of architectural elements and prototypes, as well as their future architectural possibilities. Both positions embody realist requirements for truth, fidelity in material content, and so on. However, the immediacy and accessibility of the neorationalist position probably consistently conveys, ceterus paribus, a greater sense of realism. As Michael Benedikt proposes in *For an Architecture of Reality*, a sense of "realness" is conveyed by four aspects: presence, significance, materiality, and emptiness. In contracted form, "realness" is assertive, catches one's attention, is substantial, and has a certain quiddity or lack of contrivance.[84]

A concern for advancing the medium also raises the issue of what "advancement" means and what kind of advancement should be involved. Clearly, at some basic level "advancement" must mean progression by way of a certain invention and not a reliance entirely on tried-and-true practices. It is a call for some amount of innovation, which in architecture can mean either "work on the language," to borrow Peter Eisenman's phrase for a moment, or some other formal investigation. Both aspects can and have been involved in realist projects. The use of familiar symbols or figural references, so much a part of neorealist and later populist positions, was a linguistic preoccupation, but one that went beyond mere appropriation. Vernacular practices and popular symbols were transformed in the work of Muratori and, to a lesser extent Venturi, in a manner that enriched architectural expression, rather than simply becoming a decorative appliqué. Similarly, developments aimed at enriching the repertoire of formal architectural types and other essential properties—a hallmark of the neorationalist preoccupation with genre—also advance architectural expression.

The simultaneous requirement for a "verisimilitude of content" and a "verisimilitude of genre" automatically requires interaction between these two important aspects of a realist architectural project. As already observed, it is often difficult to differentiate between these aspects anyway. Work on a language, for instance, necessarily implies some concern for content. In fact, it is hard to imagine one without the other. What is important in a realist project, however, is the trading-off and balancing between a concern for content and a

concern for medium. As noted, too much emphasis in one direction results in art for art's sake, whereas too much emphasis in the other results in a dogmatic portrayal without sufficient artifice. The debate surrounding the neorealist housing projects just discussed well illustrate this balancing test. At the Tiburtino there was a very strong presence of social interest, vernacular references and a homage to organic traditional townscapes. There was, as Tafuri and others have observed, little advancement in more strictly architectural terms. The architecture at Tuscolano, by contrast, was far less figural and easily identifiable, although vernacular references were made nonetheless. There was, however, a substantial attempt to incorporate these references into the architecture, as well as some very real experimentation with building types and forms of public space. In the end, if a judgment had to be rendered, the architects of Tuscolano probably succeeded more in effecting an appropriate balance between "content" and "genre." Their critical analysis also appears to have been more acute. By offering inhabitants of their project considerably more than familiar surroundings—through a range of accommodations that would stretch their imaginations—the differences in housing with other upwardly mobile groups in Italian society could be narrowed appreciably.

In a final analysis, both projects were well precedented, although the architecture and planning at Tuscolano was considerably more innovative. Architects in both places employed known references and formal techniques derived from well-established vernacular or high-architectural traditions. This merger was of new interest and gave the projects a strong sense of realism. By extension, the step toward a "less precedented realism" requires far greater attention to specific design conditions and situations than to general architectural preoccupations that are brought to bear repetitively. It is at root a highly situational form of realism to be found, for instance, in the recent Sicilian projects of Rodolfo Machado and Jorge Silvetti.[85] In proposals like Porta Meridionale of 1987, the focus and symbolic characteristics are, strictly speaking, without many architectural precedents. Certainly there were no highway interchanges of the same ilk. The project does, however, relate to an immediate experience of the place and to a conviction that cities can be appreciated directly and objectively as cultural facts. Far more than simply contexturalism in a passive sense, Machado and Silvetti's projects actively engage and ennoble everyday experience. The invented and heterogeneous nature of the cultural subtexts they draw upon are not about one walk of life or another. Rather, while quite apparent as things in themselves, they are not easily pigeonholed into preexisting or familiar categories. The promise of such a less precedented approach to realism is the immediacy of experience it can render, as well as the safeguard it can provide against falling into cliché.[86]

Even now, in the search for a concise definition of architectural realism, it is difficult to say much else in the absence of specific circumstances and programs of action. The philosophical relativism that served to introduce this discussion still retains some influence. Whether a project is realist or not still depends on criterion supplied by a specific time, place, and circumstances. Introduction of civic space as the focus for realism eliminates the vagueness still further. We immediately find, for example, an interest in everyday *public* life and the places where individuals meet or encounter one another, as well as where civil society and the state transact their business. Also immediately apparent is a certain familiarity or knowledgeability about surroundings probably with a preference for civil modes of conduct. In addition, civic realist projects might be required to go beyond a ready accommodation of function by materially enriching and even ennobling a particular aspect of everyday life. To say still more, however, requires more attention to the role of the individual and public places.

"What's real?" muttered Lidia to herself, mirroring the flatness of contemporary discontent. "I hardly know anymore—what with all these theories and abstract crap floating around, anything's possible. The trouble is, nobody knows what's good or even what's right," she mused to herself fitfully, pulling a strand of her tousled hair across her face and poking out her tongue in concentration.

"How's the drawing going?" asked Giovanni a little apprehensively from the neighboring desk, sensing her distracted mood. "You know this project is really important for the cause," he went on. "What bloody cause?" thought Lidia skeptically. "How come Giovanni and the others are so damn sure about what they are doing? Things are so complicated—it was probably much easier in Nonna's day," she said to herself, thinking of the well-established rituals of everyday life, the practical reckoning with need, and the help that always seemed to be at hand. "But then again, perhaps it wasn't."

"I'm almost finished, Johnny," said Lidia, concentrating on the last lines. Then she looked up and noted the obvious satisfaction on his face by her use of the Anglo diminutive of his name.

—Piero Monteverdi, *Tornare a Casa**

4

Individual Spaces and Collective Places

A cast-iron loft building in New York's SoHo district (page 124).

Hector found the solitude of the roof a welcome respite from the complications of the street below. Slowly he watched in the twilight as an airliner banked over Manhattan and continued its descent into LaGuardia across the river. "Yo Hector, my man, what's up?" hailed Luis, stepping gingerly over the debris and construction irregularities around the stairwell. Hector stiffened, startled by the sound of the voice behind him. "Great suit," he said noncommittally, filling in time. "Yeah, fourhundreddollahs," replied Luis, pirouetting, as much to make a rhetorical point as to show off the line of his suit. "Strictly legit, man," he went on. "That store I work at on West Broadway—got it on layaway. You could do the same, man." "Yeah! Put da fame behind me, huh!" Hector muttered sarcastically. "But dat place over dere man, it's a freak'n foreign country!"

Randall glanced out of the window as he stuffed the flight magazine in the pocket of the seat in front of him. "I like it when they take this route in over the island," he said to himself. "It's hard to believe the ground plan is the same all over, with all those different sizes and shapes of buildings," he mused. "I hope Martha remembered to water the plants and bring in the mail. Oh well, I should be home in about forty-five minutes, depending on traffic." Then, continuing the thought: "The trouble with SoHo is that it's like Eurobar—too many damn tourists. Soon it's going to ruin the neighborhood." God, am I tired! Too much travel!" he continued to himself, yawning, stretching and shutting his eyes for a moment.

Peter Kleinewolfe, *East, West, and Center**

From the vantage point of a blimp, airplane, or satellite, late twentieth-century New York City resembles a varied yet well-ordered grid of streets and blocks. This was not always the case, however. In 1806 the city requested the state legislature to appoint commissioners to lay out a plan for the development of Manhattan Island beyond the existing urban area, which corresponded approximately to today's "downtown" district. Shortly thereafter, three commissioners were appointed— Gouverneur Morris, Simeon De Witt, and John Rutherford—and a plan was approved in 1811, extending a single rectilinear grid over all existing rights of way, agricultural holdings, hills, marshes, waterways, and small settlements on the island, all the way up to 155th Street.[1] The primary basis for this plan was to encourage the city's development in an orderly fashion, and little to no provision was made for parkland or for the setbacks and viewing points usually associated with prominent public buildings. Parkland may well have seemed unnecessary, given the abundance of open space at the time, and the commissioners probably assumed or desired that the city would retain its early nineteenth-century scale and variety, consisting mainly of relatively affordable small-lot developments on 20 to 25 foot frontages. Care was also taken to align the more numerous streets in an east-west direction, with the wider avenues running north-south. Again the presumption seems to have been that most land traffic would be concentrated along the waterfront, requiring frequent inland access. Broadway, alone among the existing streets, was allowed to intersect the grid, forming a diagonal route across the island.[2]

In addition to becoming the infrastructure for real-estate speculation and building development, the self-same grid of streets and blocks became embellished, over time, by street facades, squares, spacious avenues, and parks. In fact, it acquired a palpable urban-architectural presence unlike anywhere else in the world, which at least by the turn of the century projected strong public-spirited collective meanings and associations. New York was a place bursting with civic pride. Simultaneously, the grid and its interstices were also the sites of other unofficial and even unauthorized activities, as well as the places individuals sought to adapt to their own peculiar circumstances. Above all, it became a matrix for a heterogeneous population of rich and poor, ethnically similar and dissimilar, each one inhabiting the same overall space, but more often than not separate spheres. Like few other cities there was and still is one entity—"the Big Apple"—and yet many New Yorks.

TRANSFORMATION OF SPACE INTO PLACE

The space we occupy, work in, dwell in, and otherwise live in, according to the French intellectual Henri Lefebvre, is essentially produced by social processes and practices.[3] Usually people rent or buy a dwelling according to their means and consequently often find themselves in a community of like minds, interests, and economic circumstances. Over time, apartments, houses, and other physical characteristics of an urban neighborhood are modified or constructed until the space of the community becomes a place with its own distinctive characteristics and aura. Other people sometimes take riskier steps and move into run-down districts of cities—attracted by perceived amenities such as once-grand spaces—and struggle to make them over into their own image. The so-called gentrification that often ensues is usually aided and abetted economically by a rent gap between the current value of properties in deteriorated and disinvested conditions and the potential of a much higher value under a new use. Typically the greater the gap, the more intense become pressures for redevelopment and economic revitalization. The new use also tends to vary with the focus of the pioneering spirit of those involved. Sometimes it is a matter of historic preservation of an area close to where they work, or it may be adoption of specific spatial characteristics offered by existing nonresidential uses and even pursuit of a certain anonymity within the greater life of a city. This process is invariably complicated. Quite often, unfortunately, economic revitalization can lead simultaneously to social devitalization, as one upwardly mobile social group displaces others from an area. Immigration and occupation of certain districts of cities by specific ethnic or national groups—linked by prevailing linguistic, economic, and other cultural conditions—is also a common phenomenon, especially in established cities like New York. Frequently, this phenomenon also recurs in the same place. East Boston, for instance, was a "port of entry" and "zone of emergence," to borrow sociological terminology for a moment, first for Irish, then for Jewish followed by Italian immigrant populations.[4] Today it performs the same function for Latin American communities. Each wave leaves its own cultural imprint, transforming the found space, at least for a time, into a socially and culturally recognizable place.

The reciprocal relationship of space defining social practice also pertains to most urban-environmental circumstances. The preexistence of space in a particular form does condition a person's actions, perceptions, and exchanges with others, as well as affect competence and performance in these functions. A ready availability of mortgage money within an area, for instance, can substantially facilitate people's acquisition of dwellings. Conversely, discriminatory market practices can prevent otherwise eligible people from choosing where to live. Generally, at least under capitalist conditions, pricing and the values assigned to property substantially affect the social geography of cities. Specific physical characteristics also materially affect social practices. The broad availability of parks, for example, probably promotes outdoor recreation and at least certain kinds of game playing. High traffic volumes on streets, by contrast, impede many forms of children's play, whereas a game such as "box ball" was developed as a vertical version of "stick ball" in many New York neighborhoods, where highrise developments and confined spaces replaced more open lower-rise configurations. The size and geometry of prominent physical features of an urban landscape—such as the dimensions of a standard street grid—can also have a substantial impact on socioeconomic processes of subdevelopment, as well as the practiced use of spaces within blocks. The Manhattan grid, described earlier, with its comparatively short and long sides (800 feet by 200 feet) promotes—largely as the original commissioners had intended—linear aggregations of buildings with considerable emphasis on street fronts and little or no activity, other than service, within the interior open space of each block. The grid structure in the central business district of Melbourne, Australia, by contrast, is about 620 feet by 320 feet, or considerably wider, although shorter, than New York's.[5] Consequently, one finds numerous arcades and alleys crisscrossing each block and offering scope for an entirely different form of pedestrian activity. Likewise, each city, depending on its physical conformation, has its own peculiar arrangement of sites for official and everyday functions, as well as for unofficial and unauthorized activities.

Generally, and again according to Lefebvre, each society offers up its own particular space. In ancient times, for instance, there was the Greek *polis*.[6] Nowadays major cities incorporate what he referred to as "bourgeoise space," with an emphasis on spaces of exchange and commerce.[7] Quite often, especially under sociocultural conditions where economic rationality and performatory function are valued highly, what one designates as space is very often what one gets. The idea of "residence," with many of its niceties beyond simply dwelling, for example, can quickly become conflated to housing and then built as such.[8] Indeed, the spatial domain of the residence historically has gone through many variations, resulting in quite different places conforming to prevailing social practice at the time, even though the basic program of spaces has remained little changed. Similarly, the recurrence of social phenomena in certain places can take on a different though no less effective form than simple economic determinism. Luc Sante, for instance, refers to the "underground tributary of tradition" whereby prejudice is perpetuated for a specific area, sometimes even in outright contradiction to actual conditions there, resulting in a lasting stigma.[9] Meanwhile other places, again for Sante, seem to be "magnetized by a genus loci which makes them thick with recurrences," such as Tompkins Square Park on Manhattan's Lower East Side, for instance, where there are still flurries of anarchistic or antiestablishment activities as there were in the later nineteenth century.[10] By contrast, more conventional civic spaces seem to offer members of society an image of that collective membership which, in the end, is more faithful and enduring than their own personal view. Clearly, at work here are the twin processes, as Lefebvre puts it, of exaltation and repression, and the resulting image is a deliberately simplified or codified view of prevailing social conditions.[11]

One place—returning to New York and the Manhattan grid—where several of these social processes and practices have played themselves out, and where the physical character of the environment itself became a strong determining factor, is the district now referred to as SoHo. The results by most standard measures can also be called civic, at least during three moments in time, coinciding respectively with the original construction of stately homes, development of the late-nineteenth century warehouse and manufacturing district, and today as a renovated loft environment. In fact, SoHo is an acronym, stemming from the district's recent redevelopment, standing for "South of Houston" and describing a forty-three-block area in Manhattan, bordered on three sides by the major arterial roads of Sixth Avenue, Canal, and Houston, as well as by the equally distinct neighborhood of "Little Italy" on the other side.[12] During the early period of development in the first half of the nineteenth century, the area adjacent to Broadway became a fashionable middle-class neighborhood with gracious houses, the best department stores, and fine restaurants and hotels.[13] Among other amenities, the short walking distance to lower Manhattan's working environment made it a popular place in which to reside. Subsequent streetcar and even later subway improvements altered this locational advantage in favor of places further uptown, away from the expanding commercial hustle and bustle. Still, for a period of about twenty years—roughly between 1830 and 1850—this segment of the Broadway corridor helped project the civic virtue and aspirations of the rapidly expanding city, and was a project that involved the municipal government as well as citizen groups.

After 1850, or thereabouts, decline from this exalted position was rapid. Many of the stately homes became brothels and were cut into apartments for the poor. Some on Greene and Mercer streets even predated this general decline. The 1850s also saw the metamorphosis of Broadway from a street of small brick stores into a boulevard of marble, cast-iron, and brownstone commercial "palazzos." Major hotels were constructed, such as the Union Hotel, the City Hotel, and the luxurious St. Nicholas Hotel. Musical halls and theaters—sites of popular entertainment—also multiplied, so much so that the strip of Broadway between Canal Street and Houston became known as the entertainment center of the city. Minstrel Hall, the Olympic, and Brougham's Lyceum were just a few of the outstanding theatrical venues, which together with Niblo's pleasure garden and Harry Hill's dance hall further on up Broadway stood out as local meccas for New York's night crowd. Even the notorious politician, Fernando Wood, used the Mozart Hall, again on Broadway, as a headquarters for many of his activities.

Consolidation and a further shift in function occurred around 1879, as once gracious homes, now dilapidated, were replaced by loft buildings providing space for mercantile and manufacturing businesses, again in collaboration with the city, particularly to the west of Broadway. Proudly trumpeting their existence and vying with each other for attention, the result was the largest concentration of full and partial cast-iron facades in the world. Although the ironmonger Daniel Badgers's Venetian Renaissance facade on the Haughwort and Constable and Co. buildings of 1857 might be said to have started things off, it wasn't really until the 1880s—well after the economic panic of a decade earlier—that construction of the stately edifices began in earnest. The Cheney brothers, for instance, one of the world's foremost silk manufacturers at the time, built offices and storage space, around 1880, at 477–479 Broome Street, in the form of a neoclassical cast-iron building by Elisha Sniffen.[14]

Cast-iron facades were competitive economically with plain masonry walls, but had the advantage of readily incorporating vastly more ornament and the appearance of a desired level of opulence. Consisting of precast panels, the cast-iron facades were also much quicker to erect, at least to a height of about six or seven stories. Height beyond that required special attention to substructure, and with it, added time and expense. Other prominent architects were also at work in the district.[15] Richard Morris Hunt, for example, designed the elegant 478–482 Broadway—later to be destroyed—and I. F. Duckworth was responsible for a number of "commercial palaces," such as 72 Greene Street, with its ten-bay facade fashioned in the manner of the French Second Empire style. Henry Fernbach was another architect working prodigiously in the area, well known for the elegance of his facades and the efficiency of his construction practices. Henry and Isaac Meinhard's warehouses at 133–137 Greene Street, for example, were completed in just ten months, between 1882 and 1883. Architects, however, were probably not employed to design many facades. Instead, castings of so-called neo-Greek, French Second Empire, French Renaissance, and Italianate styles were shared and became standard fare delivered by the foundries. Undoubtedly this aspect of "monumentality by the yard," imitating as it did structures of granite and marble, appealed to many merchants' and factory owners' desire to flaunt their good fortune—but at a reasonable price. The cumulative result, nevertheless, was impressive and fashionably uniform, providing the streets of the commercial district around Broadway with a new-found civic monumentality. As one observer put it, "one was supposed to walk down the streets to see the beauty of the Renaissance, revived in modern iron."[16] Furthermore, an explicit awareness of a larger, more civic identity for the area was clearly visible in spite of individual competition. In fact, the appearance today of large uncompleted monumental corner edifices or sections of a block bears witness to that common sense of identity.

Although the last full cast-iron facade was constructed before the turn of the century—largely because of the structures' unfavorable fire resistance and the difficulty of constructing taller buildings—the commercial and manufacturing district, in what was to become known as SoHo, enjoyed economic prosperity well up until 1920. The two major industries were garment manufacture and the fur trade, until they departed uptown in the vicinity of the "thirties" and Seventh Avenue, in search of better locations and more modern facilities. What remained were firms dealing with low-value paper products and textile wastes. Subsequently, with a small reprieve during World War II, the district declined significantly between 1920 and 1950 as a viable commercial and industrial area. It even acquired the label of "Hell's Hundred Acres" during this time because of a demonstrated potential for fires, and remained in limbo, caught between the office boom to the south, in lower Manhattan, and the institutional growth to the north, around New York University. Still, a core of enterprises remained and continued to operate. In 1962, for instance, around 650 business establishments could be found in a twelve-block area, employing about 12,600 people, mostly as blue-collar workers.[17] Industrial lofts spaces and even entire buildings, however, were also abandoned, as the area slipped further into economic decline and disrepair.

Fortunately, reasons for decline can also become reasons for revitalization. While the relatively narrow and tall lofts, together with a less direct access to markets, were unfavorable for modern industry, they were favorable to a group of pioneering artists.[18] From early in the 1960s, Minimalists, as well as proponents of Fluxus, Op, and Pop began developing studios, and in the process the district acquired its current name. The open loft spaces of SoHo permitted artistic experimentation on a grand scale with, for instance, the heavy load-carrying capacities of floors being well suited for heavy sculptures, and easily reached by freight elevators. It was also a cheap place to live, away from the urban crowd, and a place where relationships could be struck up easily with neighboring manufacturing industries and related blue-collar workers. Strictly speaking, all of this occupation was illegal and clandestine, as the district officially remained for some time an industrial and commercial zone. Nevertheless, this designation would change as the pattern of loft occupation and conversion intensified and the voluntary organizations of civil society began to emerge. First, the Artists in Residence program of the 1960s made it legal for artists to occupy loft spaces. Second, the SoHo Artists Tenant Association was formed in 1968, serving the dual purpose of dealing formally with municipal government over property rights and services, as well as further developing and augmenting unity within the community. Finally in 1971, the zoning was changed, largely in response to this coherent organization and as a de facto response to what had already happened. A little later, in 1973, the *SoHo Weekly*—an organ for presenting community issues—began publishing, and the Landmarks Preservation Committee designated a large segment of the district as a historic site.[19]

Other related activities followed a similar pattern. In 1968 Paula Cooper opened the first commercial art gallery on Wooster Street and many others quickly followed, making SoHo a center for art distribution as well as production. In short, key elements of both civil society and the state seemed to be conspiring to preserve the architectural character of the area and to change and revitalize its use. Today the SoHo Partnership continues in this direction and, among other activities, employs people—some from the ranks of the homeless—to work in the neighborhood, clean the streets, and shovel snow.

With the increasing momentum of this civic undertaking other circumstances began to change as well, but not necessarily for the better. Speculators began to take over from "risk-oblivious" early pioneers, promoting an alternative and not inexpensive lifestyle of loft living. The attractions of a bohemian lifestyle, as at other times in New York's past, brought tourists, chic boutiques, and fancy restaurants to the area. This was all well and good except for the gradual displacement of the district's remaining blue-collar jobs and the economic pressures placed on less well established artists, many of whom began migrating over the bridge into Brooklyn. Caught between a perceived need to halt illegal conversions, reach building code compliance, and generally introduce rational bureaucratic procedures while simultaneously protecting the rights of individuals already dwelling in places like SoHo, government officials eventually promulgated the Loft Law of 1981.[20] Unfortunately, these ends often proved to be at odds with one another. Current occupants simply stayed and "squatted" as normal renters, interminably delaying efforts by owners and others to improve dilapidated conditions. In spite of these setbacks, however, today SoHo stands as a vital and distinct community within New York's Manhattan borough, with a civic sensibility about its streets and public domain that is both palpable and unique. It also stands as a testament to a varied social and economic history of both individual and collective enterprise spanning more than 120 years, of which, remarkably, almost all have involved occupation of an urban space by the same buildings and street right-of-ways. The urban architecture of SoHo has made a lasting impression and, as much as anything, has been responsible for molding the social and cultural character of the area.

By contrast to the city edifice's effect on its populace, in parts of the nearby Lower East Side, social processes and practices have been decisive in converting space into place, although often tragically. As the population of New York grew rapidly—almost doubling each decade during the latter part of the nineteenth century—development within the grid expanded generally in a northerly direction toward "uptown."[21] This expansion, however, was not by any means evenly distributed, and for lower-income residents spaciousness and an abundance of open space was not one of its virtues. Immigrants, coming by boatloads well up until World War I, settled where they could, usually close to places of employment and other economic opportunities. Vast districts of tenements sprang up, consisting of narrow five- to six-story buildings with meager openings providing the minimum of light and ventilation, often crowned—hypocritically—with a well-composed genteel street facade. By the 1890s, fully 60 percent of New Yorkers dwelled in such tenements, with the Lower East Side as one of the first segments of the grid to develop in this manner. In 1910, population of the district peaked at 500,000 people, who were mainly Jewish immigrants from Europe.[22] As one might expect, local ethnic institutions developed and flourished alongside of housing. Stores and other commercial enterprises also thrived, especially along the broader and well-traveled avenues. Over time, one wave of immigrants gave way to another, and eventually a Hispanic-American population began to dominate. Unfortunately, the area also suffered economically and, together with urban renewal during the 1940s and 1950s, caused the population to decline in numbers appreciably. By 1980 the number of residents was about 149,000, or only 30 percent of the 1910 peak.[23] Hardest hit was *Alphabet City*, so-called because of the designation of north-south avenues by the letters A, B, C, and D, where population declined during the 1970s by around 67 percent, with most of those remaining existing well below the poverty level.[24] The early stigma of overcrowded tenements continued to play itself out, although now with the cruel irony that many had been torn down, leaving a desolate urban landscape of many vacant lots and abandoned shells of buildings.

At present, *Loisaida*—as it is called in Spanglish—is a poor, tough area, full of drug dealers and users, and occupied primarily by Puerto Ricans. It is also slowly being gentrified. In fact, the term "Alphabet City" only began to be used when gentrification made its first incursions into the neighborhood during the 1980s.[25] For those there beforehand, and especially for the Puerto Ricans who had been coming there since the 1940s and early 1950s, it has remained Loisaida. Geographically, the neighborhood extends roughly from First Avenue in the west to Avenue D on the east, and from Houston on the south to East 14th Street on the north. At its center, between A and B Avenues, is Tompkins Square Park, the site of numerous political demonstrations as well as celebrations over the years, together with attempts by outsiders to clean up the area and make it appear more prosperous and respectable. The overall grid of blocks and streets is surrounded on two sides by post–World War II public housing projects and abutted on the south by a much earlier and narrower grid centered on Delancey Street, with the East Village's matrix of commercial establishments, institutions, and apartments to the west. Most of Loisaida is comparatively low-rise, in the Manhattan tradition of townhouses and tenements, although a few towers loom over the area, as part of institutional complexes like hospitals and public housing.[26]

An overall scarcity of material wealth, however, does not prevent the Puerto Rican community from embellishing their lives with a rich array of symbols and rituals. On the contrary, the slender margins of existence and struggle for survival almost seem to demand tokens of identity and belonging. Parish churches, for example, celebrate the "Stations of the Cross" each Easter within the neighborhood, using particular locations with other sociopolitical meanings as the places for these commemorations. Often a teenage boy, for example, plays the role of Jesus Christ, and the actors and musical accompaniment are transported from place to place throughout Loisaida on the backs of trucks.[27] Tompkins Square Park, for one, is usually a point of celebration, as much as anything in recognition of the homeless housing struggles that have taken place there. Hence parishioners and others in the neighborhood celebrate both religious and secular aspects of their lives simultaneously. Memory walls—commemorating the death of someone, often from drug-related violence—have a similar function, although "hip-hop" graffiti art is also used to respectfully adorn—albeit with a socially critical edge—places of cultural significance, including cafés where poetry readings are held regularly and several local live theaters. Chico is a well-known local graffiti artist; together with others, he paints on commission, often in the case of memory walls at the behest of family members.[28] In a similar vein, vacant lots are appropriated to construct club-houses—*casitas*—and to install productive urban agricultural gardens. Many casitas, like those further uptown in the Bronx, are constructed in a makeshift manner and yet are lovingly adorned and often demonstrate an ingenuous use of found materials. Less visibly perhaps, neighborhood cliques are now also involved in a transition from organized street hustling to coordinated and alternative forms of street government. Happily, in some places at least, the *bomba* of Latino reality has taken an outward civic turn in the name of community solidarity and identity.[29]

     The results on urban environments of these social practices are—to use a musical analogy—invariably heterogeneous scores, or aggregations of cultural references, in both major and minor keys. Through much of this century, the symbolic environment of the Lower East Side—Loisaida, or if one prefers, Alphabet City—was constantly being both written and overwritten like the proverbial palimpsest. The outcome—in a major key—was a dense representation of different individual and collective declarations and ambitions. Awnings and other street signs, for instance, advertised the role of specific firms and yet added up to the conveyance of a common cultural heritage. Over time, however, this plurality did acquire a certain critical civic dimension, as parts were edited out by both design and neglect, while others were reinforced. Use of common realms between buildings, for example, were often intensified and portrayed as both public and community property, whereas the explicit language of one culture was simply wiped out by the next, or continued in ways that altered its meaning. By contrast, in SoHo social processes and practices, although instrumental in the formation of the environment at one level, are in a minor key when compared to the overall physical edifice of the place. Substantial functional distinctions, for instance, between publicly accessible galleries and private domiciles don't usually register on the broad and stately facades of loft buildings. The predominate promenade at street level has the twofold function of allowing passersby to see and be seen without serving too many other purposes. In fact, there is even a coherence to the crowd, especially given the propensity of habitués to wear monochromes or simply black and white. Nevertheless, both Loisaida and SoHo, in major or minor keys, are civic and real in their respective representational traditions. Indeed, they might even be seen to illustrate polar opposites of essentially the same impetus. One—Loisaida—represents a collective through its variety rather than through sheer difference. The other—SoHo—adopts or imposes upon its community a more or less uniform physical structure.

Certainly the more arcane theoretical observations of Rem Koolhaas and Bernard Tschumi are borne out by these two examples. Architectural form and program, over time anyway, don't necessarily—if even usually—conform to each other. As Koolhaas points out eloquently in *Delirious New York* and Tschumi recounts in the *Manhattan Transcripts*, the spatial order of a contemporary city is without any single intellectual construct.[30] To paraphrase Tschumi, many complex relationships between space and use are removed from conventional architectural representations. The question is whether this lack of conformance between form and program is an excuse for the willful invention of form, given that program doesn't seem able to be controlled in any reliable fashion. The answer, presumably is no, it is not. Going back to Lefebvre, genuine social space—and therefore any place within the narrower confines of this discussion—is made up of an ensemble of vital characteristics.[31] First, it is a matter of accommodating social practices, including necessary performance criteria

Tompkins Square Park in New York's Lower East Side.

and standards of competence—to be able to promenade down a street, for instance, without having to concentrate unduly, or avoiding bumping into other people, or falling into open basement areas. Second, it is a matter of having a sufficient "representativeness" to the space in question by way of signs and other codes, so that it is legible, imaginable, and so on. In short, it is to not mistake a church for a dry cleaners, for instance. And third, social practices require representational spaces embodying complex symbolisms about, for example, identity, ownership, or civic pride. In civic realist terms—going back to earlier definitions—this means creatively making environments for those practices involving the state and civil society in everyday life, which are either widely regarded or warrant distinction. Certainly SoHo qualifies, through the collective efforts of refurbishing historic buildings, the remaking of streets and entranceways with people in mind, and the maintenance of a variety of land uses. More urgently, so does the open publicity against gang violence and the community support of neighborhood parks and social facilities to be found in Loisaida, together with an affordable residential infill of once desolated areas. In both instances, the efforts of individuals—publicly motivated or not—promotes a quality of environment that offers more to a city than otherwise would have been the case.

RESISTANCE, MANIFESTATION, AND NEW YORK'S GRID

When comparing New York to Rome, the French philosopher Michel de Certeau made the point that "New York has never learned the art of growing old by playing on all its pasts." On the contrary, "its present invents itself from hour to hour." [32] He went on to say that a distinction can be made between the "geographical space" of urban theorists, cartographers, and planners—the aloof construction of some "voyeur god" on high, as he puts it—and the "anthropological space" of everyday life. [33] Several other related distinctions follow quickly. In the difference between "place" and "space," for instance, a "place" is an ordered arrangement representing a certain tendency and community-held orientation for its experience. When referring to such and such as a place, we are usually referring to a selective, semi-official ensemble of characteristics. A place that marks a center of a city, for example, is usually highly accessible and defined in a very evident if not monumental manner. The Piazza del Campo, as we saw in the first chapter, is such a place. A "space" by contrast is what de Certeau refers to as being a "practiced place"—an individual trajectory and a specific spatial experience. The inscription of the space of a window shopper, or a voyeur walking along a street with placelike qualities, are two common examples. Usually, ordinary practitioners in space escape the panoptic view referred to earlier and, in some instances, clearly transgress the formalizing tendencies that make spaces into places. "Keep off the grass" is not only an admonition but a collective state of mind about a place as distinct from a space. The "Place de la Concorde does not exist," Malaparte said. "It's just an idea."[34]

Other distinctions include the difference between "map" and "tour," where a map—as in common parlance—refers to an abstract and independent depiction of many specific trajectories and spatial experiences of an area.[35] It is about "geographical space," whereas a tour describes a specific itinerary or trajectory and is about "anthropological space." From these distinctions it also follows, according to de Certeau, that the act of "seeing" belongs to both map and place, referring to the performed, or intended, perspective or view to be taken of a space for the purposes of coloring, controlling, or otherwise influencing specific actions within it. "Acting," or "acting out," in turn, is defined and determined by stories made up of tropes, metaphors, or other linguistically analogous actions on behalf of city inhabitants. In this regard, to paraphrase de Certeau, walking is to urban systems as the speech act is to language.[36] The implication, of course, is that there are various styles and uses of walking and various kinds of walkers. The walking rhetoric—to continue de Certeau's linguistic analogy—of New Yorkers on the midtown avenues, for instance, is bound to be varied, including the self-confident bounce of a young executive going to work, the stop and go of the window shopper, and the neck craning, sweeps, and ambles of the tourist. These concepts, in turn, also allow us to distinguish behavior or activities "proper" to a place from those that are transgressions—in other words, to separate those spatial practices that conform to the intended underlying order and general tendency of a place from those more clearly at odds with it.

A literary example where both the practice of space and the tour converge occurs in Paul Auster's *New York Trilogy* when one of his characters, Peter Stillman, makes an inscription of letters spelling out _OWEROFBAB__(TOWER OF BABEL) by tracing a certain path through the orthogonal grid of Manhattan's Upper West Side, followed at a distance by another character, Mr. Quinn.[37] With less deliberation, two other characters in a later story experience a great sense of release, even abandonment, on their respective tours of many of the self-same streets. As Auster eloquently puts it, "He rides the subway, rubs shoulders with the crowd, feels himself lunging towards a sense of the moment . . . giving way to where and how the crowd takes him . . . suspending responsibility for actions."[38] Clearly, in the conceptual manifold of the moment and the space, euphoria is, or can be, a reward for being in the city, and a way of overcoming the history and circumstances of the place.

The point of this conceptual apparatus, in de Certeau's general philosophical framework, is to describe "resistive practices," as he calls them, by which inhabitants of a city can assert their own individuality and personality, or simply lose themselves for a while.[39] For him, the very real problem with convenient totalizing accounts of cities—inhabited as such accounts of cities invariably are by universal and anonymous subjects or so-called rational persons—is that they deprive cities of their essential humanity. More dangerous still, such accounts can become accepted as reality and used to fashion other places, as well as sometimes to justify coercive actions, ridding cities of their genuine anthropological spaces. For unrepresented groups like the homeless, for example, this can have extremely serious consequences, often driving them literally underground in a city like New York into more practiced spaces where acting becomes more possible, to use de Certeau's terminology for a moment. Although he doesn't say so explicitly, it also probably follows that there can be a relative tightness or looseness of fit between anthropological and geometrical space, from which it further follows that a generous place is one that can accommodate many practiced spaces. The streets of SoHo, among the two earlier examples, are probably generous in this regard. At least the walking, loitering, and meeting "rhetoric," which can be both tolerated and accommodated there, is likely to be varied and comparatively equally valued. Street artists, for instance, can hawk their wares, tourists can hang out and take pictures, and locals can converse politely without much bother. By the same token, the prevailing sense of *moral suasion* against transgressions of the place by alternative spatial practices is likely to be both strong and immediate. Not only are the streets well under the rule of law, well maintained and well surveilled, but they have a physical shape, spatial coherence, and scale that seems to say that this is a place for some activities but not others. By contrast, at least on some streets in nearby Loisaida, there is a less relaxed tolerance of variety in practiced space—arising from suspicion of unusual things—as well as a collective physical and social sense of *suasion* that is less strong and less immediate. Unfortunately, the results are often more permissive, transgressive, and even violent. Suburban streets, while appearing to be somewhere in between, are in fact often oppressive, by being both less tolerant of the variation in spatial practices and stronger in the immediacy of response toward transgressions.

The criterion that emerges for good civic space is tolerance of a real variety of social practices within limits that are well defined by both custom and the physical attributes of the place itself. Instructive in this regard is the controversy, at this writing, surrounding use of the *sagrato* in Milan (the broad band and steps in front of the *Duomo*, or cathedral). Intensive bivouacing by immigrants and some tourists blocked the space and prevented use of the cathedral and other areas of the piazza. Attempts by authorities to preserve access, however, immediately met with a public outcry over the undue curtailment of civil liberties. Nevertheless, clearly both activities upset the civic character of the place. After all, it always had been the gathering place for all manner of people, though not to the deliberate exclusion of some others. The broad steps invite one to sit and linger, in good weather, by providing a vantage point from which to survey the rest of the piazza. They also provide access to the cathedral beyond and form a symbolic dias for the whole edifice. One function is not necessarily more important than the other, because they both seem to lie within the bounds of customary and expected use, but both must be able to occur comfortably. One of the advantages of "resistive practices," in this kind of instance, is that over time they often ensure that other practices can occur. In Milan a balance was struck finally, through the provision of alternative sitting places in the form of benches, and broad planting beds the sides of which could be sat upon also. Essentially, further place making was needed to preserve and expand—at least by one—the variety of spatial practices that could be accommodated within the piazza. Yet the recent modifications may spawn still other unforeseen resistive practices, resulting in further resolution, and so on.

In a vein not too dissimilar from de Certeau, the two British sociologists, Stanley Cohn and Laurie Taylor, chronicle various ways in which we build up stable constructs of the world and present ourselves to that world as individuals.[40] Living in a contemporary society involves people in "reality work," as they call it, and "identity work." In reality work larger frameworks, like life plans, systems of goals, career plans, and so on, are created and reinforced.[41] In identity work elements of the individual are revealed and cultivated. Thus the twin problems of life, according to Cohn and Taylor, are structuring and maintaining a day-to-day existence and simultaneously constructing an individual identity. In traditional societies the discrepancy between reality and identity was narrowed significantly when individuals could display themselves by showing commitment to the arrangement and routines of everyday life. What people did and who they were, for instance, was never very far apart. In contemporary life, however, there is often both a reflexivity and a relativity that promotes a separateness between reality and identity. At times, people happily accept versions of reality as identity, like membership in a club, while at other moments there is a strongly felt need to distance or separate themselves in identity from such reality. Alienation in the workplace is one such example of the separation of reality and identity. Far from being entirely relativistic, however, such positions do carry additional weight. Paramount reality, for instance, refs to the overall and pervasive conditions of everyday life that seem to press in on people and determine their actions. It is the world of timetables, routines, duties, and responsibilities. As one humorist quipped, "Reality is a nice place to visit, but I wouldn't want to live there!"[42]

According to Cohn and Taylor, "momentary slips through the fabric of reality" are entirely necessary for human psychic well-being and the conservation of any common sense of reality per se.[43] These momentary slips take a variety of behavioral forms. Fantasy, for example, or daydreaming, usually conjure up in the mind's eye territory within an alternative world. Straightforward awareness of the master scripts, which determine so much of what people do and how they do it, can also be an effective resistive practice. Even travel and leisure-time pursuits allow people to escape, as it were, to a freer zone. Role distancing also brings self-awareness and at least a partial dislodgment from ongoing social commitments and obligations. Nevertheless, in the long run fantasy, role distancing, script evasion, escapes to free areas, and so forth both conserve and support reality. The stock of most fantasies, for instance, is taken from patterned cultural themes.[44] The summoning of daydreams relieves the tedium of daily routine but, in so doing, allows reality to continue. Vacations and leisure-time pursuits can have similar effects. Master scripts are defined, by and large, by popular culture and provide the fictional backing necessary for a reality of acceptable behavior. Conversely, while the civic aspect of city life clearly places a premium on reality work—stressing the advantages and responsibilities of membership in a society—there must also be room for identity work. The respite of a park, or the sudden release of being able to amble uncaringly down a street, are part and parcel of the civic experience. After all, people usually better understand official versions of things by virtue of their own slightly subversive stories.[45]

One of the richest examples of de Certeau's idea of "practiced space," within the generic framework of New York's grid of blocks and streets, is city play. Performed on by youngsters and adults alike—suggesting further distinctions within civil society among the worlds of teenagers, children, etc.—the play area quickly becomes the site for both identity and reality work, as well as an effective way for momentarily converting space into place and developing a stronger neighborhood sense of community. "Play," according to Johan Huizinga in his classic work *Homo Ludens*, "is a voluntary activity executed within fixed limits of time and place, according to rules freely accepted but absolutely binding, having its aim in itself and being accompanied by a feeling of tension and joy."[46] As such it stands outside of ordinary life, although it is often difficult to understand everyday life without play and the spell that is cast over things during a game. For children the preparation for later life is undeniable in terms of strategy, manual dexterity, creativity, and so on, although these attributes are certainly not lost on adults either. Above all, the concept of a controllable "turf" is paramount, and play spaces, although often subject to public scrutiny, become private spaces, at least for those involved in the game. Ready incorporation of the features of the urban landscape is almost necessary, as is the transformation of the detritus of urban life into playthings. Indeed, a true measure of the civic responsibility of a city like New York is the extent to which it can nurture and protect the core activity of game playing. Certainly, as we saw earlier with the Piazza del Campo, it was of extraordinary significance to the Sienese and their civil way of life. Not only do players in the city become the poets of their own acts, but the games themselves help define and formalize relations among elements of public authority and civil society.

In New York the incorporation of the physical conditions of the city into games is diverse and often ingenious. For most, the basic unit of urban geography is the block. In fact, in most quarters block life and a sense of neighborhood are synonymous. Every block is like a village, giving rise to the legendary provincialism that regards some other place a few blocks away as if it were a foreign land. Important also in this regard is the distinction between "street" and "block."[47] A block connotes the enclosed space of the street, delineated by street corners. The street, on the other hand, refers to the outside world of hustle, bustle, noise, and traffic. To be "streetwise" is to be able to negotiate one's way in the world beyond the block, away from the familiarity of the place, apart from neighbors and relative safety. In a similar manner, the term "street kids" usually refers to those who spend time away from their immediate neighborhood and block.

Within the block as a general theater of play, a number of physical appropriations can be made. Stoops, for example—derived from the Dutch word *stoep* and common to many rowhouses in New York—are ideal for stoopball, jacks, or just plain sitting or hanging out.[48] Lampposts, fire hydrants, and stair railings on stoops can allow two persons instead of three to skip rope, even allowing them to perform the intricate patterns of "street double dutch." They can also serve as outfield markers for games of stickball, once widely practiced on many New York blocks. Naturally enough blank walls can become the site of handball or, as mentioned earlier in the case of tall buildings, "boxball"—a vertical version of stickball, played in confined spaces. Rooftops form both a refuge and a gathering space, in summer often referred to as "tar beach" because of sunbathing. Far more complicated and time consuming are the elaborate rituals of pigeon flying from tenement roofs, whereby the birds of different owners are encouraged to mix and then return home with the aim of capturing— through their confusion—birds for another flock. It has sometimes been said that the pigeon flyers' spirits rise with the birds and that the pasttime is a very effective release from the cares and worries of everyday life.[49] Finally, the hard concrete, stone, and asphalt surfaces of city streets and squares are ideal for the chalked inscriptions of hopscotch, for roller blading, spinning tops, and playing whiffle ball. Once upon a time, "skelly boards," drawn on the pavement allowed the old game of marbles to move on to hard, slick surfaces. Even today the raised curb along streets is often a convenient site for games of "two-up."[50]

For some time now, street life and the games people play have intersected with mass media and eventually made their way into mainstream culture. In Cohn and Taylor's nomenclature, they have become important components in the development and evolution of the master scripts by which people direct and live out some aspect of their lives. Car culture—the "low riders" and "cruising," for instance, was a way of seeing and being seen within an urban context, competing, receiving recognition, and asserting an identity. It was an escape from the humdrum of everyday life and yet a conservative factor in ritualizing antiestablishment tendencies. Recently this was explicitly recognized in New Mexico by no lesser figure than the governor, Gary Johnson, who called attention to the positive social effects of low-rider afficionados.[51] Another by-product—now well accepted in special car shows and the automobile industry as a whole—was the car itself as an exuberant thing of beauty and surprise. Certainly, Juan Vaca's highly modified 1988 Honda Civic and Javier Zamora's customized 1976 Chevrolet Camino pickup are cases in point.[52]

The recent phenomenon of "hip-hop" culture has also influenced the cultural mainstream. Since its onset in the 1970s, rap music, breakdancing, "scratching," and graffiti art are its major forms, and "fame"—the notoriety of having done something well—is its chief reward. Like many such phenomena, in the beginning it was at odds with polite adult society and official authority. Some aspects remained that way, like the graffiti art that vandalized New York during the "style wars" of the 1970s, while simultaneously finding its way into the institutionalized art scene of well-known galleries. Others, like rap and breakdancing—originally a way of avoiding street fights—are now integral parts of the entertainment business. "Scratching," perhaps the least well known of the hip-hop contributions, is the practice of moving the stylus on a phonograph record at will to produce interesting amplified effects.[53] Often conducted in parks and other open areas, scratching is also a celebration of absolute control over the serial quality of recordings, which now is only partially available with the modern technologies of compact and laser discs.

Nonconformance with accepted norms was also the hallmark of New York's bohemians who gathered for a time in the vicinity of Greenwich Village.[54] Pfaff's, a tavern on the west side of Broadway above Bleecker Street, was reputedly the first bohemian haunt in New York City, whose greatest living asset in the pre-Civil War period was Walt Whitman. Later on, Washington Square became a bohemian nexus, drawing literary luminaries such as Mark Twain, Jack London, and Upton Sinclair. According to Ada Claire, the self-appointed Queen of Bohemia, "The Bohemian is by nature, if not by habit, a cosmopolite with a general sympathy for the fine arts, and for all things above and beyond conven-

The Esplanade at Battery Park City in New York by Hanna-Olin.

tion. The Bohemian is not, like the creature of society, a victim of rules and customs."[55] Not surprisingly, a utopian air pervaded Greenwich Village as many worked to remake this part of New York, calling for a "free territory untrammeled by convention." All this quickly ended, however, around 1919 if not before, due to anti-German hysteria, the "red scare," and Prohibition (officially brought on by the Volstead Act).[56]

On a far darker side of human existence, New York has also played host to groups of people with mental maps and habitual trajectories that are completely at variance with official versions of the city. The hiding places and safety zones, for example, so necessary for the homeless and other vagrant outcasts of society, are unknown to the general population.[57] Dwelling in what amounts to a separate sphere, the destitute now often occupy the niches of subway tunnels, abandoned cuttings long forgotten and uncharted, the caves at Inwood, and the alcoves under large bridge supports. At one extreme are the "mole people," whose lives are almost entirely subterranean, and at the other are drifters on park benches and in the Public Library, whose vagrancy brings them into fuller contact with other populations. In all instances they occupy a practiced space within the city, by necessity and the abject poverty of their personal circumstances. Though not without a sense of community, there is nothing civic about their existence, as both the public authorities and civil society leave them neglected.

While not altering people's itineraries or maps of a city, at least in the short run, popular outbreaks against perceived social injustices are a manifest challenge to official order and civil circumstances. New York's Draft Riot of 1863, for instance, was an insurrection on a vast scale involving tens of thousands of people objecting, among other things, to the unfairness of the Union Army draft, which could be avoided with payment of the sum of three hundred dollars.[58] For the poor living in the Lower East Side and elsewhere in the city, however, such a payment was unimaginable. As alluded to earlier, over the years Tompkins Square Park, a ten-acre formally landscaped area in the middle of the Lower East Side, has been the scene of a number of civil disturbances, primarily around themes of poverty and homelessness. In 1874, at a time when

New York had around 10,000 homeless and 110,000 unemployed because of post–Civil War scarcity, a march by those affected ended in a riot in the park, which was put down forcefully by police.[59] During 1877—sometimes known as the Year of Riots—similar uprisings occurred. On July 24 at Tompkins Square Park, police mistakenly charged a peaceful though tense political rally as demonstrators came into the park from Avenue A.[60] Unfortunately, much more recently there was a similar occurrence, when on August 6, 1988, baton-wielding police tried to rid the area of homeless "residents," only to be thwarted months later by the efforts of housing activists and antigentrification organizations. For several years thereafter the park remained a liberated space. On Memorial Day in 1991, however, a park concert under the slogan "Housing is a Human Right" led to further rioting and clashes between police and park users. These disturbances finally came to an end in June when 200 shantytown park dwellers were evicted.[61] Both the practical and symbolic role of Tompkins Square Park should not be underestimated, for these events draw further attention to the way places acquire meanings. The park was a sizable area of accessible public open space with amenities and services, as well as a capacity to support a considerable number of squatters. It was also located at the center of an area perceived by many to be economically depressed, although with sufficient public exposure, through adjacent gentrification, to effectively signal the plight of the homeless. In addition, the park was the historical site of this kind of protest, thus increasing rather than diminishing its symbolic political value.

ACCOMMODATION OF A PLURALITY OF INTERESTS

Historically, one of the remarkable features of New York City has been the diversity and multinational origins of its population. In 1910, at the peak of European immigration, 41 percent of the city's population were foreign born, as compared to 15 percent for the nation as a whole, up slightly from 37 percent and 14 percent, respectively, a decade earlier.[62] The National Origins Quota Act and the Johnson-Reed Act went into effect before World War II, and by 1950 the foreign-born population declined to around 24 percent for New York and only 4 percent for the nation.[63] With eradication of discriminatory quota systems in 1965, family reunification became a central principle, and the number of foreigners entering the city rose once again. At present, in comparison with other large and established U.S. cities like Chicago and Philadelphia, New York stands out in its diversity. The total Hispanic population in the five boroughs, for instance, rose by 27 percent during the 1980s, and the Asian population by more than 100 percent.[64] In fact, by 1990 no single race or ethnic group formed a majority among the city's inhabitants, with almost 30 percent being made up of immigrants.[65] Given this background, it is hardly any wonder that there has been a constant struggle to create public space available to all ethnic groups, as well as to rich and poor alike.

Chief among these creations was Central Park, the large 840-acre landscaped preserve that sits in the middle of Manhattan, between 59th and 110th streets, providing a peaceful respite from the hustle and bustle of the surrounding grid of streets and blocks. A primary motivating idea behind the park was to somehow restore the emotional and civic coherence that nineteenth-century New Yorkers saw vanishing under the onslaught of rampant commercial development. Between 1830 and 1860—roughly the time it took for the Central Park idea to come to fruition—New York City expanded almost fourfold, from around 200,000 people to over 800,000, primarily in a northerly direction above Canal Street.[66] For New Yorkers at the time, the park was also a place where, as Eric Homberger suggests, antebellum elites could mingle with immigrants to the city away from the frightening confusion, strangeness, and uncertainty of densely packed city streets.[67] It was also a way of literally providing "breathing room" in the urban congestion, so necessary for improving public health. John H. Griscom, the City Inspector in 1842, was one of many who believed in the miasmic diffusion of disease and the particularly beneficial effects of ventilation and exposure to fresh air. In addition, moral sensibilities also motivated the creation of a great park, not least of which were the didactic benefits of being exposed to nature, and the duty one generation owed to the next in development and management of the city.[68] Despite the closeness of open countryside, there were few places of any size in New York during the 1840s for convenient leisure-time activity and recreation. Unlike the much-admired cities of Europe, the prevailing civic impetus at the time seemed to be far too much in the direction of commercialization. Thus by the mid-nineteenth century, the provision of public parks was an attractive idea with wide support and a strong congruence with prevailing social and culture thought.

In 1850 both candidates in the New York mayoral election stood strongly in favor of the construction of a major park in Manhattan island, in anticipation of burgeoning development. Indeed, Ambrose Kingsland, the Whig who defeated Democratic candidate Fernando Wood, quickly announced the city's official interest in such a park, precisely because of the northward urban expansion and the lack of suitable places for recreation.[69] Not long after this pronouncement two potential sites emerged, each with forceful proponents, including those most likely to gain financially from adjacent development. They were Jones Wood, a large wooded tract on the East River, roughly bounded by 66th Street, 75th Street, and Third Avenue, and an even larger area of land at the center of the island, running between 39th Street and the Harlem River. In 1852, a special committee of New York City aldermen recommended the idea of a "central park"—introducing the eventual name for the first time—although legislative plans to acquire Jones Wood continued. Concurrently, Griscom proposed a third solution, with the idea of creating not one but eight or even sixteen smaller parks of around 100 acres each.[70] He saw this arrangement as being both a more democratic solution and a way of avoiding the unfortunate side effects of the speculative boom a large central park would almost certainly create. In spite of its logic, however, Griscom's proposal received little attention, and the idea of creating a large park persisted and even gathered further momentum. After furious lobbying by proponents of both proposals, in 1853 legislation was formally passed to acquire the land for Central Park, and in 1854 the Jones Wood proposal was repealed. Fernando Wood, now ensconced as mayor, gave the idea a further political shove, and in 1856 Egbert L. Viele surveyed the park land for the Board of Commissioners; during the process, he prepared a preliminary park plan. Actual acquisition of land proved to be a time-consuming and expensive affair, taking almost three years to complete at a cost of more than $5.5 million. In 1857 control of the park project was removed from local politicians and Frederick Law Olmsted was appointed as Central Park Superintendent, under Viele as the Engineer-in-chief. Not satisfied with Viele's earlier design proposal, the Board finally organized a design competition in 1858 and construction of Central Park began in earnest.[71]

Olmsted and Calvert Vaux's winning scheme—selected from among some thirty-five entries—was distinguished on a number of counts. In spite of the straightjacket of competition requirements, with an emphasis on patriotic parades, didactic landscapes, and the symbolic representation of culture, theirs was an elegant uncluttered solution, which steadfastly avoided much of the kitsch of other entries.[72] The "Greensward Plan," as it was called, was one of the very few that assumed that the park site would eventually become surrounded by intense urban development and therefore stressed future needs as major criteria for the park's conformation. The ingenious device of sinking the necessary transverse roads below the level of the park in places allowed the continuity of internal paths and carriage ways to be preserved. In addition, the creation of a tree-lined barrier around the edges further served to perceptually isolate the park from the city beyond. The result was described as a "refreshing break" from the formal repetition of the gridiron of streets and blocks, with the bold reliance on landscape serving to reinforce those essential differences at every turn. Olmsted, like Andrew Jackson Downing before him, firmly believed in the capacity of Central Park to soften and harmonize the rude experience of city life, as well as to create "a pleasant drawing room for the whole population."[73] By insisting on a well-turned merger of town and country, Olmsted and Vaux were able to successfully fuse the otherwise competing progressive and pastoral ideals so important to later nineteenth-century cultural life. Central to this fusion was the assumption that access to nature—light, open air, wildlife, and scenery—could be an effective remedy to the sensory deprivation of teeming urban life. In short, a place like Central Park, in their view, could resolve the emerging modern tensions between technological progress and the need to be in nature.

Construction of Central Park took twenty years to complete, involving movement of over ten million cartloads of stone, earth, and topsoil. At the time, the site was one of the ugliest and most commercially useless stretches of land on Manhattan, dotted with refuse dumps, swamps, shanties, and rock out-croppings. At least two settlements had to be displaced: an Irish-American community to the south and an African-American community further north. Both were given short shrift in the name of civic progress and a higher public good. Nevertheless, the social costs involved were not insignificant, in spite of a scheme for property compensation.[74] Over time further improvements were made to the park. In 1912, for instance, the gravel paths were paved, together with an entire playground, "The Heckscher," in 1926. During the 1950s large building elements were added—like the Wollman Memorial Link, the Delacorte Theatre, and the Children's Zoo—as the facilities of the park responded to increased and changing user demands.[75] Overall, as intended by Olmsted and Vaux, the landscape remained varied and perceptually interesting. Generally, the southern half of the park has a pastoral image, whereas the northern portions represent a rougher, picturesque wilderness. Crossed by the four transverse roads mentioned earlier, running east-west at 66th, 81st, 86th, and 97th Streets, the park is over two and a half miles long (extending from 59th to 110th Street) and over half a mile wide (fitting into the Manhattan grid between Fifth Avenue and the extension of Eighth Avenue along Central Park West). Three large water bodies are incorporated inside the park—the Lake, the Receiving Reservoir, and Harlem Mere—together with smaller aquatic areas, such as the Conservatory Pond, the Pond, and Belvedere Lake. Specific landscapes are numerous, including: the Sheep Meadow, the Great Lawn, Center Hill, the Ramble, the Glade, North Meadow, and Pinetown all made in the fashion typical of nineteenth-century romantic gardens. Also included is the Mall—a splendidly formal area with large trees—and Charles Vaux's adjacent great terrace, offering a spectacular outlook over the center of the park.

Almost from its opening to the present day, Central Park has lived up to the expectations of its creators. It is a place in New York where people from every walk of life go to recreate, take a leisurely stroll, sit at peace by themselves, or do nothing in particular. By now, programmatically there is something for almost everyone, with the level of improvisation sometimes reaching dizzying and outrageous heights. Puppeteers, stilt walkers, and fire eaters mingle in the crowds on good weekends, although as Olmsted would have hoped, there is also ample room for solitude, introspection, and sublime reflection. Except for periods when the park is poorly maintained and security becomes lax, use by all is relatively unencumbered and unrestricted. It is certainly large enough and varied enough to easily accommodate a plurality of interests. The park's didactic influences, such an important part of its nineteenth-century conception, are still intact—albeit in more casual form. Still, when walking along the Mall, one is a little more self-conscious about affecting a positive bearing and gait, and a certain unmistakable sense of decorum seems to descend over people observing sailboats on the Pond. The feelings of having fun but also being on good behavior often commingle in park users. It is not like playing on the block or hanging out on the roof. It is another place entirely, on a higher civic plane.

Putting on one's "Sunday best," to use the time-honored phrase, usually implies a certain conformity with the modes and manners of a day, although as a general civic orientation it can have a long-lasting and positive effect. As we saw, the opulent cast-iron structures of SoHo and even the well-proportioned facades of many tenements were recognized for their civic value long after the original occupants had left to go up or out of town. Central Park also has a grandeur and a civic presence that transcends the more casual environments of everyday play, and yet as a place to go it can be just as accommodating. A manifest desire on the part of occupants to constantly conserve and conform with the surrounding environment, which exists in all these places, appears to be an essential part of their civic character and eventual value. Moreover, here the profoundly centering effect, or cultural focus that these conservative and conforming tendencies have about them, is undoubtedly a key ingredient. While accommodating and even promoting variation in human activity, there are also recognizable limits involved. Conservation and conformation usually serve or stem from compelling and well-bounded ideas. There is often a sense of stasis, from which vantage point a certain amount of proselytizing can follow. "This is good for you," the symbolic and representational realm of Olmsted's Central Park seems to be conveying. Moreover, the idea of "once good, always good" seems to follow quickly.

From the more dynamic standpoint of a civic realm constantly in the making, Manhattan's grid of streets, blocks, and parks is also a most remarkable place. First, there is a transparency to its civic reality that is second to none, including those aspects that are undoubtedly positive and those that are sadly lacking. The crude geographical outcome of processes that bind entities of the state and civil society, for instance, are clearly evident in the disparity between the rich in their penthouses and the homeless on the pavement below, as well as among the neighborhoods occupying various parts of the grid. The physical and spatial outcome of processes representing socioeconomic and cultural trans-actions, again among various entities of the state and civil society, are also obvious, as is the role the physical environment plays as a starting point for these transactions. In particular, three broad processes stand out: the appropria-tion of space by way of expansion, succession, or gentrification; a resistance to official versions of a place by way of role playing, nonparticipation, or even insurrection; and the accommodation of differences among people and groups through the finding of common ground. Throughout, the role of the grid remains slightly paradoxical. On the one hand, its relative uniformity and lack of speci-ficity provides a comparatively unencumbered, although partially organized, field for human interaction. On the other, it is precisely the specificity of certain intense and localized periods of development that forms the real armature for the city's ensuing social and cultural geography. Heterogeneous groups, after all, are not looking for flat, featureless planes, but rather for a varied and distinctive territory within which to live. Finally, it cannot be concluded that all grid layouts possess these same characteristics—far from it; the grid's geom-etry, for one, is peculiar. As noted, the narrowness of the Manhattan grid pushes activities outward toward the street, and the length practically requires multiple development of blocks, almost regardless of scale. More important though, New York and Manhattan is a unique historical occurrence, the space and timing of which makes it a place like no other.

It was crowded on the East Drive as you move down toward the park entrance near 72nd Street. Hector, arms swinging gracefully at his side, surged forward, gliding this way and that, passing one skater and then another. He loved the fluid smoothness of the ride, the exhilaration, the feeling of the space around him and yet all the other people, the fame! "You can't come close to this down on Sixth Street," he thought to himself. Then, suddenly this Anglo babe in front of him began to fall backward, her feet moving quicker and quicker in short movements as she tried to keep her balance. Sensing what was about to happen, Hector almost reflexively swooped down and grabbed her around the waist, picking her up as he sped by, smiling at her startled look. "Hey, thanks a lot," exclaimed Randall as he also arrived at Martha's side a fraction of a second later. "It's cool. No problem, man!" Hector shot back, quickly pushing forward again. "Drive safe!"

Peter Kleinewolfe, *East, West and Center**

5

Representation and Constitution of Spatial Meanings

A model of Ljubljana showing the old town, the Ljubljanica, and Castle Hill (page 162).

The eerie silence, which had extended over the city since mid-morning, was suddenly shattered by the scream of the jet fighter overhead, swooping low toward the city center. Nearby inhabitants, and especially the irregulars overlooking the closed army barracks, waited, transfixed by this unexpected aerial intrusion. Then it came—a loud explosion, as the plane's vapor trail continued off toward the horizon. "Oh no, not the bridges!" cried Miloš with sudden dread. "Damn! They wouldn't bomb the bridges!"

Prešeren Square was jammed as it had been on similar occasions in the past. Revelers spilled out along the embankment, and the lights they were carrying provided an additional festive decoration to the floodlit setting in red, white, and blue. "Why do you think the tanks simply went away like that?" inquired Marianne of her husband. "They probably thought it wasn't worth the fight," replied Aleš, "at least that's what everyone's saying." "Anyway, it's a big relief," continued Marianne after a pause. "Think what might have happened to all of this had they stayed," she went on, gesturing toward the river.

Tuby Ratesele, *Mostovi I Trgovi**

It is clear, at least from chapters 2 and 3, that concerns for daily life and the ennobling capacities of civic realist projects can have different expressions. Furthermore, these seem to apply both within and between different times and places. The minimalist abstraction of the Plaça dels Països Catalans in Barcelona, for instance, is radically different in outward appearance from other more traditional public places constructed within the same city at roughly the same time. It is also substantially different from equally modern public projects in Rome, inspired by vernacular traditions.

At the source of these differences there exists a genuine question about the extent to which architecture and urban design can be expected to represent sociopolitical ideas or preferred modes of public conduct unambiguously, even under the most favorable of circumstances. In the first place, the relative arbitrariness of urban-architectural expression, as a precise system of signs, makes representation difficult outside of the autonomous realm of the discipline itself. In the second place, temporal gaps often exist between particular sociopolitical conditions and related cultural enterprises. For one thing, the relative permanence of public urban-architectural projects, in relationship to the socioeconomic and political circumstances that brought them into being, is usually far greater and thus prohibits any mirroring of more temporary political activities. Nevertheless, an insistence on anything approaching a total arbitrariness of architectural signs would not only render impossible the conveyance of meaning outside of architecture itself, but would also seem to be unwarranted. We do, after all, manage to negotiate the functional if not broader cultural realm of most cities largely unguided. As a matter of fact, when occasions permit, a reasonable conformance can be found between unifying sociopolitical ideas, even replete with a moral tone to move forward with our lives, and the expressive form of public works.

Fortunately, the interwar years in Ljubljana—the capital of the emerging nation-state of Slovenia—was one such occasion, when the city was transformed by, above all, the architect and native son Jože Plečnik. If nothing else, his projects showed that urban architecture could be an integral part of a broader civic project on the part of society, in both a constitutive and representational manner. Here, especially in retrospect, any practical and intellectual separation of urban-architectural expression from sociopolitical experience—other than in purely representational terms—seems to be particularly misplaced. Plečnik's work, and most notably his improvements to the public infrastructure of Ljubljana, clearly set a civic tone for public life and helped establish and celebrate the course of Slovenian cultural autonomy during the years that followed. Indeed, it is with an emerging sense of regionalism or even nationalism that we seem very likely to find architecture clearly being pushed in these representational and constitutive directions at once. This was certainly the case with modern Paris and contemporary Barcelona, although with Slovenia and Plečnik's Ljubljana such developments were almost entirely without precedent, and therefore all the more interesting.

REGIONALISM AND PLANS FOR A CITY

The end of the nineteenth century and the beginning of the twentieth was a period of intensifying Southern Slavic pressure on the hegemony of the Austro-Hungarian Dual Monarchy toward regional independence and unification.[1] At least by 1870, the *Yugoslavian idea*, though still fluid, was a reality and many of the modern political parties that formed during the 1880s coalesced popular opinion against this hegemony. The year 1903 ushered in a period of particular internal crisis, and when Austria-Hungary annexed Bosnia-Herzogovina in 1908, the situation for the Dual Monarchy deteriorated still further. By 1912 revolutionary pro-Yugoslavian activity was rife, including student-worker strikes and open expression of the idea of a violent break-up of the dynastic states. When Archduke Ferdinand was assassinated in Sarajevo in 1914, Austria decided to attack Serbia and, although the attack failed, most of the rest of the western world was plunged into World War I. Some four years later, as the Allies and Serbian armies broke through enemy lines to the south, the

Austro-Hungarian political hegemony over the Slavs to the north finally disintegrated. Simultaneously, deputies representing the Croats, Serbs, and Slovenes formed a National Council in Zagreb, proclaiming both unity and independence on 1 December 1918.

The Kingdom of Serbs, Croats, and Slovenes was proclaimed by Alexander Karadjordjević of the Serbian royal house, acting as a regent for his father, King Peter.[2] International recognition quickly followed, granted first by the United States in early 1919, although it wasn't until 1924 that the frontiers of the new state were agreed upon, a decision prolonged primarily by border disputes with Italy to the west. Carinthia, an area to the northwest heavily populated by Slovenes, decided to join Austria under an Allied-controlled plebiscite. In brief, the new nation finally consisted of at least five different components: the Kingdoms of Serbia and Montenegro, the Slovenian lands of Austria and Istria, with the just-noted exception of Carinthia; Croatia-Slavonia, formerly under the Hungarian crown; several other former parts of Hungary, including Vojvodina and eastern Slovenia; and the recently annexed Austro-Hungarian condominium of Bosnia-Herzegovina.

The emergent Yugoslavian state was based upon two revolutionary principles at the time: the self-determination of people, and the transfer of ownership of land to those who tilled it.[3] Yet in spite of these lofty ideals and considerable agrarian reform, much of Yugoslavia remained in a chaotic and economically underdeveloped state for some time to come. Vast areas were depopulated by a total of as many as 2 million persons, mainly from the incessant warfare between 1912 and 1918. Economic life was at a standstill in many areas, or highly disorganized, and the landed peasantry was in a revolutionary frame of mind. Severely damaged urban areas, unemployment, inflation, and extreme food and housing shortages also produced dire conditions of privation in many parts of the country. Unfortunately, agrarian reform, especially among the larger estates of the northern provinces, though socially desirable and politically unavoidable proved to be of doubtful economic value, resulting in farms that were too small to be productive using modern agricultural techniques.[4]

The first general elections for the Constituent Assembly were held on 28 November 1919, with 65 percent of the electorate going to the polls to elect over 400 deputies from among a number of political parties.[5] Without a clear single-party majority, a coalition consisting primarily of the Serbian Radical Party, the Democratic Party, and the Moslems formed an interim government, strongly favoring highly centralized unification around a constitutional monarchy. The Radical Party stronghold was in Serbia, where it was especially well established among the peasantry. Although now far less radical than during the late nineteenth century and certainly since 1903, the Radicals were the strongest single and largely homogeneous political force. The Democratic Party, by contrast, represented Yugoslavs from all parts of the country, consisting roughly of urban intellectuals, Slovene liberals, dissident young radicals, and the Croat-Serbian coalition, all rejecting religious, provincial, and other sectarian interests. In opposition there was mainly a coalition of the Croatian Peasant Party and the Communists. Again, as the party names suggest, the Peasant Party was for a firm sense of Croatian identity, with membership mainly from Croatia, whereas the Communists, like the Democrats, represented Yugoslavs from many different areas and strongly favored a republican form of federalism.

After much heated dispute, strife, and even boycotts, the Constituent assembly adopted the so-called Vidovdan Constitution on 28 June 1921. Finally the Democrats, Radicals, and others had coalesced to enact an electoral law and a constitutional monarchy based on provincial proportional representation, universal male suffrage, free elections, and titular leadership of the Serbian Karadjordjević household under Prince Alexander. In short, the constitution of 1921 was a triumph of the unitary, centralist, and largely Serbian political tradition. Local governments were also made centrally accountable through the delegated authority of provincial prefects and subprefects.[6]

Upon King Peter's death in July 1921, Alexander ascended to the throne. During the subsequent elections, held every two years, Pašić's Radical Party, in coalition with a variety of other parties, managed to hold onto the government.[7] Acts of terrorism and assassination, particularly during 1921, turned the public mood strongly against the Communists and, together with government sanctions, almost forced the party into virtual extinction during 1922. By and large, urban intellectuals parted company with the peasants, as well as with other rural interests, and provincial advantages were followed wherever possible, resulting in some surprising concessions and reversals in political viewpoints. During the Vukičević government, which had succeeded that of Pašić, and after the closely contested elections of 1927, complete pandemonium broke out. There were two fatal shootings of Croatian deputies and the wounding of three others, including Radić—the leader of the powerful opposition Croatian Peasant Party—who later died of his injury. On 6 January 1929, amid the political lawlessness and confusion, King Alexander dispensed with parliament and entered a period of personal rule. Genuinely patriotic, Alexander was a soldier who disliked politicians, had grown impatient with Serbian and Croatian particularism, and was dismayed by the limited sectoral vision of most parties.

As might be expected, King Alexander and his appointed government continued the unitary, centralist policies of the preceding parliamentary majorities—a program of Yugoslav nationalism seen by many Croats as a more efficient version of Serbian centralism.[8] In the remainder of the country there was little protest of the royal coup, which was widely viewed as only temporary and necessary to preserve some semblance of civil order. Indeed, by the summer of 1931, the King himself thought his extraparliamentary rule had lasted too long. A new constitution was drawn up with a bicameral parliament of a senate— largely of appointees—and a national assembly elected universally by male suffrage. The King, however, retained the right to appoint all government ministers.

Amid a worsening economy, now in the grips of the Great Depression, civil unrest broke out. During the banking crisis of 1932 through 1936, the Yugoslav *dinar* was depreciated substantially, and the country once again went through the privations of food shortages, brought on this time by several harsh winters.[9] Diplomatic relations with Italy and Hungary also deteriorated, pushing Yugoslavia into an alliance with France. A short time later, in October 1934,

King Alexander was assassinated in Marseilles by an agent of the *ustaša*—a Croatian insurrectionary movement—to be immediately succeeded by the regency of Prince Paul. Loyal to both the family and the old causes, Paul continued to pursue King Alexander's policies, but now against considerable opposition to what was widely perceived as veiled authoritarianism and pseudo-representation. The situation eased slightly with a government of reconciliation under the newly formed Yugoslav Radical Union—a merger of Serbian Radicals, Slovenian Populists, and Moslems—and with improvement in the economy.[10] By the beginning of 1936, however, Yugoslavia was becoming increasingly dependent on Germany as a trading partner and a source of needed foreign exchange. A commercial agreement was concluded with Italy in 1937, and Yugoslavia appeared to draw closer to the emerging European Axis Powers, especially with the signing in 1941 of a tripartite pact. Finally, on 25 March 1941 a bloodless coup overthrew the government and proclaimed Peter—not yet of age—the King. Incensed by the turn against the Axis powers, Hitler attacked Yugoslavia on 6 April 1941, together with armed forces from Italy and Hungary, beginning a harsh period of occupation that lasted until 1945. Of the approximately 1,750,000 people who died during World War II, more than half were killed by other Yugoslavs in what amounted to a civil war.[11] Finally, after long years of fighting, Tito's resurgent Communists gained the upper hand and created an entirely new governmental order.

Throughout the interwar period Yugoslavia struggled to secure national stability and make its way into the modern world. The constant debate was between a centralist, unitarist form of unification and a federalist, dualist position.[12] More concretely, the debate and, in the end, the open conflict pitted the Serbian and Croatian political traditions against each other, with the Serbian position eventually emerging victorious, although at the cost of unification itself. The task of national reconstruction, which began optimistically in 1918 with sweeping land reforms, floundered in the face of rising parochial interests and the immensity of the very real socioeconomic differences between one part of the new nation-state and another. The illiteracy rate, for example, which was about 51 percent in 1919, decreased only relatively slightly to about 40 percent by 1941.[13] Real income, in all employment sectors, declined against prewar levels. For agricultural workers, for instance, the decline was around 32 percent and as much as 45 percent for public employees.[14] In the contemporary terms of other developed European economies, Yugoslavia failed to generate much of a private supply of capital throughout the country, and thus become too dependent for its own well-being on foreign sources of capital and the state monopolies of the public sector. Together with a lack of progress toward real unification, both dependencies were gradually to prove ruinous, bringing Yugoslavia full circle, as it were, to a condition of occupation and external control.

The province or state of Slovenia, an active participant in these events, shared many aspirations and outcomes with other Yugoslavs, but also with some important differences. Slovenian nationalism was awakened relatively early—during occupation by Napoleon Bonaparte's forces between 1809 and 1813—giving rise to the so-called French Illyrian Ideal of an indigenous Slovene culture with Etruscan antecedents.[15] This in turn stimulated considerable advancement in Slovenian language, literature, education, and cultural life generally, especially in Ljubljana the provincial capital. The national awakening was short-lived, however, under subsequent intensified periods of economic and cultural Germanization, and the continuing political presence of the Hapsburgs and the Dual Monarchy. Ever the cautious minority and relatively loyal to Austria, Slovenes favored *Trialism,* or the notion of a semi-autonomous state as a part of Austrian feudalism, to outright independence.[16] Nevertheless, this political leaning was to change rapidly and opportunistically after the outbreak of World War I, when a Yugoslav solution appeared to offer the Slovenes more chance of national freedom than continued hegemony under the German-minded Austrians.

In the attempts at Yugoslav unification and reconstruction that followed creation of the Kingdom, Slovenes enjoyed their share of government responsibilities, although they tended to align with the Croats around a "federalist" and "dualist" position with respect to the question of national unity. Less doctrinaire than many of their southern neighbors, however, the Slovenes generally sought compromise to keep the Yugoslav idea alive, and cultural expansion to press forward their own parochial claims toward Slovenian nationalism.[17] They suffered the same fate as other Yugoslavs during World War II, through civil war, and by being overrun and harshly subjugated by invading German, Italian, and Hungarian forces. Ljubljana, for instance, was occupied by the Italians on 11 April 1941, and under the orders of Count Ciano, the Italian foreign minister, an attempt was made to obliterate the Slovenian identity by annexing Ljubljana and its surrounding territory to Italy as the *Provincia di Lubiana*.[18] In 1942, all Slovene organizations were promptly abolished, Italian taught at all levels in the schools, and the city itself entirely encircled in barbed wire, bunkers, and checkpoints.[19] With the eventual Italian armistice in 1943, German occupation continued until the allied and partisan liberation of the city and countryside during 1945.

In many other important respects, however, especially for the rapid redevelopment of Ljubljana and Plečnik's eventual influence there, Slovenia was different from the other Yugoslavian provinces and would-be nation-states. The population, for instance, was relatively small and homogeneous in comparison to many other provinces, numbering about 1 million Slovenes in 1921 out of some 12 million Yugoslavs.[20] Historically, Slovenia was on the western Catholic side of the east-west split, which has so fundamentally divided what was now Yugoslavia for centuries. Germanic influence was very strong, with Germans occupying most prominent administrative and business positions within the community throughout most of the nineteenth century and at least up until 1918. Demographically, the Slovenian population was also different from that of many other Yugoslav provinces, especially in the south, with a natural increase in 1939 of 9.9 persons per 1,000 population, compared to a national average of 11.0 and a high, in Bosnia, of 20.2 persons per 1,000 population.[21] As with neighboring Croatia, the resulting demographic profile of Slovenia was more consistent with that of other parts of western Europe.

Economically, the differences between Slovenia and the other Yugoslavian provinces was even more distinct. Indeed, by the beginning of World War II, real structural differences began to emerge, particularly when it came to the relative balance of industrial and agricultural development. Comparatively well endowed with natural resources, Slovenia hosted fully a quarter of the nation's industrial development in 1918, amid less than 10 percent of the total population.[22] Agricultural employment, though important, was far less overwhelming than in the rest of the country, and farm holdings were far larger on the whole and more productive, certainly until the economically unsound agrarian reforms of the interwar years. By the beginning of the Axis occupation, Slovenia's gross national product was divided roughly in the proportions of 27 percent for agriculture, 37 percent for industry, and 36 percent for the remainder, including the service sector. Comparable statistics for Yugoslavia as a whole were 41 percent for agriculture, 25 percent for industry, and 34 percent for remaining activity, with the least economically developed province, Vojvodina, having a distribution of fully 61 percent in agriculture, 17 percent in industry, and 22 percent in other forms of production.[23] Perhaps even more striking, the per capita income for Slovenia was fully 63 percent above the national average and 50 percent above the income levels of the next most prosperous province, Croatia.[24] Both statistically and in reality, the levels and types of industrial and economic development in Slovenia reflected those of more developed nations. A high-speed road, for instance, was built between Kranj and Ljubljana, and the first airline company was started during the interwar years. No doubt this was due, at least in part, to technical and related economic influences from Germany. Nevertheless, it certainly stood in marked contrast to the otherwise agricultural and underdeveloped areas of Yugoslavia.

As might be expected with this profile of economic development and the presence of substantial private capital, the institutional structure of Slovenian civil society was also well developed, again in contrast with most of the nation where substantial government monopolies were the rule rather than the exception. Commercial and savings banks flourished, particularly in Ljubljana, recalling another period of strong economic development and trade during the Baroque period after 1650. A cooperative economic system was also established, principally by the Catholic Slovenian People's Party, as a form of mutual aid particularly for the betterment of workers and landed farmers. Cooperative savings banks and credit unions, for instance, were formed totaling some 500 in number by 1938, with approximately 156,000 subscribers.[25] Consumer and producer cooperatives also managed to break the German monopoly on trade and manufactured goods during the same interwar period. A Slovenian University was created in Ljubljana in 1919, along with the National Gallery and other museums, a National and University Library, and a radio station broadcasting, for a change, in the Slovenian language. Other characteristics of modern civil society also began to appear. New housing estates, for example, tended to be spatially segregated, with workers' housing in places like *Rožnadolina* and housing for the emerging white-collar workers in locations like *Mirje* and the new *Prule*.

At the center of much of this activity and Slovenian nationalism was the Roman Catholic Church. Traditionally, Slovenian national leaders and educators came from the ranks of the clergy, especially during the periods of intense Germanization during the nineteenth century. Although by no means the only Catholic area in the new Yugoslavia, the clerical and anti-Communist influence in Slovenia was unusually pronounced. In 1905 the influential Slovenian People's Party was organized largely out of the older Catholic Political Association, in order to provide a necessary roof, as they called it, to protect all manner of cultural, educational, religious, social, and economic activities of the Slovenian Catholics.[26] In the succession of national elections that took place during the parliamentary period of the 1920s, the Slovenian People's Party increased its proportion of the Slovenian vote from 36 percent of the total to 60 percent. Moreover, from 1923 onward it held a significant absolute majority of voters.[27]

A further mark of both the Catholic and the distinctive character of Slovenian regionalism was the vigorous prosecution of Communist radicalism within Slovenia after World War II. In what remained of the civil war and the fight for the ideological control of the country, particularly hard hit were the comparatively large anti-Communist Slovene detachments of the Nationalist Front and especially the Home Guards concentrated around Ljubljana. Slovenia, as noted, also provided the largest portion of the national income and was also seen, by the Communists at least, as most vulnerable to western influence, given its geography and historical ties.

Concentration of Slovenian civil society during the interwar years was in and around the provincial capital of Ljubljana, which by then had reached a population of some 40,000 people. Understandably, the economic boom that propelled Slovenia into a well-developed economy during the 1920s and 1930s, if not before, changed the character of the city substantially. An earthquake, which devastated the town in 1895, also provided broad opportunities for redevelopment and, as the remaining parcels of improved land were quickly occupied, the formulation of plans for new development and outward urban expansion became necessary.[28]

The aftermath of the earthquake provided the first and perhaps primary impetus for developing a long-range plan for Ljubljana as a modern European city. At that time Ivan Hribar, the city's first Slovene mayor, invited prominent architects to prepare plans for Ljubljana. The two most prominent entries in the competition were those of Camillo Sitte and Maks Fabiani. Sitte's plan followed the aesthetic urban design principles set out in his opus, *Planning According to Artistic Principles*, a copy of which accompanied his submission. Basically, the plan respected and reinforced the traditional quarters of Ljubljana, including the remains of the early Roman town of Emona, the medieval neighborhoods around the castle hill, the Baroque additions, and the eighteenth- and nineteenth-century residential developments along major regional roads.[29] Whenever possible, the logic of existing patterns was projected into nearby areas as a basis for new development. The plan also delineated several major vistas toward the castle—by far the most prominent feature in the urban landscape.

Fabiani's plan, produced in collaboration with I. Jager, also took into account the old and established areas of Ljubljana, but with a distinct focus on Prešeren Square (St. Mary's Square), and with a grid system of streets and land parcels projected toward the north—*Bežigrad*—to accommodate new development.[30] The most prominent feature of Fabiani's plan was undoubtedly the ring-road concept, based on the well-known Viennese prototype. In addition, two prominent north-south streets were incorporated into the plan: Miklošičeva leading north from St. Mary's Square, and Prešernova running in parallel further to the west. Miklošičeva effectively formed an axis for the new development around the railroad station, and Prešernova gave the city the overall appearance of a high-quality residential and office precinct. Along both streets, formal squares were located as the setting for major institutions, and between 1902 and 1906 Fabiani himself designed several buildings with towers in the Secessionist style (Art Nouveau) to mark the corners of Marxov Square on Miklošičeva Street. Several other architects, such as Ciril Metod Koch and Friedrich Sigmundt, also contributed to what had now become a collective task of planning and developing modern Ljubljana.[31] In fact, Koch's plan was an attempt to synthesize many of the existing schemes and represented the general direction city authorities felt predisposed to follow.

A little later in 1913, Alfred Keller began reconstruction of the river banks of the Ljubljanica, the water course that effectively bisected much of Ljubljana at the time, with the old medieval city on the right or easterly bank, around the castle hill, and the newer developments on the left or westerly bank, stretching off toward some flat, low-lying areas.[32] Although playing an important historical role for defense, transport, and as a food source, the Ljubljanica and its upstream tributary, the Gradaščica, were also erratic in both the volume and duration of stream flow—so much so that in the eighteenth century a channel, the Gruber cut, was made on the eastern side of the castle hill to relieve the rather constant threat of flooding.

When Jože Plečnik arrived in 1921, at the invitation of Ivan Vurnik among others, to take up the chair in architecture at the newly founded University of Ljubljana, he effectively became the city architect as well, and shortly thereafter he involved himself in formulating a more definitive set of plans for Ljubljana. In all, Plečnik prepared two drafts—one in 1928 and the other some time later, in 1943—and both recognized the work of his able predecessors.[33]

For instance, he clearly followed Koch's map for Ljubljana, a copy of which he had purchased on a previous trip home, and the influence of both Fabiani and Sitte is evident, respectively, in the major street layout and harmonious squares and the visual variety, neighborhood scale, and focused vistas.

Apart from a synthesis, however, Plečnik's unique contributions were the creation of a land axis, a water axis, and an extensive northerly extension of the city in the Bežigrad district.[34] The land axis effectively extended Miklošičeva Street south, through Prešeren Square, along Vegova Street in the former old town and across the Gradaščica tributary into the residential neighborhood of Trnovo. The water axis took up the problem of the utilitarian concrete channel and flood-control improvements proposed by Keller for the Ljubljanica and Gradaščica, transforming them into an organizing spine through the city and a place of extraordinary civic amenity. Plečnik also proposed at least three river crossings that greatly improved accessibility and effectively supplied three transverse axes within his overall plan, roughly perpendicular to both the land and water axes. Finally, the plan for the extensive northerly extension of the city was based primarily on Garden City principles prevalent at the time and was intended to be developed in a fanlike shape, with greenbelts and large areas left for future residential development.

Historically, one can only speculate about what might have happened to the plans for Ljubljana in the absence of both Yugoslav and Slovene nationalism. Clearly the planning efforts were initiated at a time when the Slovenes and many other Yugoslavs were under the hegemony of the Austro-Hungarian Dual Monarchy. Nevertheless, once the plans began to really shape the city during the later 1900s, political opposition and a strong sense of at least the possibility for far greater local autonomy were becoming universal. Certainly by the time of Plečnik's arrival in Ljubljana, the Yugoslavian nation state had been formed and Slovenia, although politically subordinate to the central government in Belgrade, was rapidly developing a distinctive socioeconomic and cultural identity. Economic prosperity alone seems unlikely to have produced the programmatic opportunities presented by the prolific creation of the national

Tromostovje, or the three bridges, in Ljubljana by Plečnik.

institutional development that took place in Ljubljana and propelled its plans. Moreover, the very act of remaking the city so forcefully and enthusiastically into a relatively coherent new image had all the hallmarks of the contemporary and prevalent sense of national destiny.

Establishing a sense of national or regional identity inevitably invokes a process of differentiation across broad political, social, and cultural characteristics. Sometimes it is a matter of language; on other occasions it is a question of geography, and in still others one of a shared history. Often, as in Slovenia, all of these factors come into play. Once established, this sense of identity quickly becomes a strong unifying force, defining interactions between the state and civil society on matters of the civic realm. In the end it is a complex ensemble of political and cultural messages, conveyed by all manner of expressive paraphernalia, of which architecture and the physical layout of cities and civic spaces are but a few. Constantly involved in such enterprises (particularly those involving public architecture) are attempts to invoke a certain admiration of the emerging regional or national state of affairs through the size, scale, formal composition, and iconography of buildings, as well as the process of justifying distinctions of identity through references to preordained authorities and sources. Thus architecture as the indicator of both the miranda and credenda of regional or national identity and power has a significant role to play.

PLEČNIK'S WATER AXIS IN LJUBLJANA

Of all the aspects of Plečnik's plans and architectural contributions for the city of Ljubljana, his water axis and infrastructural improvements to the Ljubljanica River and the Gradaščica tributary are the most coherent and well established, as well as strong purveyors of Slovenian identity and civic presence. As mentioned, the Ljubljanica River was conceived by Plečnik as a backbone to his overall plan. More specifically, he saw it as a linear sequence of places and spatial experiences that would unite the old medieval town on the right bank with the newer town on the left bank, as opposed to the barrier to development and access presented by Keller's utilitarian flood-control project of a deep concrete-lined channel.[35] In fairness to Keller, from at least the middle ages onward, the Ljubljanica—with its walls along the left bank—had formed a defense barrier in front of the town. Nevertheless, Koch, in agreement with Plečnik, clearly appreciated the modern change in circumstances, as reflected in his pointed commentary about the inappropriateness of the river divide presented in his own map for Ljubljana. Plečnik had a similar reaction to the plans for cleaning up and rectifying the Gradaščica, drawn up by the city's Building Control Office in 1913.[36] Instead of converting it into a narrow channel, Plečnik proposed the idea of a linear park, designed in a countryfied, natural fashion, emphasizing and complementing the peaceful and rather haphazard residential character of surrounding neighborhoods.

With these overall purposes in mind—unifying sections of the city, harmonizing new projects with surrounding areas, and taking up the opportunity to convert an infrastructure project into a civic monument—Plečnik set about designing and constructing various riverine improvements. In all, at least six major projects were involved, forming what is today a strong sequence of public events.[37] They are: the embankments and Trnovo Bridge of the Gradaščica (1929–1932), the Shoemaker's Bridge (*Čevljarski Most*) on the Ljubljanica (1931–1932), the Three Bridges (*Tromostovje*) also on the Ljubljanica (1931–1932), the embankments of the Ljubljanica River itself (1932–1940), the market (*Tržnice*) on the left side of the river (1939–1942), and the sluice gates (*Pregrada*) further downstream on the Ljubljanica (1939–1943). Several other bridges across the Ljubljanica were also planned, including the Butcher's Bridge in conjunction with the market complex, but were never built. The sequence can also be seen to extend further upstream at least to the Prule Bridge beyond the Gradaščica tributary, with long and broad sweeping stone steps and terraces forming one side of the Ljubljanica, together with hedgerow and tree improvements along parallel avenues.

Within the overall concept of a countryfied, linear park, Plečnik's embankments of the Gradaščica gently sloped down to the channelized water course, where the undulating grassy sides contrasted with the strong linear, concrete-clad alignment of the river bed proper. The outer margins of the linear park were planted with rows of trees and hedges, and several landings, or "washing stages," were incorporated along the length of the stream. At those points the river bank became strongly defined by the architectural features of a vertical stone wall and balustrade at the street level, together with an arched opening in the wall itself and stone steps leading down to a stone platform where the washing could take place conveniently. The whole composition was symmetrically composed on both sides of the stream, with some detailed variations in the sizing and placement of decorative stone elements. The Trnovo Bridge formed the major crossing in this sequence of improvements, placed on axis with the Trnovo parish church at the end of Karunova street, effectively linking the adjacent Trnovo and Krakovo residential districts. The bridge itself has a wide platform, roughly square in plan, and is supported from below by a stone arch. An avenue of birch trees planted along the bridge deliberately obscures the bridgelike quality at street level and is complemented by pyramidal elements at the corners and stylized vaselike elements used as balustrades. At the center of the bridge there is a statue of John the Baptist on one side and on the other, a slender pyramid reportedly commemorating Baron Žiga Zois, the eighteenth- and early nineteenth-century supporter and proliferator of the Slovene language and other national cultural interests.[38] The "double reading" that one gets of the bridge from below and at grade was to become characteristic of many of Plečnik's river projects. Finally, a broad curvilinear sweep of terraces, capped by a clump of willow trees, forms a well-scaled jetty and marks the confluence of the Gradaščica with Ljubljanica.

The Shoemaker's Bridge, continuing the sequence, was located downstream from the already existing St. Jacob's Bridge, around which Plečnik also made some civic improvements, linking the left bank of the Ljubljanica embankment with *Podtrančo* on the east or right bank. As the site of the former Hradecky's Bridge built in 1867, on which first butchers and later cobblers had their premises, Plečnik made a very wide crossing—approximately a double square in plan—virtually constituting a well-delimited urban square suspended across the river below. The inherent grandeur of the spatial experience was further enlarged by the relatively broad and short streets at either end of the bridge, today marked out in the form of public plazas by bollards and concrete planters. A twofold impression of the structure, similar to the Trnovo crossing, becomes very apparent from further away on the embankment, where the bridge appears as a very light plank thrown straight across the river, supported from below by slender columns at the center. Ornamentation takes the form of six stylized Corinthian columns along the sides of the bridge, each capped by a round ball, and two Ionic columns at the center, capped with tall cylindrical light fixtures. The balustrade, like the Trnovo bridge, is generous in its massing and ornamentation, while the entire columnar arrangement further serves to define a strong sense of place within the bridge platform, aided by a homogeneous use of reinforced concrete and stone. Indeed, early drawings by Plečnik show that the columns were originally to have supported a roof, somewhat like Palladio's covered bridge at Bassano.[39] However, the financial constraints of the earlier 1930s made this additional construction impossible.

The Three Bridges, the next crossing downstream, was originally seen as another wide platform to replace the original stone bridge by Fransisco Camolo, built in 1842.[40] Always very insightful and respectful of context, Plečnik changed his mind, however, overcoming the traffic-carrying inadequacies of Camolo's bridge with two additional pedestrian bridges on each side. This rather ingenious solution also allowed Plečnik to contribute constructively to Prešeren Square, on the west bank, and to palpably convey the essential idea of building across from one side of the city to the other. By splaying the new pedestrian bridges out in the direction of Prešeren Square, a fluid funnellike effect was created spatially, recalling the much earlier importance of the site as a major gateway and market area at the entrance to the old medieval town. Together with the two symmetrical palatial structures by Leopold Theyer on the east bank, and the varied yet harmonious grouping of buildings around Prešeren Square and the Franciscan Church on the west bank, Plečnik's bridge focuses and completes the entire composition at this very important center of daily life in Ljubljana. The importance of the site is further marked by an accessible lower gallery level along the river bank on the western side. Here a closed-arched stone loggia opens out on each side to a habitable open terrace, with public toilets beneath the formal line of the bridge proper, again emphasizing Plečnik's attention to programmatic details and the easy incorporation of mundane yet necessary functions alongside a higher-minded orientation toward civic monumentality.

When designing the embankments of the Ljubljanica, Plečnik also strove toward monumentality, not inappropriately coinciding with the several bridge crossings and the functional flood-control demands for a deep channel. The segments in the upstream vicinity of the Shoemaker's Bridge, for instance, and downstream, past the Three Bridges to the existing Dragon's Bridge, are highly articulated and replete with architectural details. Throughout, Plečnik cleverly subdivided the otherwise monotonous deep-channel profile and steep, high embankments with small ledges, riverside galleries, and small viewing terraces supported on stone pilasters. Lush planting coincided with these interruptions, effectively producing a highly varied and stratified effect, including virtual extension of the palatial facades fronting the river down toward the water level many meters below. Bi-level occupancy of the embankment was also achieved, in addition to the loggias and terraces flanking the Three Bridges. Lines of trees, some grandiose steps, distinctive lights, street furniture, and a fluted columnar folly at the *Gledališka stolba*—announcing passage through to the prominent Congress Square—also lined the urban river embankment. Similar spatial themes were introduced on the downstream side of the Three Bridges, although here as elsewhere along the Ljubljanica the embankment section was asymmetrical. Specifically, the curving line of the market complex, with its rusticated base, formed a relatively sheer wall along the eastern side of the river, whereas the bi-level terrace, with long lines of trees at both levels, was continued on the western bank. Beyond the Dragon's Bridge, the stream channel

assumed a straightforward, rectilinear utilitarian quality—an unfinished reminder of what might have been constructed without Plečnik's inspired and
sensitive improvements.

As built, the market project, between the Dragon's Bridge and the
Three Bridges, was part of a much larger project, originally to have included a
monumental curved Butcher's Bridge (*Mesarski most*) at its center and substantial improvements on both sides of the river.[41] As it stands now, the market
follows the line of the former town wall, presenting a two-story edifice on the
river side consisting of a half-rusticated wall with small arched openings at the
lower level and gracious larger openings at the upper level. At the center, a
five-bay columnar porch and a shallow classical entablature projects slightly
out into the river channel. On the street side, the market consists of an alternat-
ing closed and open colonnade, beginning with a beautifully proportioned neoclassical gatehouse near the Three Bridge crossing. The curving, columnar,
double-height arcade, of particularly high quality, now forms the outer edge of
a tree-lined street paralleling the river and an open marketplace with a further
square beyond and behind the cathedral. Not inappropriately, the spatial feeling
of an agora is quite pronounced adjacent to the street side of this complex.

Finally, the Pregrada sluice gates, completed just before the Germans
called a halt to city construction in 1943, allowed the water level of the
Ljubljanica to be brought under control, giving the maximum effect to Plečnik's
river improvements. The sluice itself has three monumental towers, with sloping
walls terminating in massive entablatures and roofs lower down, which entirely
cover the mechanisms for raising the gates. As in many of his designs, Plečnik
was more interested in the symbolic appearance of the gate structure—subsequently likened to the great Egyptian temples in the Nile—than in the essential
architectural source material of mechanical devices.[42] In both effect and affect,
the sluice was conceived of as a triumphal arch and a watergate to the city.
Furthermore, in Plečnik's original conception it was to be flanked by two parks
beside Ambrožev Square on the right side of the river, and by Vrazov Square

on the left. Doubtless, ornamentation on the columns and towers of the sluice by Božidar Pengov is more literal than on the earlier river projects, although the overall form remains stylized.

Plečnik most probably viewed the various elements of his water axis as part of a well-orchestrated sequence, somewhat like a piece of music or a poem, with a definite beginning, distinct phrases, and an end. Town planning from a cartographic perspective was almost certainly alien to him. Contemporary accounts contend that Plečnik formulated his plans for Ljubljana during daily walks from his home in Trnovo, near the site of his first riverine improvements. In common with Sitte, he had a strong interest in the sensible effect urban design compositions might have on passersby, and again like Sitte, Plečnik was often content to edit and augment existing circumstances. Rather than being a radical designer or master planner, his approach was more organic, taking into account what was already there and seeking a better synthesis.[43] Nevertheless, Plečnik's water axis is far more than mere contextualism or opportunistic picturesque speculation. The sequence of projects begins strongly on one side of town with a linear park, which has had more effect in constituting the surrounding residential neighborhoods over time than vice versa. The succession of projects then peak in scale, monumentality, and civic ambition around the Three Bridges and the market before concluding with the Pregrada sluice gates on the other side of town. Not incidentally, the linear parks intended by Plečnik in conjunction with these gates would have concluded the sequence more or less as it began, in a countryfied atmosphere. Furthermore, if taken as a civic cross-section through Ljubljana, the sequence of projects also seems to suggest models worthy of emulation in other parts of the city. Given his organic manner of working, Plečnik probably saw the river sequence as one of many programs for subsequent improvement and beautification.

Several other themes emerge from Plečnik's plans for Ljubljana and the extensive body of urban-architectural works that followed. First, there is the rather obvious interplay between a strong overall sense of structure and variety in the local public spaces and buildings. Second, the design approach is invariably conservative in at least a couple of related respects. Both in style and representational program, Plečnik's projects often recall aspects of Ljubljana's history. More often than not, the sensitive manner in which the context of each work is approached not only preserves some familiarity and continuity with the past, but also allows Plečnik to take advantage economically of what is already in place. Third, a considerable amount of programmatic invention seems to have taken place beyond a project's primary function. The inclusion, for instance, of washing ledges and public bathrooms within the considerably more monumental framework of the river terraces and the Three Bridges is both practical and extends the scope of the works from the mundane realm of daily activities to celebratory sites aimed at providing a strong sense of civic identity and dignity. Fourth, the style of Plečnik's work is characteristically eclectic, even radically so. On the whole a mannered, and some would say Italianate, neoclassicism is at work, with a strong interest in both antiquity and the vernacular of Slovenia through its craft tradition, indigenous building materials and use of rustication. Also present is a clear modern influence in the use of contemporary materials and construction techniques (although nowhere to the same extent as contemporaries like Vurnik and Šubic) as well as the use of geometrical reduction and abstraction. These influences reflect Plečnik's formation as an architect, ranging from an early upbringing in the home of his father, a cabinetmaker, work in the *Wagnerschule* in Vienna, and a sojourn in Italy that accompanied his winning the Rome Prize in 1898.[44] Finally, Plečnik was obviously an ardent student of architecture and not disinclined to draw on references close at hand that he admired. To name just a few that played a role in the Ljubljana water axis, there was the Wagnerschule *Donau Kanal* project, Friedrich Ohmann's 1906 terraces in the Vienna *Stadtpark*, Peter Paler's Karlsbridge across the Moldava in Prague, and Palladio's bridge at Bassano, mentioned earlier.

Important though these results may be, the functional outcomes of better access, orientation, and choice for Ljubljana's citizenry do not adequately reflect the full import of Plečnik's urban work. Nor does the historicism, attentiveness to surrounding circumstances, programmatic inventiveness, and stylistic eclecticism fully support his efforts on behalf of his native city. Far more at stake seems to have been celebration of emerging Slovenian regionalism, the making of a state capital, and the construction of a dignified framework for civic life.

To begin with, the idea of an overall public order in which there can be individual private identity—as reflected architecturally in the concept of variety within a strong spatial structure—had a particular sociopolitical relevance for Plečnik and many other Slovenes during the interwar years. Plečnik's design principles, as well as his project titled "Houses Under a Common Roof," clearly recalled the Slovenian People's Party dictum cited earlier, of providing a *roof* under which (Catholic) Slovenes could prosper.[45] Moreover, this was no coincidence of ideas, but the self-same ideology. The architect was, after all, a devout Catholic and very committed to the national (Slovenian) cause. His return to Ljubljana in 1920, just as the national movement was openly getting under way, was in fact more than coincidental.

Plečnik's interests in archaeology, history, and antiquarian conservation were also highly selective and nationalistic. Of the monuments he created, including the pyramid commemorating Žiga Zois at the St. Jacob's Bridge, the Illyrian monument to the French Revolution in the square of the same name along Vegova Street, and the work on Congress Square, almost all have a strong orientation toward periods of the Slovenian past relatively unencumbered by foreign domination. So also do his well-known preferences for the Baroque period in Ljubljana, dating from around 1650—a time of free trade within the city and relative freedom from outside influences. This proclivity can then be quickly contrasted with Plečnik's avowed adversity to the nineteenth-century building in Ljubljana, which he regarded as boring, unimaginative, and symbolic of foreign domination at the hands of Austria and Hungary.[46] The city's Roman ruins, although reflecting a non-Slavic past, do recall the foundations of Ljubljana—then known as Emona—and evoke a pride in roots and sources of civilization independent of the more immediate Germanized past. Plečnik also apparently believed that the Slovenes were direct descendants of the Etruscans

The market along the Ljubljanica by Plečnik.

and therefore of a Mediterranean culture.[47] If nothing else, this somewhat fantastic belief supports the nationalistic claim being made by the adoption of a Roman past. Furthermore, in the location of projects—like the market along the old wall, the Three Bridges at the old gate in the wall, and the Shoemaker's Bridge on the site of a former medieval crossing—Plečnik is clearly distancing the city from its most recent occupiers, if not oppressors, by recalling a much earlier and more autonomous period of existence.

Programmatically, Plečnik's inventiveness and embellishment of necessary functions allowed many works to have a sense of purpose and meaning for all Slovenians, wholeheartedly embracing and redefining many aspects of daily life in Ljubljana. The bustling marketplace is a clear case in point. Moreover, the range of accommodation made by Plečnik in his projects was often considerable. By considering the bridges across the Ljubljanica, for instance, as places where people could linger, rather than as momentary stops along a route, allowed the city to be recentered both practically and symbolically away from its immediate past, orienting it instead toward a new Slovenian future and sense of wholeness. The creation of architectural monuments out of what were at some basic level only infrastructure improvements also aggrandized the city and reinforced the idea of something grand and befitting a nation-state. Here again Plečnik makes reference to ancient Rome, but he breaks with emerging modern architectural ideologies north of the Alps—the source of previous cultural domination—by deliberately concealing nearly all manner of mechanism, material, and engineering function in his public works projects. It is not that the bridges, canals, and sluice gates are uncontemporary in operational terms—they simply don't appear that way, and for good reason.

Stylistically, Plečnik's widespread use of an Italianate neoclassicism allowed him to give dignity and appropriate civic stature to his public works projects while avoiding the prevailing and, to many, pompous Austro-Hungarian style of monumental building. Apart from expressively distancing his works from the earlier dominant foreign culture, this choice also enabled Plečnik to present a more sober image for the city, consistent with the birth of a new nation in modern times. As mentioned, constant references to the Slovenian craft tradition and vernacular style of building were woven into the architectural language of the projects, giving them a strong nationalist cast. Particularly conspicuous was the inventive and seemingly spontaneous use of local materials and a penchant for the use of rustication and for the colorful display of natural materials. A certain modernism is also evident, largely through the use of contemporary materials like reinforced concrete and geometrical reduction and abstraction in the profiles of building elements. Both aspects imbue Plečnik's works with a progressive character, again supporting the idea of a modern nation-state. Beyond simply matters of style and expression, however, there is a classical humanistic perspective to be found in many of Plečnik's projects, centered mainly on the likely experience of a person in the street and clearly aimed at providing ready access, guidance, and a sense of dignity.

CONSTITUTIVE AND REPRESENTATIONAL ASPECTS OF PUBLIC DOMAINS

Slovenian regionalism and civic pride were clearly conveyed by Plečnik's public improvements to Ljubljana. Today, precisely at a time of renewed national fervor—although this time without reference to a larger Yugoslav confederation—Plečnik's projects are viewed both as obvious symbols of Slovenia and as firm bases for conducting and projecting the idea of civic life in a new democratic state. The constitutive and representational qualities required of that civic life include a monumentality appropriate for a regional capital and an architectural expression that is, above all, local and ennobling as well as being a sober setting for day-to-day conduct. If anything, the formal qualities and appearances of Plečnik's projects put people on their best behavior. One can easily impute a formal, slightly ritualistic mode of preferred behavior, but without any sense of undue constraint. They provide a beautifully appointed and yet familiar public realm, which both expresses and evinces a conviction in the comely public display of private contacts among the populace.

Some other more recent projects that have this same familiar, centering, and sobering effect, although without quite the same national import, are the public open-space improvements to New York City by the Philadelphia firm of Hanna-Olin. In particular, there is the reconstruction of Bryant Park in midtown, and the Esplanade alongside Battery Park City on the Lower West Side. Design of the new Bryant Park retained many aspects of the earlier neoclassical scheme, but simplified the complexity of the annular adornments of planting beds, herbaceous borders, and paths. In the manner of the Jardin de Luxembourg, Parisian-style furniture, balustrades for leaning on, and broad open spaces for watching and being seen are generously provided in place of the former more closed subdivision of outdoor spaces. Similarly, a strong intention behind design of the Esplanade lining the approximately one-mile river edge of the 92-acre residential and commercial development at Battery Park City was to provide public access and an area full of New York commonplaces. A cleverly organized cross section, with two major avenues of trees and zones of movement and occupation, provide the setting for a great variety of public outdoor activity within a relatively short distance. Like Plečnik's work, in both places a certain expressive eclecticism is evident, but with a less radical and stronger quotidian orientation and concern for making places appear familiar. Also, like Ljubljana, both places in New York are the outcome of joint efforts by the public and private sectors to improve the quality of the city's civic space. Indeed, a special quasi-private administrative district was created around Bryant Park to assist the government with adequate provision of services. A so-called business improvement district was created in 1985 by a group of local businesspersons known as "the Partnership."[48] Chartered by state law, this authority had the power of mandatory taxation once the district was formed by a majority of property owners. Assessment fees were then spent on sanitation, security, and open-space and street improvements, as well as a homeless outreach program. Likewise, in Ljubljana, Plečnik tried to redress the public-private balance, only this time in favor of the public sector and its right to take property for projects of a perceived public benefit.

Robert Hanna's and especially Laurie Olin's interest in the ordinary seems to stem from a conviction that commonplace and everyday environments—provided that they are of a certain quality—can bring people most directly into contact with the essence of things and thus provide them with an excitement about the world they inhabit. Furthermore, if daily spatial experience can be well rendered in ordinary terms, both the meaningfulness and congeniality of public life will be enhanced appreciably. Far from being merely mundane, this ordinary spatial experience provides a close natural relationship to the world and a broad basis for turning back nagging doubts about the existence of that world—nowadays a rather persistent philosophical problem about meaning. Put more prosaically, an interest in the *ordinary*—a decidedly quotidian orientation—can be a very useful basis on which to resolve the otherwise "undecideable" aspects of expressive meanings, to return to the problem described at the beginning of this chapter.[49] Accordingly, a common sense of place and conviviality, together with the collective well-being that usually follows from such feelings, can be established, especially in those public domains of cities that probably matter most and yet often seem to suffer most from neglect.

One way in which Hanna-Olin's designs for both the Esplanade at Battery Park City and Bryant Park approach this rather particular ordinary condition is through the apparently effortless, seemingly preordained, expected, and familiar character of their proposals. They appear to have been in place since time immemorial, and with the same sense of acceptance and affection that goes with a favorite pair of shoes or with a kind, familiar face. In reality, however, nothing could be further from these perceptions. Battery Park City was created—roughly between 1979 and 1983—out of raw landfill on Lower Manhattan's West Side, and the construction documents for Bryant Park—a 5-acre restoration around 42nd Street and Sixth Avenue—were completed as recently as 1988.[50] Nevertheless, both projects seem to follow on from their time and place and readily adopt New York's urban tradition in a manner that belies their newness, although not necessarily their contemporaneity.

Part of this natural, preordained, quotidian appropriateness also comes by way of Hanna-Olin's choice of solution type or paradigm for the public places under consideration. There was nothing at Battery Park City by way of historical or archeological evidence to suggest as esplanade and associated open-space system. There is by contrast, ample precedent for imagining and even expecting grand public walks alongside large bodies of water—like the Hudson River—to have the character of a promenade or corniche. In short, it is within the underlying expressive power of given site circumstances and programmatic needs that certain widely recognized types can emerge within landscape design. In practice, Hanna-Olin, like Plečnik, are particularly adroit at this form of conceptual appropriation. In a much earlier project at the Arco Corporation, for example, both the genius loci of the site in Pennsylvania and the idea of a research and development campus become merged into a single idea: the concept of a large country estate. Of broader theoretical and practical interest here, however, are the emphases on relatively familiar themes, organically making the most of what is already on site, and a conviction that a relatively small number of typological concepts can adequately underlay most public space improvements.

Not unexpectedly, even with a broad appeal to familiar precedents, there can also be a capacity within a project to convey more of an expressive meaning than authors intend. By now, for instance, we are quite aware of the multiple interpretations that can be given routinely to commonplace things. Certainly, things are often commonplace or not depending on the context. In other words, concern about the "uncanny" aspect of the ordinary—in philosophical terms—together with "undecideable" aspects of meaningful expression, probably can and should be relaxed somewhat.[51] In fact, in Hanna-Olin's projects, as well as many of Plečnik's more radically eclectic projects, there appears to be a certain trading on the vagueness or slipperiness of precise references. Throughout, they all seem to be well aware of the capacity for architectural forms to express more than authors intend, but still remain broadly compatible with authorial intentions. Indeed, one might quickly claim this capacity for all great civic works. Wherever possible, good designs seem to err toward redundancy and multiple interpretation, especially with respect to both functions and specific meanings, while maintaining a certain consensus about broad collective understandings. In the work of both Plečnik and Hanna-Olin, the expressive slipperiness that is usually so much a part of their versions of eclecticism is played to advantage, although only up to a point. As we have already seen, the general meanings and civic aspirations of Plečnik's urban projects are far from vague. Conversely, within the otherwise strong and expressively clear framework of Hanna-Olin's New York projects, a certain ambiguity and redundancy go a long way in producing perceptions of comfortable familiarity and generous accommodation. People bring their own activities to these public places rather than the places dictating the activities. Both Bryant Park and the Esplanade at Battery Park City are settings largely for unpredetermined activity, as for that matter are the banks and terraces of the Ljubljanica. Clearly these places, like Central Park, are better suited for certain forms of behavior than others, but they possess a robust character that facilitates other extemporaneous and less well imagined uses. In so doing, they have the capacity to draw people in and to engage them, rather than simply appearing as expressive figural fixtures or adornments within the city, like so many waving flags or flashing neon signs. Success lies in a very real capacity to constitute civic life in the city. At Bryant Park, for instance, the imaginative opening of the space to clear view and access effectively removed the earlier barrier that had tragically made the place a haven for drug pushers and muggers.

Finally, a moral directive emerges through all this work. On balance, it is an admonition toward sobriety, propriety, and the harmony that comes from being synchronized with the broader ambitions of one's world and one's day-to-day existence. Although not exactly straightlaced, it is a moral directive that, if perhaps a little old-fashioned to some, resonates loudly in favor of dignified play and extemporaneous invention as a way of bringing us constructively into closer contact with ourselves and our world. In these regards a communitarian view seems to be expressed, through which guidance and a constructive framework are given to daily practices and the lasting conduct of civic life, rather than a distinctive expression or style.

"What are you going to do now?" asked the foreign journalist. "You can only have so many Plečnik retrospectives!" "The important thing is to move forward," said Miloš thoughtfully. "The city has many needs, it's true, but more important, we have to find our own way. One that people can identify with." "What does that mean?" inquired the journalist, a little skeptically. "I dunno—I guess a little of this and a little of that," countered Miloš, although quickly becoming dissatisfied with his own answer. "This is an interesting place, you know," he went on, a little defensively, "and we should work with that, as well as looking into ourselves somehow."

Tuby Ratesle, *Mostovi I Trgovi**

6

The Practice of Civic Realism

Pregrada sluice gates in Ljubljana by Plečnik (page 198).

"Maman, look at the blue elephant!" cried the little girl with glee, rushing ahead of her mother, her crinoline skirts flying. "Fait attention! Isabelle!" shouted Madame Hardelin, now more than a little exasperated at her daughter's antics and lack of decorum. Certainly the Pays des Fées, outside of the Exposition gates on the Avenue Rapp, was becoming a very popular attraction. Nevertheless, there were appearances to maintain. "We can't have everyone running about all over the place, simply as they please," thought Madame Hardelin to herself. "What will all these nice visitors to Paris think!"

"Ooh! My tummy feels funny!" exclaimed Isabelle, squeezing her mother's hand more tightly. "When is it going to stop?" she inquired anxiously. "We'll be there in a minute," answered her mother, although she herself was quite unused to the rapid ascent of the elevators up this massive, somewhat outlandish modern structure, with all its metal beams, brackets, and trusses. "Still, the food is excellent, and that's what counts. This is France, after all," she thought to herself smugly.

"Please can I? Please, maman, can I?" Isabelle was now quite literally trying to fly by herself, while simultaneously reaching out for the small balloon into which her mother was carefully inserting a note with her name and address on it. "Please! Isabelle! Just a minute! How often do I have to tell you to be a little more patient?" remonstrated Madame Hardelin, although she herself thought it would be fun to let the red balloon and its personal contents sail off the tower into some stranger's hands below. "He could even be foreign," she thought to herself, her pulse quickening.

Pierre Grimmonde, *De Plus en Plus Fort**

Almost without exception, the contemporary instances of civic realism discussed so far could have been used interchangeably to make similar points. Like the Piazza del Campo, they are all well-rounded examples and not as sharply focused as the earlier presentations might have suggested. Through their sheer scope and diversity, for instance, the urban public places of Barcelona or the grand projets of Paris could have been used to illuminate practically any underlying theme. Although used to demonstrate the representational and constitutive aspects of urban-architectural space, the improvements in Ljubljana could just as easily have been employed to characterize settings for both individual and collective behavior on the part of the city's populace. Likewise, the civilizing and moral direction provided by New York's Central Park was touched upon, even though the bulk of the presentation concerned efforts to resolve differences among a heterogeneous population in the construction of a single recreational venue. A convergence also began to appear among several of the book's primary conceptual terms. In the use of both "civic" and "real" there was an insistence on everyday life, away from the private realm. By the same token, both terms, in their more favorable uses, implied something socially critical and not simply state dogma or accepted private sector practice. They also usually connoted settings for public conduct that were somehow ennobling and often dignified. As much as anything, civic realism could be seen as attitudinal and a practical habit of mind conducive to making places of collective significance. Given the evolutionary descriptions of places like SoHo or Loisaida in New York, there also appeared to be no such thing—necessarily—as a civic realist project in the conventional relatively instantaneous sense of those terms, and some aspects of civic realism probably exist in many places, whether we choose to acknowledge and valorize them or not. Urban-architecturally speaking, the civic realism depicted in this book is certainly not a style nor a specific aesthetic ideology. In essence, it is at first a descriptive state or condition of being in the world, and second, an orientation and set of conceptual balancing tests or principles to be adopted and applied when making urban architecture into something that is about civic as distinct from simply public or personal experience.

THE CIVIC, THE REAL, AND THE SPECIFIC

To summarize, the civic realm—roughly speaking—lies somewhere between the more strictly public and private aspects of our lives, although it tends to be produced by both. As much as anything, it derives from networks of associations within society, many of which are informal. Consequently, the term civic is usually highly correlated with the idea of civil society, which as we have seen is also neither strictly public nor private. In Habermas's and others' theoretical formulations, it is usually the middle term in a tripartite political formulation consisting of "public, civil, and private," and a tension is presumed to exist between civil society and the state, which in turn stands apart from the more intimate and personal relations of the private realm.[1] Within this tripartite scheme considerable debate exists around how specifically civil society should be defined in relation to the other realms of our lives. For some, like Cohen and Arato, it consists primarily of voluntary associations, social movements, and public communications, with offshoots like political and economic society essentially arising out of civil society itself.[2] For others, including Habermas, it also embraces economic transactions more formally described by markets. Far from being static, the relative importance of civil society usually waxes and wanes. According to the political analyst Robert Putnam, for instance, recently there has been a downturn of civil interest within American society. His leitmotif of "bowling alone" rather graphically depicts this phenomenon by statistically describing the current situation where more people than before engage in the leisure-time activity of bowling, although the number of groups participating in the sport has declined, relatively speaking.[3] The upshot appears to be a weakening of both the variety and extensiveness of voluntary networks, with a corresponding withdrawal into the private, and to a lesser extent, the public spheres.

A central assertion in this book has been that the most productive opportunities for creating civic spaces, urban-architecturally speaking, arise across the conceptual divide between the state and civil society. This creation entails interpreting the community interests of the private sector and including all of the inherent tensions, particularly when the broader social aims of both the public and private spheres is high and the embrace of both—especially vis-à-vis disenfranchised and marginalized segments of society—is broadest. Indeed, many of the examples cited so far represent circumstances that at least approximate these ideals. Unfortunately this assertion also carries with it the implication that good civic space cannot be manufactured on demand, as it were, without favorable social and political conditions. As most modern political analysis makes evident, civil society is often seen as a way of backing out of statism, in its various forms, and away from both excessive liberalism and the hold of neoconservative market-oriented forces. Cohen and Arato, for example, have rather clearly demonstrated that the contemporary problem of civil society and its desirable evolution is sufficient development of autonomous forms and institutional frameworks, away from conservatism and an overly influential economic sphere on the one hand, and statism or governmental cooption on the other.[4] In architectural and urban design terms, this would seem to suggest the need for resistance of the whims, idiosyncrasies, and egocentric tastes of private developers, as well as the consumerist pabulum of market forces, while simultaneously avoiding cooption by states in the form of grandiose projects, propaganda, and standardization in the name of dubious pluralist interests. Rather than seeing the social, political, and cultural realms of our lives as somehow separate, or indeed separable, an architecture that somehow resists both positions would at least seem to support the broader project of a movement toward a stronger autonomously based and self-organized civil society.

Mostly, the term civic also represents a point of view about public conduct. Certainly that was the case for Hannah Arendt.[5] For her something civic was edifying and worthy of being seen and heard in public, as well as being something we would be proud to pass on to future generations. From this vantage point, to be civic is a position that requires, at heart, some kind of convergent or communitarian concept to which people's conduct can correspond. It requires an authoritative account of sorts, but at least in this day and age, one that can be sustained with the utmost tolerance and respect of others' beliefs and traits. In contradistinction to some other definitions, here the term civic does not seem to be appropriate for projections of personality, aristocracy, theocracy, or despotism of any kind. Consequently, as we began to see in the earlier examples, it applies within the western world, most broadly anyway, during periods like the Greco-Roman republics, the autonomous medieval city-states like Siena, and the modern enlightenment democratic nations. If anything, most recently the term goes along with the rise of bourgeois society, although as Gramsci was quick to remind us, it could be applied to a socialist hegemony under the right conditions of autonomy and self-organization within a society.[6]

Realism, at least in aesthetic terms, is also concerned with a public nature of things often distinct from the state per se, and excludes as legitimate purely subjective responses. Although not necessarily naturalistic, a figurative dimension is required, referring to some aspect of a thing capable of being shared and appreciated in common, situated outside of the exclusive purview of the work itself. The rural village references of Tiburtino, for example, or the heraldry and iconography associated with the Campo clearly meet this criterion, as does the detailing of Plečnik and the plaza duras of Barcelona, even if in somewhat abstract architectural terms. Furthermore, although a realist depiction or project might well deal with what is familiar, recognizable, or commonly understood, there is also an impetus toward advancing various media and their effects. In short, as we saw in the comparative discussion of Tiburtino and Tuscolano within Italian neorealism, there is a concern with both the verisimilitude of the common place and the verisimilitude of genre. Overall, the subject matter for realist projects are drawn from daily life—often unavoidable in architecture—although not in any universal or classical manner. Issues of shelter and housing, for instance, at a particular moment and in a particular place— rather than simply in general or in principle—can be the stuff of a realist project, even though those same aspects might later take on certain transcendental qualities. Finally, the depiction, celebration, or constitutive aspect of everyday life must be either ennobling or critical, and not merely a matter of portrayal. In architecture, the former qualities might seem conceptually easy to achieve, whereas architectural embodiment of an act of being critical appears more complicated, probably less likely to happen, and even perhaps less appropriate to attempt to satisfy than other architectural responsibilities. The idea of celebrating at least quasi-democratic rule in medieval Siena, and hence resisting more singular despotic forms of governance, was rendered forcefully by the heterogeneous interests underlying expression within the Piazza del Campo. Similarly, the sheer pluralism of programs and expressions among the urban public space projects in contemporary Barcelona certainly called into question any preordained, state-directed way of doing things. The sheer generosity of different settings and possibilities for multiple use within places like Central Park or the Parc Citröen constantly present challenges to singular authoritative construals of civic space, even though society, at one time or another, might be verging in those directions.

Philosophically and artistically, when the terms civic and real are taken together, a dynamic concept emerges that cannot be defined with any precision a priori. Both terms are inherently relativistic, at least up to a point. Almost by definition, civic involves interaction between civil society and the state, or between the public and private sectors of our lives through civil society. Even in the most stable of moments, both arrangements are constantly in a state of dynamic equilibrium. In philosophy, according to scholars like Hilary Putnam and Nelson Goodman, as well as Linda Nochlin in art history, reality depends in large measure on the conceptual scheme one adopts.[7] Fortunately this has a familiar ring to it. We tend to see things as being most real when they are directly in front of us and of most concern to us at the time. There is therefore a certain immediacy associated with realism and, by extension, with civic realism. Both terms, ceteris paribus, converge on the everyday and the familiar. This quality may, however, be extended to include something that can be less literally familiar and present, but that nevertheless is expected. Special civic celebrations, for example, could hardly be excluded from the realm of civic realism. Indeed, the calendar of contemporary life is replete with examples, which sometimes involve official holidays, are related to religious observations, or are tied to seasonal events. As we also saw, civic realism, in more strictly artistic terms, is related to the relative development of various artistic genre or media. If, for instance, one of the stipulations of a realist project is some sense of development within a medium or genre, then a certain relativism will pertain. As we observed in the celebrated Brecht-Lukács debates, who might be correct and who incorrect depends on how various means of expression are valued in both expressive and historical or developmental terms. If we believe, as Brecht seemed to, that photodocumentary media are truly of the moment, then they should be used in the depiction of socially relevant daily circumstances rather than other less contemporary media.

One problem posed for us by this relativism is the comparatively enduring and static quality of architecture. It can hardly be expected to metamorphize in step with definitions of civil society, which change rather more quickly, or as the temporary frames of reference defining particular other forms of reality come and go. The conditions for temporal narratives of these kinds are usually highly restricted if not precluded from an architectural work. Thus the question emerges: how can architecture and urban-architectural design rise to such inherently relativistic occasions? Certainly from what we have seen, it can do so by appearing to be very specific and palpable at a particular time and place. On balance, architecture is probably more constitutive of people's lives than strictly representational of their actions, as we saw in chapter 5. In short, because a particular reality and its corresponding architectural presence stands a good chance of being remembered during one period, it probably means it will be recognized under somewhat different social or political circumstances in another period, and thus continue to help define emerging senses of civic realism. Although iconographically locked mainly in the fourteenth century, the Piazza del Campo is an example of this enduring capacity to continually define an important aspect of civic realism, in spite of the terminology's inherent relativism.

Paradoxically perhaps, this requirement of specificity in a civic realist project seems to argue against the abstract, open-ended, and deliberately nonspecific proposals of the 1960s and early 1970s, which were attempting to create so-called democratic environments by providing, in essence, merely a framework for action (urban proposals like Runcorn and Milton Keynes in Britain, or the Title VII New Towns in the United States, immediately come to mind).[8] Primarily they were extensive armatures of infrastructure for further investments, around which market forces were supposed to provide most community facilities and services. Nevertheless, the requirement of specificity in planning and place making also seems to point in the other direction as well, toward a broader frame of reference than simply producing projects. Bohigas's remonstration about "projects and not plans" is all well and good when there exists a strong urban circumstance like the *Eixample* in Barcelona to react against. Likewise, Plečnik was drawing on enduring geographical circumstances, persistent cultural features, and an iconographical—albeit idiosyncratic—interpretation of both past and present to create a place that could both symbolize and constitute a strong sense of Slovenian nationalism.

This capacity to be continually admired, and therefore continually capable of constituting a viable civic aspect to our cities, not only holds for the Piazza del Campo and Plečnik's Ljubljana, but for the other projects we have investigated as well. It certainly holds for Rockefeller Center and, although the jury is still out, the same qualities are promisingly present in the Parc de la Villette and the Parc Citröen in Paris, as well as among the recent public space projects in Barcelona. Once etched in a populace's mind, they tend to take on almost mythological qualities of their own, which create in turn an enduring aura of civic realism. Without anthropomorphizing too much, these projects effectively become actors, or at least significant stage sets for actors in a much broader play of sociopolitical forces. Tompkins Square Park, for instance, has persistently been a place of both protest and celebration in New York City, and thus of helping to better define civic life. Moreover, the capacity of New Yorkers to continually define and redefine turf in the otherwise ubiquitous Manhattan grid is testament to the need for specificity, locality, and just plain realism in their urban-architectural environments. In short, the architectural and urban

The Parc de l'Espanya Industrial in Barcelona by Peña Ganchegui and Ruiz.

structure of cities, as well as specific artifacts and places within them, effectively have the capacity to cheat the otherwise highly relativistic connotations of both the "civic" and the "real" in favor or more lasting, valuable, but nevertheless highly specific urban qualities.

CIVIC REALISM AS A CONSTELLATION OF CONCEPTUAL DIMENSIONS

By breaking down further the broad conceptual framework of civic realism we find a constellation of concepts embracing well-known entities like: characteristics of a state, voluntary associations, special events, everyday life, urban environments, visual forms, and so on. As noted earlier, rather than being identifiable or definable by way of fixed categories, civic realism is variable and relatively independent of both style and particular appearance. Moreover, civic realism fundamentally and explicitly involves personal interaction with a particular urban place and therefore takes its measure from this interaction. Nevertheless, four normative dimensions are involved, the rough intersection of which constitutes civic realism. They are: a dimension that can be graduated from abstract to naturalistic with regard to shape and appearance; a dimension that can be graded from individual, everyday, and ordinary occurrences to collective and transcendental experience; and a dimension that spans from simple representation of authority, power, and related social facts to the physical constitution of a place for similar effects; as well as a dimension that allows comparative differences in the sponsorship of urban projects between civil society and the state to be reflected fully. In short, civic realism is conceptually defined by the four dimensions of appearance, experience, effect, and sponsorship. Although each dimension is more or less independent of the others, there are some obvious overlaps. The statist or collective ends, for instance, of each dimension like appearance, effect, and sponsorship are likely to be highly correlated. Particular dimensions may also be understood in different terms. The abstract-naturalistic aspect of the dimension of appearance, for instance, may be interpreted better as the interaction between a verisimilitude of both genre and of content. Here, among the examples described, La Villette would favor genre, while Tiburtino would certainly lean toward content.

Subject to reasonable interpretation, all the urban examples discussed so far can be arrayed relative to one another along the four conceptual dimensions of civic realism. By comparison to the SoHo loft environment, for example, La Villette is clearly more abstract in appearance, although involving less entrepreneurship on the part of civil society than state sponsorship. The SoHo environment is largely a collective expression without quite the same latitude for individual experience and outward bodily expression as La Villette, whereas both examples are probably as much representational in their outward appearance as they are constitutive of people's behavior. The urban projects of Barcelona tend to be rather evenhanded products of the state and civil society, with a concern for everyday functions as much as special events. On the whole they also tend to be abstract, although understandable and even familiar in appearance and architectural expression. Plečnik's projects in Ljubljana, by contrast, are overtly nationalistic and therefore collective and statist in their overall effect. They are also somewhat naturalistic in appearance, at least by comparison with projects in Barcelona. Of all the examples, Central Park in New York is probably the most overtly constitutive of social behavior and practice, as well as being naturalistic in appearance, although it was very much the artifact of intense interaction between the state and civil society. Clearly the salient characteristics of Rockefeller Center and other examples could also be plotted among the four conceptual dimensions in essentially the same manner. Here we would find, for instance, an appearance that is naturalistic at the smaller scale of doorways and lobbies while abstract overall, an experience that is concerned with everyday life, and an effect that is certainly representational of social forces while simultaneously constitutive of both public and private occasions. Sponsorship of the center was primarily by way of the private sector and civil society, although the role of the state in guiding and framing development should not be underestimated.

The obvious question arising from this kind of formulation is whether a particular example could fail to qualify along one or several of the four dimensions, that is, not be a part of the constellation of dimensions defining civic realism. The simple answer is yes. An exclusive private housing enclave, for instance, would lie well outside the conceptual realm defining a productive interaction between the state and civil society. Conversely, many realist totalitarian state monuments would also escape definition within the acceptable limits of the conceptual constellation. As we saw, dogmatic socialist realism in art would fail the test with respect to appearance by lying too far to one side of any advancement of the media of representation and by overinflating the realm of everyday experience. Nevertheless, while many projects and parts of an urban environment are undoubtedly precluded from a civic-realist characterization, fortunately many others at least have some modicum of potential for being so valued and encouraged. Moreover, this potential is precisely the point of the present argument. As much as anything, civic realism is not a quality of urbanity that can be identified so often or so easily without some work of introspection on the part of an observer and participant. It is certainly not an ideology about urban architecture that is nostalgic for lost places and urban sensibilities now somehow rendered obsolete by the everyday practicalities and spatial production of contemporary society. On the contrary, it is a way of thinking through matters or urban-architectural design along well-prescribed but nevertheless broadly applicable dimensions and of coming to know and understand urban places, as well as being in a position to say something meaningful about what might be needed there. Such introspection necessarily leads to assessment and, based on that assessment, ultimately it can lead to some form of action and continued reciprocity between a space and its use. As we have seen, people create spaces through social processes and thus convert space into place. This was certainly the case in Loisada and Central Park in New York. By the same token, certain places also continually affect people, such as the recent inhabitants of SoHo, further reinforcing particular senses of the same place. Unfortunately, as we know, once vibrant places may also devolve back into space, as the characteristics and values embodied in the various dimensions of civic realism either ebb away through neglect, abandonment, and decay or are terminated more violently and abruptly through disinvestment or destruction. Like most arts or even habits of mind, civic realism requires practice and constant vigilance.

A second obvious question arising from this kind of formulation is whether the central region among the four conceptual dimensions is the best domain for civic realism. In other words, if we plotted the characteristics of a given project along each of the four dimensions and found that they connected with the central point of the conceptual constellation, would that necessarily represent an ideal case of civic realism? Interestingly enough, the answer probably is no, on several counts. Technically, as noted earlier, several dimensions are probably well correlated among many actual examples, such that interpretations from a broad universe of urban projects would reveal that the dimensions of the conceptual space defining civic realism are not independent of one another. This is not necessarily a serious problem for application of the formulation, nor for interpretation, but it does tend to exclude the notion of a single central point corresponding to a uniquely ideal instance of civic realism. Rather, a relatively localized domain within the conceptual space would seem to define such an ideal more plausibly, and this potential technical result has a satisfying intuitive ring to it as well. Given what has been said so far, a dynamic tension, rather than a condition of static equilibrium, is to be valued within and across the conceptual dimensions. Equal parts participation by the state and civil society, for instance, does not necessarily make for a better project than a condition in which one side has at least a slight upper hand, through which a constructive tension can be maintained. Moreover, construal of where a project lies within the conceptual framework likely will change with time and the intervening processes by which a sense of place is produced socially. There is nevertheless, going to be a domain within this conceptual constellation—rather than some Archimedian point—within which better examples of civic realism can be either found or produced.

Finally, five important balancing tests emerge for both defining and maintaining civic realism and for initially helping to bring its qualities to the fore during the social production of urban space. First, civic realism represents or expresses a pluralism of attitudes, credos, and other human characteristics inherent in society and yet also fosters a convergence or distinctiveness of viewpoint about what the urban realm should be like. In short, civic-realist projects are inclusive but affirmative and relatively singular. Like the Piazza del Campo or Central Park they deliberately reach out through program, shape, and iconography to various constituencies of society and yet also propose something for society as a whole. Another more recent example that comes to mind is the town hall in Logroño, Spain, by José Rafael Moneo. His approach to public buildings is based on the principle, as he puts it, "that the larger the commitment of the public building, the more general its design should be."[9] The town hall was conceived of as an extension of the city itself: the façades were designed to be rather unassuming and purposely diverse, and the building complex's openness and accessibility was meant to exemplify the "social and democratic principles" of post-Franco Spain.[10] Completed in 1981, the town hall is located on the site of a former army barracks and programmatically integrates 25,000 square meters of governmental functions, administrative offices, and a large meeting hall. By far the most significant feature, however, is a large paved plaza, surrounded on two sides by a generous loggia, which is usually populated by habitués seeking communion with fellow citizens around the benches. While dissolving the inherently public image of the town hall, as such, in favor of simply a place to be, Moneo also enframed this place of individual activity with a noble colonade and underpinned it with a common paved area. In short, the project is simultaneously both inclusive and affirmative in the manner in which it deals with the idea of the state in relation to civil society.

Almost as a corollary to this first test, civic realism presents a challenge and a critique to established orders and prevailing authority, yet also expresses a sense of common accord. As we have seen, any literally critical and didactic dimension is difficult to embody in architecture. Nevertheless, it has been equally evident that a viable critical dimension can be carried in an architectural work by what is included, excluded, expressed, celebrated, or downplayed in more strictly sociopolitical terms. Again Moneo's town hall is a good example of this capacity. The expression of a singular authority is often far easier to achieve; houses of government, for instance, and palatial estates have expressed and helped project state power and authority for centuries. By contrast, the design of U.S. courthouses reflects an active critique of prevalent forms of social justice, and attempts have been made to express a sense of common accord. In the courtroom itself, there has been a certain amount of experimentation with the spatial relations of the actors in a judicial proceeding, sometimes with the aim of helping to realign the perception of power and authority. In a recent proposal for the new U.S. courthouse in Boston, Harry Cobb attempted, as he put it, "to give voice through architecture to those aspects and beliefs that underlie an American system of jurisprudence,"[11] especially with regard to every citizen's right to equal access before the law. This ambition is evident in the arrangement of the twenty-seven courtrooms around an expansive semicircular enclosed space, facing central Boston from the courthouse's four-and-a-half-acre site on Fan Pier. The elaborate glazing and transparency of this façade further signifies the relatively direct connection between jurisprudence and society at large, reinforcing the issue of access and equality. The stately overall proportions of the building and its roughly symmetrical composition single out the courthouse as an important institution in everyday life—one that should be accorded a certain dignity, if not solemnity. By skillfully revealing the idea of pluralist interests within the scope of a singular institutional framework, Cobb in effect highlights an important issue confronting today's society while simultaneously affirming the need for common accord. It is therefore through the architectural assertion of a well-articulated sociopolitical position that the difficult critical dimension of civic realism can be broached

successfully. Or, at the very least, sufficient clues can be provided in the architecture to potentially sustain such an interpretation.

As a third test, civic realism is capable of reflecting many changeable
aspects of society and yet possesses a certain transcendental quality, by giving
those in a society a sense of something permanent in common. In effect, there
is a enough of an architectural framework provided to accommodate different
functions, modes of behavior, and expressive proclivities as well as to maintain
a lasting and significant presence beyond those specific functions, modes, and
proclivities. From the examples cited so far, it appears that this can be accomplished in several ways. Certain adaptive reuse of extensive urban precincts,
like SoHo in New York, almost by definition embraces this characteristic. So
too does the Parc del Clot in Barcelona, with its strong remnant landscape
recalling bygone times. The use of "heterogeneous texts," mentioned in relation
to the "unprecedented realism" of Machado and Silvetti's projects, can be deployed to represent and constitute different sociocultural needs and aspirations
while providing for more enduring urban-architectural qualities. Usually this is
accomplished either by amalgamating different distinctive elements in some
manner, or through specific iconographic themes. Plečnik's work in Ljubljana
can be seen effectively in this light. On the one hand, it is a collection of
environments and symbols that support a wide variety of activities, including
both the ephemeral and more permanent aspects of day-to-day life. Here, Plečnik's aphorism about variety and order are clearly apposite. On the other hand,
this collection has also portrayed Slovenian regional and nationalistic ambitions, well beyond the contemporary circumstances of Plečnik's time. Still another approach is to create, almost literally, a sufficiently bold and permanent
architectural frame of reference to accommodate, ameliorate, and guide future
changes in function and use. Aldo Rossi and Carlo Aymonino's Gallaratese
project in the Milanese Monte Amiata complex, of 1969 through 1974, has this
type of architectural presence.[12] In a similar manner so too does Fernand Pouillon's project for perimeter block housing, commerce, and public open space in

Climat de France, Algiers, of 1953 to 1957.[13] There, both the environmental colonnade and sectional resolution of the building's spaces, in cross section, has remained constant and largely constitutive of the place, while specific functions have been allowed to change appreciably.

The fourth important test of civic realism is an essential concern with everyday life and its depiction, and yet with a concomitant advancement in the art of a particular medium of expression. As we have seen over and over again, it is not enough for civic realism simply to represent or accommodate functions and symbolic programs of one kind or another. Such tasks must be undertaken in a manner that is not nostalgic, mundane, or stifling, while still maintaining a certain familiarity and recognizability in their formal expression. Among the everyday living environments considered so far, Tuscolano in Rome stands out as embodying both of these qualities. It is familiar in appearance, but not simply as a regurgitation of past practices without any architectural development of the building types involved; there is at Tuscolano a convincing verisimilitude of both genre and content. Similarly, the urban-architectural qualities of El Silencio, in Caracas, Venezuela, by Carlos Raúl Villanueva, from a little earlier time period—1942 to 1945, to be precise—are deeply concerned with the accommodation and portrayal of everyday life among *Caracaños* in a familiar manner, and yet they also occur under the rubric of modern perimeter-block housing and mixed-use development.[14] The resulting eclectic combination of traditional forms and ornamental motifs, quoted, as it were, within an otherwise contemporary modernist style of planning, construction, and architectural expression, allows the complex to symbolically connect ideas about life in a rural town and life in a contemporary city. More recently, and in a less figurative vein, is the so-called dirty realism of the Kunsthalle in Rotterdam by Rem Koolhaas. Completed between 1987 and 1991, this project adroitly incorporated commonplace materials and elements, like corrugated fiberglass sheeting and a large billboard sign, befitting the building's location on a major thoroughfare, with traditional materials like stone and an overall formal language that is classically elegant in its references to other modern institutions of the same general type. Further incorporation within the scheme of a pedestrial path leading down and across the levee on which the building stands not only usefully divides the program of accommodations in two, but underlines the idea of public accessibility to state institutions.

Finally, the fifth test of civic realism is that places provide for collective practices and rituals, while remaining congenial for individual habitation and experience. As we have seen, the Manhattan grid in many of its particular incarnations and locations within the city of New York exemplifies this quality. So do far more particular urban accouterments and spaces like the traditional *zócalo* of the Latin American town, as in the example of El Silencio. Such a square or central gathering space was certainly prescribed in the Law of the Indies under which most Spanish colonial towns in Latin America was settled, like Oaxaca in Mexico, Antigua in Guatemala, and Coro in Venezuela. Nevertheless, each square was developed in quite a specific manner, particularly in the way in which an annular arrangement of spaces with different furnishings and other landscape features occurs as one moves into the center of a zócalo from the inevitable arcade around its perimeter. There both individual and collective activities could and can still be accomplished with graceful ease. Getting a shoe shine, drinking coffee, reading the paper, chatting, listening to a concert, attending a political rally—all can be accommodated, surprisingly, sometimes simultaneously. Like the contemporary version of Bryant Park in New York, though, the zócalo is a place that usually puts us on our best behavior. For other less dignified or congenial forms of individual or collective behavior, we would obviously have to go elsewhere.

In summary, a good work of civic realism is at once familiar, pluralistic, and critical—at least to the extent that this last quality can be sustained architecturally. It is also specific, socially relevant, transcendental, and concerned with everyday life, including matters of both individual and collective experience. Furthermore it is inextricably bound up with the continual advancement of the expressive means by which it is made and elaborated.

El Silencio in Caracas by Villanueva.

TOWARD A WELL-GROUNDED CONTEMPORANEITY

At this juncture the question arises as to how architecture and urban design can contribute to the practice of civic realism, especially by addressing the preceding five balancing tests and by resolving the inherent paradoxes found there. As often noted, architecture is a "weak" device—in Vatimo's philosophical sense—for dealing directly with sociopolitical criticism.[15] There is an arbitrariness of signs involved in architecture and urban design that makes them less expressively specific, in many regards, than other arts. Both architecture and urban design are usually involved with multiple agendas and programmatic requirements, often deflecting attention away from highly specific expressive foci and symbolic precision. Furthermore, some conceptual contradictions require special attention. The inherent idea of a strong local urban-architectural tradition, for instance, often implies various forms of contextualism, the use of vernacular, the search for some form of genius loci, and so on. When such tradition is primarily a source of cultural continuity, this local orientation can be well worth pursuing and perpetuating. When, however, this resort to tradition results in nostalgia and making a fetish of the past, it is clearly an undesirable course to follow.

Fortunately, this last path was not taken in the timely renovation of two of Mexico City's remaining historic areas. Xochimilco, the last remnant of a glorious Aztec past, when the early settlement floated in an expansive lake on *chinampas*—a woven composite of organic and mud materials—has been reclaimed recently as a public park and ecological reserve.[16] Slowly perishing through years of neglect, its magnificent channels clogged by vegetation and debris, this essential feature of Mexico's cultural heritage was rescued from the brink of almost total destruction by the aggressive efforts of city officials and community leaders. However, instead of replicating historical circumstances—and therefore leaving in place the potential for the preserve's decline—new uses and new park landscapes were incorporated into the overall plan. Mario Schjetnan's designs for a new lakeside park are daring reinterpretations of the site's myths and realities, readily incorporating archaeological discoveries into the park's broad educational and environmental themes. In short, a landscape architecture of contemporary Mexico was well integrated with the traditional way of doing things: cultural relevance and the park's former splendor were recombined in what promises to be a lasting manner. Concurrently, the extensive historic center of Mexico City has undergone careful, incremental renovation under the skillful direction of Jorge Gamboa de Buen, among others.[17] The largest existing preserve of seventeenth- and eighteenth-century buildings in Latin America, the historic center was also neglected, dilapidated, and seemingly beyond repair. Through the efforts of both the public and private sectors, including cooperation among the institutions of civil society, inventive new programs were found for old structures, and traditional and contemporary styles of architecture were combined with unusual wit, flair, and facility. The result preserved a significant aspect of Mexico's cultural heritage, while breathing new life into the city's center.

Another idea inherent in the balancing tests, of a contemporary approach to architecture and urban design—which in itself usually implies a reasonably inclusive orientation—may result, under the influence of excessive pluralist pressures, in such a bowing to local interests that any possible sense of common accord or a broader permanence among things is undermined substantially. Unfortunately, recent American experiences with the local sentiment of "not in my backyard" (NIMBY) are clear cases in point. Many communities, for instance, struggle over issues of social equity and adequate provision of service and shelter for heterogeneous populations. Once, in the absence of higher levels of government regulation, some local communities went out of their way to resist development of affordable housing in the name of preserving local values. Large-lot zoning, for example, was often a ploy—albeit in environmental guise—for discriminatory economic practices. More understandably, perhaps, fierce local resistance has turned many less desirable yet necessary service facilities, like waste treatment plants and solid waste sites, into political footballs. Indeed, the expression "NIMBY" stems from the desire of some to take full advantage of a service without assuming much direct responsibility for its provision. Of necessity, the threat of regional natural phenomena, like flooding and land subsidence, can galvanize local interests around larger causes. So too can a broader sense of regional identity, especially when it is to most people's advantage and in their pecuniary interest. Earlier comments in this chapter about the need to be specific in matters of urban design notwithstanding, when specificity is taken to extremes in programmatic terms, little of lasting permanence seems likely to be created without constant and expensive modification and replacement in response to changing needs. Design specificity without social or programmatic exclusivity, by contrast, can provide a lasting sense of identity and common accord, not only for a few but for many.

Resolution and constructive exploitation of the five paradoxes usually requires, in urban-architectural terms, a tempering of any prevalent singular ideas about style or other overarching design prescriptions. Nevertheless, at the same time, any constructive approach must also avoid a slide into architectural commonplaces that are too local, too specific, and too idiosyncratic to support the broader consensual claims of civic realism. Fortunately, as we have seen, eclecticism and borrowings of various kinds, ranging from quotation—again to use a literary term for a moment—to the deliberate deployment and use of heterogeneous references, can be a fruitful way of resolving these paradoxes and of creating viable civic realms. Again the proviso is that continued work on the language—a verisimilitude of genre—must be maintained. This general approach toward civic urban architecture has been successful in the neomodernism of Paris and in the regional eclecticism of Ljubljana. Although perhaps less obvious, it was also successful in the "Catalan modernism" of Barcelona, which is not really a style so much as it is a way of working with the city's context, history, local circumstances, and social requirements. Among the broad grouping of urban open-space projects there, some were minimal—like the Plaça Reial—and others were not. Nevertheless, as at other times in Barcelona's history, when taken together, a distinctly "Catalan way" of making public places emerged. As we saw in chapter 5, a similar generality and distinction arose from the quotidian character of several otherwise disparate public places constructed recently in New York.

A certain lack of purity and singularity of architectural gesture implied in these examples, however, need not be the only way of overcoming the paradoxes implicit in the balancing tests and of successfully practicing civic realism. After all, the Eiffel Tower has neither of these qualities, at least in any abundance, and yet it would be difficult to deny its role as a civic symbol and as a realist project in terms of its faithfulness to the techno-economic realities and imperatives of its time.[18] It is certainly local. Indeed, it is one of a kind, and yet the tower clearly transcends its locality, over time becoming *the* symbol of Paris and one of the few symbols of France. Nevertheless, its importance in the hearts and minds of Parisians was not always so evident. When the tower was first proposed for the 1889 Exposition, Eiffel's design showed the iron frames sweeping up from the tower's four supports in one uninterrupted gesture.[19] Although it would have been structurally sound in this configuration, to many it seemed unstable, with the result that the intermediate platforms and the arches forming a kind of "skirt" at the base were introduced. One effect of these modifications was that a structure, the design of which was clearly intent on advancing the states of the art in engineering, was aestheticized, so to speak, well back into the nineteenth century—much to its designer's chagrin. As a civic symbol, however, it quickly gained power and a hold on people's affection that could hardly have been anticipated. Moreover, its iconographic generality and sense of belonging to everybody has allowed ample room for various individuals' own interpretations and associations with the tower. For some Parisians it might have been the site of a special rendezvous, while for others it was a place to go on weekends, or a vantage point for gauging the city's development. All in all, though, it quickly became a reminder to most that they are in Paris, and served as a symbol of the city's culture and civic life.

Through the book's examples the constant argument for the practice of civic realism turns on what might well be called a "well-grounded contemporaneity" in matters of urban-architectural design. Such a stance certainly argues against prevalent attempts to develop singular, overarching, or comprehensive expressive theories, such as modernism, postmodernism, or deconstructionism in any orthodox sense. Given the foregoing criteria, such seemingly complete positions almost seem doomed to failure, by favoring only one essentially global and potentially totalizing side of issues about people and places. Conversely, though, a well-grounded contemporaneity also argues against overly self-conscious forms of localism, regionalism, tradition, and vernacular as being potentially culturally calcifying and class-bound. Such approaches also run the rather high risk of being historicist, in the sense of not belonging to this day and age. Unfortunately, many recent attempts to reform the spatial character of the American suburb, through the so-called "New Urbanism," and to realign suburban life in civic directions have many of these traits. Instead, a well-grounded contemporaneity in architecture and urban design seems better suited to account for style, theoretical propositions, and historicism and yet transcend all three, resulting in something else, something more complex and more real. Which positions or terms in the conceptual argument should be emphasized will depend, fairly obviously, on prevailing circumstances and sociocultural aspirations.

Orthodox architectural doctrines are of only partial use in the practice of civic realism for other reasons as well. The tenets of modernism, as noted before, are usually most applicable—other than in purely aesthetic terms—on the margins of technological performance, economic operation, parsimony and efficiency of construction, functional conformance, and so on. These characteristics, however, rarely if ever pertain quite so completely to circumstances of bourgeois culture, a reasonable amount of affluence, and a laxity in technical performance. Clearly, something more is required of civic realism under these latter circumstances. Likewise, the easy consumerism and commodification that has come to characterize much so-called postmodern production is of little value to civic realism. That individual tastes and cravings are satisfied by this form of production is just the point: little remains to pass on, so to speak, toward achieving a higher cultural purpose and civic calling. Similarly, excessive identification with and celebration of various pluralist interests in society runs the very high risk of making a fetish of certain of these interests at the expense of others. The all too common recent practice of fixating on the rough underside and marginalia of prevailing social and physical situations, as a basis for producing contemporary urban architecture, is particularly misplaced. It is one thing to draw attention to problems and shortcomings in a society; it is quite another to address them and therefore productively move beyond these drawbacks in the manner that civic realism would require.

If we return to the question posed at the beginning of this section of the book about how architecture and urban design can contribute to civic realism, it is clear that one answer is to work conscientiously with what, so to speak, is in play—in short, to be in a position of reorienting the programmatic, formal, and other aesthetic judgments of a particular time and in a particular place. After all, civic realism, in the end, is not so much a thing as it is a practice. Moreover, it is both a resistive and an affirmative way of working with what is on hand and of making urban environments with that perspective in mind. This is certainly how the Piazza del Campo evolved over several generations—partly as a high-style celebration of municipal life and partly as a vernacular response to the practical exigencies of the time. It is also how the Slovenes asserted themselves through their architects and the architecture, as well as the public works, of Ljubljana. Furthermore, much the same can be said for the Catalans in Barcelona and the Parisians with their grand projets. Unconsciously or not—because after all, civic realism in these cases is a post facto conceptual reconstruction of what actually happened—everyday and even uncommon practices of urban-architectural design were leveraged significantly to achieve broader civic goals. In all cases there was an affirmation of local identity, but in a way that attempted to resist socially harmful exclusions from the grander scheme of things. As we saw, this was not always totally successful. In SoHo, for example, gentrification took its toll, and the homeless were removed from Tompkins

Square Park. Also, in all cases, extreme forms of localism and the presence of parochial interests were resisted in order to affirm, through the program and expression of the urban architecture, broader and more widely held cultural views. Furthermore, this process of resistance and affirmation was far from being conservative. In places like Ljubljana and Siena, for instance, it clearly advanced the cause of broad segments of civil society, as well as state interests. Conversely, not all social and cultural concerns were served. However, architecture almost by definition must create a particular framework or environment and therefore inevitably be conservative of certain social institutions and ways of doing things rather than of others. Through the practice of civic realism, the aim should be to be inclusive and open-ended, but without trying to be all things to all people.

What else might be done? At a more fundamental sociopolitical level, as we have seen, a society's capacity for the self-organization and propagation of associations, relations, and other transactions—which constitute civil society in the first place—must be constantly improved and strengthened. To use Robert Putnam's terminology again, we must get away from "bowling alone." As they say, "giving at the office" is no substitute for first-hand voluntary involvement. The volunteer organization of mothers uniting to save their children in an East Los Angeles wracked by gang violence is a strong and unusual example. Pico Gardens and Aliso Village combine to form the largest public housing project west of the Mississippi, the poorest parish in the Roman Catholic Archdiocese of Los Angeles, and the highest concentration of gang activity.[20] There, under community leaders like Father Boyle and Pam McDuffie, volunteers consistently stand between feuding gang members, pressure errant public authorities into action, and actively strive to bring safety, self-respect, and hope to their neighborhoods. In keeping with the liberation theology of base communities, the question they constantly ask is "*Qué haria Jesús?*," or what would Jesus have done?[21] State institutions are very active in many other places, so much so that active attempts are being made to control their size and relative influence. A few good examples notwithstanding, it is not entirely evident what other social, political, and cultural arrangements might constructively replace present institutional alignments. Although these issues are not matters of urban-architectural design, the way we design and, in particular, the way we design the public realm, can help or hinder broader efforts to create a stronger civil society of whatever particular political persuasion. In other words, urban-architectural design is a dimension of this larger concern with bringing back palpable civic qualities to our cities, and what it requires is the conscientious practice of civic realism.

"Merde! The first's the one you'd kill for," Simone mumbled to herself, as she fumbled with the matches and stumbled toward the light, still very much in a disoriented state. *"Way too much booze,"* she reproached herself, her mouth feeling like cotton wool. *"One more down and another year to go,"* she thought to herself dully, making a face. *"Oh well! Some things change and others stay the same—thank God!"* she added quickly, looking distractedly out of her dormer window at *"the colossal,"* as her mother liked to call it—a stark yet comfortingly familiar outline in the cold early morning light.

"I hope Gilbert hasn't forgotten," Simone thought to herself as she looked at her watch anxiously for the umpteenth time. *"Although for him it's still early,"* she went on. *"Why does he always have to be late? Perhaps he is waiting on the other side?"* the thought suddenly occurring to Simone that she herself might be on the wrong side of the gallery. *"I've never really understood why Gilbert likes to meet here so much. It's so obvious and overly sentimental. Still, the view is nice,"* she observed. *"The space across from the Trocadero to the Tower and the Champ-de-Mars is so vast and so noble, with all those people parading around down there,"* she continued to herself, unwittingly gesturing with her hands—certainly by comparison to her own cramped living quarters. *"Well,"* she thought, softening a little, *"I suppose I shouldn't complain too much about Gilbert's sentimentality. The Tower, after all, was the spot where Grandmama met George way back when. It had something to do with a note,"* she recalled dimly, again looking at her watch anxiously and stamping out her cigarette.

Pierre Grimmonde, *De Plus en Plus Fort**

Notes

Chapter 1

1. Giuliano Procacci, *History of the Italian People* (London: Penguin Books, 1968), 13f.

2. Ibid., 64f.

3. Ibid., 30f.

4. Ibid., 64.

5. Ibid., 32.

6. Ibid., 49.

7. William M. Bowsky, *A Medieval Italian Commune: Siena under the Nine, 1287–1355* (Berkeley: University of California Press, 1981), 1f.

8. Ibid. and Mario Ascheri, *Renaissance Siena: 1355–1559* (Siena: Nuova Immagine Editrice, 1993), 10.

9. Bowsky, *A Medieval Italian Commune*, 2.

10. Daniel Waley, *Siena and the Sienese in the Thirteenth Century* (New York: Cambridge University Press, 1991), 2f.

11. Bowsky, *A Medieval Italian Commune*, 184f.

12. Ibid., 1–22.

13. Ibid. and Procacci, *History of the Italian People*, 64f.

14. Procacci, *History of the Italian People*, 64f.

15. Bowsky, *A Medieval Italian Commune*, 20f.

16. Ibid., 22.

17. Ibid., 81f.

18. Ibid., 186f.

19. Iris Origo, *The Merchant of Prato: Daily Life in a Medieval Italian City* (London: Peregrine Books, 1963). See also David Herilhy and Christiane Klapisch-Zuber, *Tuscans and Tuscan Families: A Study of Florentine Catasto of 1427* (New Haven: Yale University Press, 1985).

20. Waley, *Siena and the Sienese in the Thirteenth Century*, 6.

21. Ibid., 12f.

22. Ibid.

23. Ibid., 8.

24. Bowsky, *A Medieval Italian Commune*, 185.

25. Ibid., 13.

26. Alan Dundes and Alessandro Falassi, *La terra in piazza: An Interpretation of the Palio of Siena* (Berkeley: University of California Press, 1975), 12f.

27. Ibid., 43.

28. The following paragraphs dealing with the evolution of the government in Siena are

based on Bowsky, *A Medieval Commune*, Waley, *Siena and the Sienese in the Thirteenth Century,* and Ascheri, *Renaissance Siena: 1355–1559.*

29. Ascheri, *Renaissance Siena: 1355–1559,* 13–14.

30. Ibid., 12.

31. Ibid., 10, and Procacci, *History of the Italian People,* 57.

32. Procacci, *History of the Italian People,* 56–60.

33. Waley, *Siena and the Sienese in the Thirteenth Century,* 5.

34. Ibid.

35. Lando Bortolotti, *Le città nella storia d'Italia: Siena* (Rome: Laterza and Figli, 1983), 35.

36. Ibid., 35f, and Enrico Guidoni, *Il Campo di Siena* (Rome: Multigrafica Editrice, 1971).

37. Bortolotti, *Le città nella storia d'Italia: Siena,* 38.

38. Ibid., 40, and Dundes and Falassi, *La terra in piazza,* 231.

39. Bortolotti, *Le città nella storia d'Italia: Siena,* 37.

40. Waley, *Siena and the Sienese in the Thirteenth Century,* 4, and Bowsky, *A Medieval Italian Commune,* 286.

41. Bortolotti, *Le città nella storia d'Italia: Siena,* 42.

42. Ibid., 40.

43. Ibid., 36.

44. Bowsky, *A Medieval Italian Commune,* 260f, and Umberto Eco, *Art and Beauty in*

the Middle Ages (New Haven: Yale University Press, 1986), 93f.

45. Bowsky, *A Medieval Italian Commune,* 289.

46. Ascheri, *Renaissance Siena: 1355–1559,* 25f.

47. Ibid.

48. Dundes and Falassi, *La terra in piazza,* 4.

49. Ibid., 1f.

50. Ibid., 7f. See also Giovanni Cecchini and Dario Nevi, *The Palio of Siena* (Siena: Monte dei Paschi, 1958).

51. Dundes and Falassi, *La terra in piazza,* 5.

52. Ibid., 48f.

53. Ibid., 185f.

54. Ibid., 199.

55. Guidoni, *Il Campo di Siena,* 56f.

56. Benjamin Woolley, *Virtual Worlds* (London: Penguin Books, 1992).

57. The "talking heads" analogy was provided by Felicity Scott.

Other references include: Jacob Burckhardt, *The Civilization of the Renaissance in Italy* (London: Penguin, 1990); Ubaldo Cagliaritano, *The History of Siena* (Siena: Periccioli, Edition, 1983); Langston Douglas, *A History of Siena* (London: John Murrey, 1902); Silvio Gigli, *The Palio of Siena* (Siena: Stefano Venturini Editore, 1960); Richard A. Goldthwaite, *Wealth and the Demand for Art in Italy* (Baltimore: Johns Hopkins University Press, 1993); Milland Meiss, *Painting in Florence and Siena after the Black Plague* (Princeton: Princeton University Press, 1951); Ferdinand

Scherill, *Siena: The History of a Medieval Commune* (New York: Commons), and Daniel Waley, *The Italian City-Republics* (New York: Longman, 1988).

Chapter 2

1. Victor M. Pérez-Díaz, *The Return of Civil Society: The Emergence of Democratic Spain* (Cambridge, MA: Harvard University Press, 1993), 55.

2. Ibid., 54–55.

3. The following descriptions of the urban public places of Barecelona are based on field observation and primarily upon: Joan Busquets, "Barcelona," *Rassegna* 37; Joan Busquets, *Barcelona: Evolucíon urbanistica de una capital compacta* (Madrid: Mapfre, 1992); Peter G. Rowe, *The Urban Public Spaces of Barcelona, 1981–1987* (Cambridge, MA: Harvard University Graduate School of Design, 1991; and M. Cristina Tullio, *Spazi pubblici contemporanei: Innovazione e identità a Barcelona e in Catalogna* (Rome: Quaderini de Au, Editrice in ASA, 1987).

4. Joan Busquets (ed.), *Cerdà: Readings on Cerdà and the Extension Plan of Barcelona* (Barcelona: Ajuntament de Barcelona, 1992).

5. Rowe, *The Urban Public Spaces of Barcelona*, 7f.

6. Busquets, *Barcelona*, 313f.

7. Ajuntament de Barcelona, *Barcelona: Spaces and Sculptures, 1982–1986* (Barcelona: Joan Miró Foundation, 1987).

8. Tullio, *Spazi pubblici contemporanei*.

9. Oriol Bohigas, *Reconstruction of Barcelona* (Madrid: MOPU Arquitectura, 1986).

10. Ibid.

11. Peter Buchanan, "Regenerating Barcelona with Parks and Plazas," *Archictural Review* (June): 32–46.

12. Robert Hughes, *Barcelona* (London: Harvill, 1992), 284–285. See also Manuel Vásquez Montalban, *Barcelonas* (London: Verso, 1992).

13. Antoni Llagostera and Maria Lluïsa Selga, *Olympic Barcelona: The Renewed City* (Barcelona: Ambit Serveis Editorials, S.A., 1994).

14. John Hooper, *The Spaniards: A Portrait of the New Spain* (London: Pelican, 1986), 22f.

15. Ibid.

16. William C. Atkinson, *A History of Spain and Portugal* (London: Pelican, 1960), 330f.

17. Hooper, *The Spaniards*, 30.

18. Pérez-Díaz, *The Return of Civil Society*, 26f.

19. Jean L. Cohen and Andrew Arato, *Civil Society and Political Theory* (Cambridge, MA: The MIT Press, 1995), 29f.

20. Hooper, *The Spaniards*, 183f.

21. Bruce Robbins, *The Phantom Public Sphere* (Minneapolis: University of Minnesota Press, 1993).

22. Richard Sennett, *The Uses of Disorder: Personal Identity and City Life* (New York: W. W. Norton, 1970) and *The Fall of Public Man* (New York: W. W. Norton, 1974).

23. David Harvey, *The Condition of Post-Modernity* (London: Basil Blackwell, 1989).

24. Hannah Arendt, *The Human Condition* (Chicago: University of Chicago Press, 1971).

25. Jürgen Habermas, *The Structural Transformation of the Public Sphere: An Inquiry into the Category of Bourgeois Society* (Cambridge, MA: The MIT Press, 1991).

26. Ibid., 2f.

27. Ibid., 19.

28. Seyla Benhabib, *Situating the Self: Gender, Community, and Postmodern Contemporary Ethics* (New York: Routledge, 1992), 104f.

29. Cohen and Arato, *Civil Society and Political Theory*, ix.

30. Arendt, *The Human Condition*.

31. Pérez-Díaz, *The Return of Civil Society*, 65f.

32. Arendt, *The Human Condition*, 57.

33. Benhabib, *Situating the Self*, 95f.

34. Georg Wilhelm Hegel, *Philosophy of Right* (Oxford: Clarendon Press, 1967).

35. Oskar Negt and Alexander Kluge, "The Public Sphere and Experience: Selections," *October* 46: 60–82.

36. Cohen and Arato, *Civil Society and Political Theory*, 118f.

37. Ibid., 142f.

38. Hughes, *Barcelona*, 374f.

39. Daniel Patrick Moynihan, "Civic Architecture," *Architectural Record* 142 (December): 107.

40. François Chaslin, *Le Paris de François Mitterand: Histoire des grands projets architecturaux* (Paris: Gallimard, 1985), and Anthony Sutcliffe, *Paris: An Architectural History* (New Haven: Yale University Press, 1993), 184–206.

41. Sutcliffe, *Paris: An Architectural History*, 184–206.

42. Ibid., 200.

43. Ibid., 160.

44. Ibid., 173.

45. Ibid., 186.

46. Apart from field research, the following description of the *Parc de la Villette* is based on: Etablissement Public du Parc de la Villette, *La Villette: A Large Urban Project, A New Calling* (Paris: E.P.P.V., December 1993); Pierre-Charles Krieg, *Cahiers de L'I.A.U.R.I.F.* (no. 90), 5–36; *Paris Projet*, "Espaces Publics" (Numero 30–31, 1993); and Toshio Nakumura, "Bernard Tschumi, 1983–1993," *A & U: Architecture and Urbanism* (March 1994).

47. Etablissement Public du Parc de la Villette, *La Villette*.

48. Richard Dagenhart, "Urban Architectural Theory and the Contemporary City: Tschumi and Koolhaas at the Parc de la Villette," *Ekistics* 334 (January/February 1989).

49. Bernard Tschumi, "The La Villette Park Competition," *Princeton Architectural Review* 2 (1983): 208.

50. Etablissement Public du Parc de la Villette, *La Villette*.

51. Ibid., 25f.

52. Apart from field research, the following description of Parc Andre Citroën-Cevennes is based on: Robert Holden, "New Parks for Paris: Landscape Art and the State," *Architecture Journal* 12 (July 1989): 57–67; and Thomas Vonier, "Non-Parallel Parking: Two Divergent Approaches to Urban Parks in Paris," *Progressive Architecture* 74, no. 10

(October 1993): 66–72. It is also based on research by Mark Edward Pasnik, then a graduate student at Harvard's Graduate School of Design.

53. Anthony Vidler, *The Architectural Uncanny* (Cambridge, MA: The MIT Press, 1994), 220.

Other references include: Nathan Glazer and Mark Lilla, eds., *The Public Face of Architecture: Civic Culture and Public Spaces* (New York: The Free Press, 1987); W. J. T. Mitchell, *Art and Public Sphere* (Chicago: University of Chicago Press, 1992); Z. A. Pelczynski, ed., *The State and Civil Society* (New York: Cambridge University Press, 1984); John Rawls, *Political Liberalism* (New York: Columbia University Press, 1993); Charles Taylor, *Multiculturalism and the Politics of Recognition* (Princeton: Princeton University Press, 1992), and *Philosophical Arguments* (Cambridge, MA: Harvard University Press, 1995).

Chapter 3

1. Georg Wilhelm Hegel, *Aesthetics* (London: Oxford University Press, 1975), 11, and Hans-Georg Gadamer, *The Relevance of the Beautiful and Other Essays* (New York: Cambridge University Press, 1986), 5.

2. Gadamer, *The Relevance of the Beautiful,* 3.

3. David Papineau, *Reality and Representation* (London: Blackwell, 1987).

4. Nelson Goodman, *Ways of World Making* (Cambridge, MA: Hackett Publishing Company), 2.

5. Hilary Putnam, *The Many Faces of Realism* (La Salle, IL: Open Court, 1987), 17.

6. Ibid.

7. Linda Nochlin, *Realism* (London: Penguin Books, 1971), 13.

8. Ibid.

9. Ibid., 112f.

10. Adam Gopnik, "Whistler in the Dark," *New Yorker,* July 17, 1995, 68–73.

11. Nochlin, *Realism,* 20.

12. Milan Kundera, *Testaments Betrayed: An Essay in Nine Parts* (New York: Harper Collins, 1993), 131.

13. Nochlin, *Realism,* 137f.

14. Ibid., 137.

15. Ibid., 17.

16. J. A. Ward, *American Silences: The Realism of James Agee, Walker Evans, and Edward Hopper* (Baton Rouge: Louisiana State University Press, 1985), 6f.

17. Ibid., 10.

18. Ibid., 7f.

19. Kundera, *Testaments Betrayed,* 131.

20. Ibid., 132.

21. Georg Lukács, *Essays on Realism* (Cambridge, MA: The MIT Press, 1980).

22. Ibid., 47f.

23. Ibid.

24. Bertolt Brecht, "The Popular and the Realistic," in *Brecht on Theatre* (London: Methuen, 1964), 107–112.

25. E. Bloch, G. Lukács, B. Brecht, W. Benjamin, and T. Adorno, *Aesthetics and Politics* (London: New Left Books, 1977).

26. Lambert Zuidervaart, *Adorno's Aesthetic Theory: The Redemption of Illusion* (Cambridge, MA: The MIT Press, 1994), 93.

27. Ibid., 95.

28. Bloch et al., *Aesthetics and Politics*, 134.

29. Briony Fer, David Batchelor, and Paul Wood, *Realism, Rationalism, Surrealism: Art Between the Wars* (New Haven: Yale University Press, 1993), 256f.

30. Ibid., 260.

31. Ibid., 263f.

32. Descriptions based on: Peter Noever, *Tyrannei Des Schöen: Architektur Der Stalin-Zeit* (Munich: Pestel, 1994).

33. Fer, Batchelor, and Wood, *Realism, Rationalism, Surrealism*, 294.

34. Peter G. Rowe, *Modernity and Housing* (Cambridge, MA: The MIT Press, 1993), 35f.

35. Ibid., 128f.

36. Ibid., 35f.

37. Diego Rivera, *My Art, My Life: An Autobiography* (New York: Dover, 1986).

38. The following description of Rockefeller Center is based on field observation and primarily upon: Samuel Chamberlain, *Rockefeller Center* (New York: Hastings House, 1949); Robert A. M. Stern, Gregory Gilmartin, and Thomas Mellins, *New York 1930: Architecture and Urbanism Between the Two World Wars* (New York: Rizzoli, 1987), 617–672, and Elliot Willensky and Norral White, *AIA Guide to New York* (New York: Harcourt Brace Jovanovich, 1988), 272–274.

39. Stern, Gilmartin, and Mellins, *New York 1930*, 639.

40. See photographic coverage in Chamberlain, *Rockefeller Center*.

41. Rivera, *My Art, My Life*, 124f.

42. Ibid.

43. Stein, Gertrude, *Everybody's Autobiography* (New York: Random House, 1937), 202.

44. Nochlin, *Realism*, 217f.

45. Jorge Silvetti, "On Realism in Architecture," *The Harvard Architecture Review 1* (Spring 1980): 12.

46. The following general description of neorealism in Italy is based mainly on Germano Celant, *The Italian Metamorphosis, 1943–1968* (New York: The Solomon R. Guggenheim Foundation, 1994); Peter Bondanella, *Italian Cinema: From Neorealism to the Present* (New York: Frederick Ungar Publishing Co., 1983), and Schwartz, Barth David, *Pasolini: Requiem* (New York: Vintage Books, 1992), as well as on conversations with Pietro Barucci.

47. Based on an analysis of data presented in Paul Ginsborg, *A History of Contemporary Italy: Society and Politics 1943–1988* (London: Penguin Books, 1990), 434f.

48. Italo Insolera, *Roma Moderna: Un secolo di storia urbanistica 1870–1970* (Rome: Einaudi, 1993), 102.

49. Ginsborg, *A History of Contemporary Italy*, 210f.

50. Based on data presented in ibid., 439f.

51. Ibid., 173f.

52. Paul Furlong, *Modern Italy: Representation and Reform* (London: Routledge, 1994), 3.

53. The following general account of political life in postwar Italy is based primarily on Ginsborg, *A History of Contemporary Italy* and Furlong, *Modern Italy*.

54. Insolera, *Roma Moderna*, 102f.

55. Details about Fanfani and the Christian

Democrats based on Ginsborg, *A History of Contemporary Italy*, 165f.

56. Ibid., 246.

57. Paul Wendt, "Post–World War II Housing Policies in Italy," (*Land Economics* (March 1962): 129.

58. Manfredo Tafuri, *History of Italian Architecture, 1944–1985* (Cambridge, MA: The MIT Press), 15.

59. Insolera, *Roma Moderna*, 127.

60. General description of *borgate* is based primarily on ibid., 127f. The term has also been used widely to refer to shantytowns and informal settlements on the outskirts of Rome, many of which grew up before, during, and after World War II.

61. Peter Bondanella, *The Films of Roberto Rossellini* (London: Cambridge University Press, 1993), 5.

62. Insolera, *Roma Moderna*, 102.

63. Description based on field observation and primarily on Giovanni Astengo, "Nuovi quartieri in Italia," *Urbanistica* 7 (1951): 9–25; Carlo Aymonino, "Tiburtino: storia e croniche," *Casabella* 215 (April–May 1957): 19–23; and Piero Ostillo Rossi, *Roma: Giuida all'architettura moderna 1909–1991* (Rome: Editori Laterza, 1991).

64. Ibid., 172. Also P. Ciorra, *Ludovico Quaroni, 1911–1987* (Milan: Electa, 1989), 92–99.

65. Rossi, *Roma*, 173.

66. Conversation with Pietro Barucci, November 1995.

67. Tafuri, *History of Italian Architecture*, 11f, and Rossi, *Roma*, 173.

68. Tafuri, *History of Italian Architecture*, 13, and Rowe, *Modernity and Housing*, 84.

69. Tafuri, *History of Italian Architecture*, 13.

70. Rossi, *Roma,* 174f.

71. Ibid., 176.

72. Ibid.

73. Conversation with Pietro Barucci, September 1995.

74. Tafuri, *History of Italian Architecture*, 30f. See also interpretative discussion in Ginsborg, *A History of Contemporary Italy*, 246f.

75. Based on data in Tafuri, *History of Italian Architecture*, 30, and Rowe, *Modernity and Housing*, 59.

76. Tafuri, *History of Italian Architecture*, 59.

77. Ibid., 30f.

78. Ibid.

79. Bondanella, *The Films of Roberto Rossellini*, 5.

80. Pier Paolo Pasolini, *Ragazzi di vita* (Turin: Einaudi, 1955) and Pier Paolo Pasolini, *Una vita violenta* (Turin: Einaudi, 1959).

81. Schwartz, *Pasolini,* 35f.

82. Silvetti, *On Realism in Architecture,* 11–34.

83. Conversations with Richard Plunz and Lauretta Vinciarelli (Columbia University), September 1994.

84. Michael Benedikt, *For an Architecture of Reality* (New York: Lumen Books, 1987).

85. Peter G. Rowe, ed., *Rodolfo Machado and Jorge Silvetti: Buildings for Cities* (New York: Rizzoli, 1989), 142.

86. K. Michael Hays, ed., *Unprecedented Realism: The Architecture of Machado and Silvetti* (New York: Princeton Architectural Press, 1995), 259f.

Other references include: G. Acasto, V. Fratcelli, and R. Nicolini, *L'architettura de Roma capitale: 1870–1970* (Rome: Golem, 1971); Sarah Faunce, *Gustave Courbet* (New York: Abrams, 1993); Francesco Garofalo and Luca Veresani, *Adalberto Libera* (New York: Princeton Architectural Press, 1992); Bernard B. Perlman, *Painters of the Ashcan School: The Immortal Eight* (New York: Dover, 1971); Giorgio Pigafetta, *Saverio Muratori architetto: Teoria e progetti* (Venice: Marsilio, 1990); and Marcello Rebecchini, *Architetti italiani: 1930–1960* (Rome: Officina Edixione, 1990).

Chapter 4

1. Christine M. Boyer, *Manhattan Manners: Architecture and Style 1850–1900* (New York: Rizzoli, 1985), 8–9.

2. Eric Homberger, *The Historical Atlas of New York City* (New York: Swanston Publishing Limited, 1994), 90f.

3. Henri Lefebvre, *The Production of Space* (London: Blackwell, 1991).

4. Robert A. Woods and Albert J. Kennedy, *The Zone of Emergence* (Cambridge, MA: Harvard University Press).

5. Based on scalar measurements from city maps.

6. Lefebvre, *The Production of Space,* 31–32.

7. Ibid., 32 and 58.

8. Ibid., 314.

9. Luc Sante, *Low Life: Lures and Snares of Old New York* (New York: Vintage Books, 1991), xiv.

10. Ibid., xix.

11. Lefebvre, *The Production of Space,* 292.

12. Landmarks Preservation Commission, *SoHo-Cast Iron Historic District Designation Report* (New York: City of New York, 1973).

13. The following paragraphs describing historical developments in SoHo are based on ibid.; Homberger, *The Historical Atlas of New York City;* and James R. Hudson, *The Unanticipated City: Loft Conversions in Lower Manhattan* (Amherst: University of Massachusetts Press, 1987).

14. Descriptions from the "stylistic history" in Landmarks Preservation Commission, *SoHo-Cast Iron Historic District Designation Report.*

15. Ibid.

16. W. Koch, "Reflections on SoHo," in Ulrich Eckhardt and Werner Düttman, eds., *New York-Downtown Manhattan: SoHo* (Berlin: Akademie der Künste-Berliner Festwochen, 1976), 117.

17. Chester Rapkin, *The South Houston Industrial Area* (New York: New York City Planning Commission, 1963).

18. The aspects of the modern history of SoHo are covered well in Hudson, *The Unanticipated City.*

19. Today there is a quarterly newsletter, the *SoHo Alliance.*

20. This legislation began at least as early as 1977 and is well described in Hudson, *The Unanticipated City,* 106–119.

21. Eric Homberger, *Scenes from the Life of a City* (New Haven: Yale University Press, 1994), 222–293.

22. Neil Smith, "New City, New Frontier: The Lower East Side as Wild, Wild West," in Michael Sorkin, ed., *Variations on a Theme Park: The New American City and the End of Public Space* (New York: The Noonday Press, 1992), 80–81.

23. Ibid.

24. Ibid.

25. Geoffrey Biddle, *Alphabet City* (Berkeley: University of California Press, 1992), and Kurt Hollander, *The Portable Lower East Side* (New York: The Portable Lower East Side, 1988).

26. Ibid., and field observations by the author.

27. Field observations by the author and conversations with John Loomis.

28. Conversations with the author on the Lower East Side.

29. Idea of cliques and phraseology based on Miguel Algarin, "Loisaida: Alphabet City," in Biddle, *Alphabet City,* 6.

30. Rem Koolhaas, *Delirious New York: A Retroactive Manifesto for Manhattan* (New York: Oxford University Press, 1978), and Bernard Tschumi, *The Manhattan Transcripts* (London: St. Martin's Press, 1981).

31. Lefebvre, *The Production of Space,* 33.

32. Michel de Certeau, *The Practice of Everyday Life* (Berkeley: University of California Press, 1984), 91.

33. Ibid., 91f and 115f.

34. Ibid., 104.

35. Ibid., 116, and Charlotte Linde and William Labov, "Spatial Networks as a Site for the Study of Language and Thought," *Language* 51 (1975): 924–939.

36. de Certeau, *The Practice of Everyday Life,* 97.

37. Paul Auster, *The New York Trilogy* (London: Penguin, 1986), 85.

38. Ibid., 189 and 195.

39. de Certeau, *The Practice of Everyday Life,* 96.

40. Stanley Cohen and Laurie Taylor, *Escape Attempts: The Theory of Practice of Resistance to Everyday Life* (London: Allen Lane, 1976).

41. Also based upon Peter L. Berger and Thomas Luckman, *The Social Construction of Reality* (London: Penguin, 1972), and Georg Simmel, *The Transcendent Character of Life* (Chicago: University of Chicago Press, 1971).

42. Cohen and Taylor, *Escape Attempts,* 30.

43. Ibid., 220f.

44. Ibid., 77.

45. Ibid., 225.

46. Johan Huizinga, *A Study of the Play Element in Culture* (London: Routledge and Kegan Paul, 1949), 13.

47. Amanda Dargan and Steven Zeitlin, *City Play* (New Brunswick: Rutgers University Press, 1990), 46.

48. Ibid., 50.

49. Ibid., 64.

50. Ibid., 40.

51. Paige R. Penland, "New Mexico Governor Gary Johnson Goes for a Ride," *Lowrider* (September 1995): 22–23.

52. As shown in *Lowrider* magazine.

53. Dargan and Zeitlin, *City Play,* 6.

54. Sante, *Low Life,* 320f.

55. Ibid., 323.

56. Ibid., 336.

57. Jennifer Toth, *The Mole People: Life in the Tunnels Beneath New York City* (Chicago: Chicago Review Press, 1993).

58. Sante, *Low Life,* 348.

59. Ibid., 354, and Smith, "New City, New Frontier," 62.

60. Smith, "New City, New Frontier," 62.

61. Ibid., 62f.

62. Homberger, *The Historical Atlas of New York City,* 162.

63. Ibid., 163.

64. Ibid.

65. Joint Center for Housing Studies, *State of the Nation in Housing* (Cambridge, MA: Harvard University, 1995).

66. Homberger, *Scenes from the Life of a City,* 219.

67. Ibid., 1–8.

68. Ibid., 212–218.

69. Ibid., 253.

70. Ibid., 253f.

71. Ibid., 253–260 and Elizabeth Stevenson, *Park Maker: A Life of Frederick Law Olmsted* (New York: Macmillan, 1977).

72. Henry Hope Reed and Sophia Duckworth, *Central Park: A History and a Guide* (New York: Clarkston N. Potter, Inc., 1972), and Homberger, *Scenes from the Life of a City,* 280.

73. Attributed to Downing in Homberger, *Scenes from the Life of a City,* 234.

74. For instance, at least two squatter settlements numbering, in total, more than several thousand people were summarily removed from the site without anywhere near complete compensation.

75. Reed and Duckworth, *Central Park,* and Elliot Willensky and Norval White, *AIA Guide to New York* (New York: Harcourt Brace, 1988), 336–341.

Other references include: C. L. Byrd, *SoHo* (New York: Doubleday, 1981); Gregory Derek and John Urry, *Social Relations and Spatial Structures* (New York: Macmillan, 1985); Claude S. Fischer, *The Urban Experience* (New York: Harcourt Brace Jovanovich, 1976); Paul Goldberger, *The City Observed: New York* (New York: Vintage Books, 1979); Charles T. Goodsell, *The Social Meaning of Civic Space: Studying Political Authority through Architecture* (Lawrence, KA: University Press of Kansas, 1988); Antonio Gramsci, *Selections from the Prison Notebooks* (New York: International Publishers, 1971); Leo Marx, "The American Ideology of Space," in Staurt Wrede and William Howard Adams, eds., *Denatured Visions: Landscape and Culture in the Twentieth Century* (New York: Museum of Modern Art, 1991), and Edward T. Spann, *The New Metropolis: New York* (New York: Columbia University Press, 1981).

Chapter 5

1. The following description is based on Stephen Clissold, ed., *A Short History of Yugo-*

slavia (London: Cambridge University Press, 1960); Dimitrije Djordjevic, ed., *The Creation of Yugoslavia 1914–1918* (Santa Barbara: Clio Books, 1980); and Stevan K. Pavlowitch, *Yugoslavia* (New York: Praeger Publishers, 1971), chapter 1.

2. The following paragraphs describing the formation of Yugoslavia between the wars are based primarily on Ivo Banac, *The National Question in Yugoslavia: Origins, History, Politics* (Ithaca: Cornell University Press, 1984), Clissold, *A Short History of Yugoslavia,* and Pavlowitch, *Yugoslavia,* chapter 2.

3. Pavlowitch, *Yugoslavia,* 55.

4. Ibid., 60.

5. The following paragraphs describing political events are based primarily on ibid., chapters 2 and 3.

6. Fred Singleton, *Twentieth-Century Yugoslavia* (New York: Columbia University Press, 1976), 76.

7. Pavlowitch, *Yugoslavia,* chapter 2.

8. Ibid.

9. Phil Wright, *The Political Economy of the Yugoslavia Revolution* (the Hague: Institute of Social Studies, 1985), 27.

10. Pavlowitch, *Yugoslavia,* 72f.

11. Singleton, *Twentieth-Century Yugoslavia,* 86.

12. Pavlowitch, *Yugoslavia,* chapter 2.

13. Ibid.

14. Based on Wright, *The Political Economy of the Yugoslav Revolution,* tables.

15. John A. Arnez, *Slovenia in European Affairs: Reflections on Slovenian Political History* (New York: League of CSA, 1958).

16. Ibid., 60–64.

17. Ibid., 140f.

18. Ibid., chapter titled *The Nazi and Fascist Occupations.*

19. The total length of the barbed-wire and bunkered enclosure was on the order of 30 kilometers.

20. Singleton, *Twentieth-Century Yugoslavia,* tables.

21. Ibid.

22. Ibid., and Wright, *The Political Economy of the Yugoslav Revolution,* 14f.

23. Ibid.

24. Ibid.

25. Arnez, *Slovenia in European Affairs,* 140.

26. Ibid., 144f.

27. Ibid., 140.

28. Breda Mihelič, *Ljubljana City Guide* (Ljubljana: Državna Založba, 1990).

29. Also referred to as *Aemona.*

30. The following planning history is based primarily on Ian Bentley and Durda Gržan-Butina, *Jože Plečnik 1872–1957: Architecture and the City* (Oxford: Oxford Polytechnic, 1983), and Peter Krečič, *Plečnik's Ljubljana* (Ljubljana: Cankarjeva založba, 1991), 4–5.

31. Mihelič, *Ljubljana City Guide,* 79f.

32. Krečič, *Plečnik's Ljubljana,* 5, and Durda Gržan-Butina, "Ljubljana: Master Plan and Spatial Structure," in Bentley and Gržan-Butina, *Jože Plečnik 1872–1957,* 28–35.

33. Gržan-Butina, "Ljubljana," 28.

34. Bentley and Gržan-Butina, *Jože Plečnik 1872–1957* and terminology in Krečič, *Plečnik's Ljubljana,* 15f.

35. Richard M. Andrews, "Ljubljana: The River Sequence," in Bentley and Gržan-Butina, *Jože Plečnik 1872–1957,* 36–43.

36. Ibid.

37. The following project descriptions are based on field observations and primarily on ibid.; Richard Bassett, "The Work of Plečnik in Ljubljana," *AA Files* 1, no. 2 (1982): 34–49; Alberto Ferlenga, "Riverbank Among the Trees: A Trip Through the Ljubljana of Plečnik," *Lotus International* 59 (1989): 6–13; and Krečič, *Plečnik's Ljubljana.*

38. Žiga Zois was the son of Michelangelo Zois, a Slovene-Italian merchant in the iron trade who became a nobleman.

39. Bassett, "The Work of Plečnik in Ljubljana," 38.

40. Andrews, "Ljubljana," 40.

41. Ferlenga, "Riverbank Among the Trees," 8.

42. Krečič, *Plečnik's Ljubljana,* 52–53.

43. Andrews, "Ljubljana," 40.

44. Richard Guy Wilson, "Jože Plečnik in Ljubljana, *Progressive Architecture* 10 (1985): 96–97.

45. Gržan-Butina, "Ljubljana," 30.

46. Ibid., 29.

47. Wilson, "Jože Plečnik in Ljubljana," 97.

48. James Traub, "Street Fight," *New Yorker,* September 4, 1995, 36–40.

49. After Stanley Clavell, *Themes Out of School: Effects and Causes* (Chicago: University of Chicago Press, 1984), 184–194

and *Conditions Handsome and Unhandsome: The Constitution of Emersonian Perfectionism* (Chicago: University of Chicago Press, 1990), 64–100.

50. Laurie Olin, "Design of the Urban Landscape," *Places* 5, no. 4 (1988): 91–94.

51. See also Stanley Clavell, *In Quest of the Ordinary: Lines of Skepticism and Romanticism* (Chicago: University of Chicago Press, 1990).

Other references include: Richard Bassett, "Plečnik in Ljubljana," *Architectural Review* 170, no. 1014 (August 1981): 107–111; François Burkhardt, Claude Eveno, and Boris Podrecca, *Jože Plečnik, Architect: 1872–1957* (Cambridge, MA: The MiT Press, 1989); Alberto Ferlenga and Sergio Polano, *Jože Plečnik: Progetti e città* (Milan: Electa, 1990); Giorgio Lombardi, "Urban Space and the Contemporary City," *Ottogono* (December 1989): 40–53; R. D. Ostović, *The Truth about Yugoslavia* (New York: Roy Publishers, 1952); and Garth M. Terry, *Yugoslav History: A Bibliographic Index of English-Language Articles* (London: Astra Press, 1985).

Chapter 6

1. Jürgen Habermas, *The Structural Transformation of the Public Sphere: An Inquiry into the Category of Bourgeois Society* (Cambridge, MA: The MIT Press, 1991).

2. Jean L. Cohen and Andrew Arato, *Civil Society and Political Theory* (Cambridge, MA: The MIT Press, 1995), 29f.

3. Robert D. Putnam, *Bowling Alone: Democracy and the End of the Twentieth Century* (Harvard University, August 1994).

4. Cohen and Arato, *Civil Society and Political Theory,* 15f.

5. Hannah Arendt, *The Human Condition* (Chicago: University of Chicago Press, 1971).

6. Antonio Gramsci, *Selections from the Prison Notebooks* (New York: International Publishers, 1971), 210f.

7. Nelson Goodman, *Ways of World Making* (Cambridge, MA: Hackett Publishing Company, 1978); Linda Nochlin, *Realism* (London: Penguin Books, 1971); and Hilary Putnam, *The Many Faces of Realism* (La Salle, IL: Open Court, 1987).

8. Simon Pepper, "British Housing Trends, 1964–1974," *Lotus International* 10 (1974): 94–103.

9. Ziva Frieman, "Shoring up the Center," *Progressive Architecture* 4 (1993): 90.

10. Ibid.

11. Ibid., 89.

12. Yukio Futagawa, ed., "Carlo Aymonino/ Aldo Rossi, Housing Quarter at the Gallaratese Quarter," *Global Architecture* 45 (1977).

13. Bernard Félix Dubor, *Fernand Pouillon* (Milan: Electa, 1986).

14. Ricardo De Sola Ricardo, *La Urbinacion "El Silencio"* (Caracas: Ernesto Armitano, 1987).

15. Gianni Vattimo, *The End of Modernity* (Baltimore: Johns Hopkins University Press, 1988).

16. Ecological restoration of the district of Xochimilco was undertaken by Mexico City between 1987 and 1995. See Jean Sidaner, ed., *Xochimilco: Imagenas de un Rescate* (Mexico City: Portico, 1991), and Alejandro Ochoa Vega, "Parque Ecológico Xochimilco," *Entorno* 6 (1993): 5–10.

17. Restoration of the Historic Center of Mexico City was started in 1988 and is still incomplete. See Monica Hallquist, ed., *Centro Historico de la Cuidad de Mexico* (Mexico City: Enlace, 1993).

18. This sense of realism persists today in interpretative art works like Chris Burden's *Another World* of 1992—a kinetic sculpture based on the fantasy of using the Eiffel Tower as a vertical armature from which two replicas of the *Titanic* are suspended. See Peter Noever, ed., *Chris Burden: Beyond the Limits* (Vienna: MAK, Cantz Verlag, 1996), 115.

19. Charles Rearick, *Pleasures of the Belle Époque* (New Haven: Yale University Press, 1985), 119f.

20. Celeste Fremon, "Tough Love," *Utne Reader,* March–April 1996, 95.

21. Ibid., and Celeste Fremon, *Father Greg and the Homeboys* (New York: Hyperion, 1995).

Fragmentary excerpts from real stories—yet to be fully told—that were heard simultaneously during the writing of this book. The imagined authors Pietro Lupino, Petro A. Lupo-Garcia, Piero Monteverdi, Peter Kleinewolfe, Tuby Ratesele, and Pierre Grimmonde are one and the same.

Illustration Credits

Index